Praise for Daniel Shapiro's *Negotiating the Nonnegotiable*

"Dan Shapiro has written a masterpiece—clear, insightful, and practical—about the most difficult and emotionally charged of negotiations: those that revolve around identity. Highly recommended!"
—William Ury, coauthor of *Getting to Yes* and author of *Getting to Yes with Yourself*

"Daniel Shapiro's *Negotiating the Nonnegotiable* is a modern masterpiece. Bold and compelling from the first page, he shines a light on the dark divisive forces of conflict while describing pathways toward peace and harmony through the power of reconciliation and affiliation. It is the ultimate proof that addressing conflict requires a courageous head as much as a collaborative heart. Every leader should read it and live by it."
—Katherine Garrett-Cox, CEO, Alliance Trust Investments

"*Negotiating the Nonnegotiable* is one of the most important books of our modern era. Dan Shapiro gives us a whole new set of tools to tackle our toughest disputes—those that threaten our identity. This brilliant book is innovative, practical, and exactly what we need in today's world."
—Jaime de Bourbon de Parme, Ambassador of the Netherlands to the Holy See

"*Negotiating the Nonnegotiable* is a fascinating read that gets to the core of all kinds of conflicts. Daniel Shapiro draws on his lifetime's work to examine processes that lead from discord to harmony and from war to peace. His book is a gripping account of how people of every persuasion can come together and find a new beginning. Anyone with an interest in the work of reconciliation, peace building, and conflict resolution should read this book."
—Bertie Ahern, Former Prime Minister of Ireland 1997–2008; conegotiator of the Good Friday Agreement

"As Commander of the NYPD Hostage Negotiation Team for over fourteen years, I have been involved in many dangerous nonnegotiable negotiations, where a tactical resolution often had to be realized. In *Negotiating the Nonnegotiable*, Dan Shapiro unlocks the strategies to reconcile strained relationships and find the hidden possibilities for resolution. An extraordinary book that will change your life."
—Lt. Jack Cambria, Commanding Officer NYPD Hostage Negotiation Team (Retired)

"Dan Shapiro has written a book that is at once both profound and practical, heartfelt and hopeful. At a time when one of our world's most alarming fault lines is the growing polarization between individuals and groups—divided by race, ethnicity, politics, religion, or class—immersion in his wisdom is a must for anyone trying to prevent or resolve these conflicts."
—Matthew Bishop, senior editor of *The Economist* Group; cofounder of the Social Progress Index

"No one has thought more deeply and creatively about the impact of emotions on conflict than Dan Shapiro. In *Negotiating the Nonnegotiable*, Dan draws on that depth of knowledge to develop a workable method that enables us to deal effectively with emotional conflicts that all too often seem nonnegotiable."

—Jeswald W. Salacuse, Henry J. Braker Professor, the Fletcher School of Law and Diplomacy, Tufts University; author of *Negotiating Life*

"A wise book—full of experience, heart, and intelligence—it will give every reader insights to consider and plans to enact. We can hope that no conflict is intractable, thanks to this book. And it has great stories."

—Susan T. Fiske, Eugene Higgins Professor of Psychology and Professor of Public Affairs, Princeton University

"What a powerful book! *Negotiating the Nonnegotiable* is both entertaining and deeply enriching, with a comprehensive content and a diversity of examples from daily life and global contexts. I wish I would have known much earlier in life about the ideas in this book, including my vertigo syndrome! Shapiro provides us with a fabulous invitation to consistently trade disharmony for harmony."

—Alain Robert, Vice Chairman, UBS Wealth Management

"This fascinating book tells us a lot about the role of identity in international conflicts and how to bridge the divide. It expands our understanding of the political reconciliation in the international system."

—Professor Yan Xuetong, Dean of the Institute of Modern International Relations, Tsinghua University (China)

"Welcome to Negotiation 3.0! Dan Shapiro gives us new eyes through which to understand even the most difficult negotiations—and a powerful new tool kit to overcome them. Negotiators from both my own country of Japan and from around the world will be inspired by this important new text and will benefit immensely from it."

—Jiro Tamura, Professor of Law, Keio University, President, Negotia Club (Japan)

"In *Negotiating the Nonnegotiable*, part manual and part memoir, Dan Shapiro offers insight into negotiation and identity culled from an extraordinary career working on critical conflicts around the world. *Negotiating the Nonnegotiable* is sure to be required reading for diplomats and peace builders alike seeking more effective practice and a broader toolbox for solving seemingly intractable conflicts."

—Nancy Lindborg, President, United States Institute of Peace

Negotiating
the
Nonnegotiable

Negotiating
the
Nonnegotiable

HOW TO RESOLVE YOUR MOST

EMOTIONALLY CHARGED CONFLICTS

Daniel Shapiro

VIKING

VIKING
An imprint of Penguin Random House LLC
375 Hudson Street
New York, New York 10014
penguin.com

Page 13: "Drawing Hands" by M. C. Escher. Used by permission of The M. C. Escher Company

ISBN 9780670015566
EXPORT EDITION ISBN 9780399564406

Printed in the United States of America
1   3   5   7   9   10   8   6   4   2

Set in ITC Giovanni Std
Designed by Alissa Rose Theodor

To Mia,
Noah, Zachary, Liam,
Mom & Dad, Maddie & Mike, Steve & Shira,
Margaret, Betsy & Peter, and Susan,
for teaching me about
life's one nonnegotiable: love.

The Challenge

EVERY GENERATION OF HUMANKIND BELIEVES THEY ARE
MORE EVOLVED, MORE SOPHISTICATED, MORE "MODERN"
THAN THOSE WHO CAME BEFORE THEM.

YET NO MATTER HOW FAST SOCIETY ADVANCES,
PEOPLE IN CONFLICT ARE, AND ALWAYS WILL BE, *HUMAN*.

THE CHALLENGE IS HOW TO BRIDGE THE DIVIDE WHEN
OUR MOST FUNDAMENTAL VALUES ARE ON THE LINE.

HOW DO WE
NEGOTIATE THE NONNEGOTIABLE?

Contents

Introduction: Why This Book?

Negotiating the Nonnegotiable introduces a new paradigm for resolving conflict—one that speaks as much to the heart as to the head. Just as scientists have discovered the inner workings of the physical world, my research in the field of conflict resolution has revealed emotional forces that drive people to conflict. These forces are invisible to the eye, yet their impact is deeply felt: They can tear apart the closest friendship, break up a marriage, destroy a business, and fuel sectarian violence. Unless we learn to counteract such forces, we will tend to engage repeatedly in the same frustrating conflicts, with the same frustrating results. This book provides the necessary tools to overcome these dynamics and foster cooperative relations, turning the most emotionally charged conflict into an opportunity for mutual benefit.

The need for a new paradigm struck me twenty-five years ago in a café in the splintering state of Yugoslavia. I had just facilitated a weeklong workshop on conflict resolution for teenage refugees—Serbs, Bosnian Muslims, and Croats—and several of us were now discussing the differences between life in Yugoslavia and in the United States. The sound of gunfire still echoed in the minds of these teenagers, but here we were, in the eye of a hurricane, drinking Turkish coffee and talking about soccer and who in our workshop had a crush on whom. Among us was long-haired, blue-eyed, seventeen-year-old Veronica, who stared straight ahead with unnerving intensity. She had said little throughout our workshop, so I was surprised when, during a pause in the chatter, she suddenly spoke.

"It happened nine months ago," she began, her gaze fixed on her plate. "My boyfriend and I were having lunch at his house. There was a knock at the door. Three men with guns entered." She glanced up for a moment, unsure whether to continue. "They pushed my boyfriend against the wall. He pushed back, but they fought harder. I tried to scream. But nothing came out. I wanted to run for help. To do *something*. But I froze."

Now her already monotonic voice flattened even further, and her eyes opened wide.

"They grabbed my shoulders, pinned me down, and held his head in front of mine. I saw the fear in his eyes. He shook to get free, but they held him tight."

She paused again and then said, "One of them took out a knife, and I watched as they slit his throat."

The noise of the café fell away. I looked at her, stunned, feeling as though I had been pinned to my chair. I wanted to comfort her, to support her in some way, but I didn't know what to say. And then, just as suddenly as Veronica had awakened to this moment of horror, she fell quiet.

My colleagues and I had only one more night in Yugoslavia; at dawn we would catch a train to Budapest. I was sad to leave the workshop participants, of whom I had grown deeply fond and who, in this nightmarish war zone, had entrusted us with their secrets. But more than sadness, I felt guilt: I would be returning to the comfort and security of the United States, while they would remain in despair.

As our car approached the train station early the next morning, my heart jumped. All twenty-four teenagers from our workshop were standing by the track, waving. Veronica was among them. She walked over to say good-bye.

"Don't be like all the others who come to help," she said. "Don't say you will remember us and then forget."

I gave her my word.

The Missing Piece

What drives humans to engage in destructive conflict? Are we psychologically predisposed to repeat the same dynamics again and again—despite the often calamitous results? And how can we resolve emotionally charged conflicts when our most cherished beliefs and values are at stake? These are the vital questions at the heart of my work.

While you may never find yourself in a situation as dire as Veronica's, you cannot avoid emotionally charged conflicts. They are part of what it means to be human. You may resent your romantic partner, hold a grudge against a colleague, or despair at deteriorating ethnic relations. The chart below illuminates some of the innumerable circumstances in which these conflicts crop up.

Illustrative Examples of Emotionally Charged Conflicts

- A **couple** wrestles over the values that should govern their shared life together. How do they negotiate divergent perspectives on finances, household roles, and politics?
- **Parents** guard against any of their children marrying outside the family religion, class, or ethnicity. Any child remotely exploring that option will be rejected.
- A **work team** divides along cultural lines and experiences internal tension over who should lead the team. Each side distrusts the other, talks about the other behind closed doors, and produces dismal results.
- **Senior corporate leaders** are deadlocked on the issue of budget allocation, split over the values that should represent their company. Should they prioritize short-term profit? Long-term reputation? Community service?
- A **neighborhood** is rocked by a local controversy that divides residents along racial or ethnic lines. Most people on one side refuse to speak to those on the other side, and there is the unspoken fear of escalating violence.
- A **community** sees itself being swallowed up by a larger "global culture" threatening its local customs and values.
- Members of a **political group** come to view competition for resources as a quest to define their collective identity; they take up arms to fight for their rights.
- A **nation** faces a values-laden debate over the erosion of national identity amid an influx of foreign cultural, religious, and secular influences.

You cannot resolve such conflicts unless you address them at the root—which stretches beneath rationality, beneath even emotions, to the heart of who you are: your identity. By default, disputants tend to define their identities in opposition to one another: It is *me* versus *you*, *us* versus *them*. We point fingers, assign blame, insist, "This is *your* fault." But this clash of identities only escalates conflict. A better approach is to collaboratively problem solve differences: to uncover each person's interests and commit to an agreement that works for both sides. Yet in an emotionally charged conflict, from a marital dispute to a clash between nations, collaborative problem solving often proves insufficient. Why?

First, you cannot *solve* emotions. Ridding yourself of anger or humiliation is a very different matter than solving a math problem. Emotions are idiosyncratic; no mathematical equation can tell you with certainty how the other side will react. Apologizing to your spouse may backfire today, but work wonders tomorrow.

Second, even if you rationally want to repair relations—with your spouse, with your boss—emotional impulses often goad you to continue to fight. In an emotionally charged conflict, something within blocks you from cooperative problem solving: a knot of resentment, an intuition that the other side is out to get you, a voice that whispers, *Don't trust them*. Whether you are in conflict with someone you love or someone you hate, an inner urge to resist cooperation can get in the way of resolution.

Finally, you cannot simply adopt the other side's beliefs as yours. In a heated conflict, your identity is on the line, but it is not a commodity you can trade away; what you believe is what you believe.

So how *do* you resolve emotionally charged conflicts?

I have spent decades investigating that very question—and have made some important discoveries along the way. This book is the result. Written here in Cambridge and at night in cafés during my research travels around the world—from Cairo to São Paulo, Zurich to Dar es Salaam, Sydney to Tianjin, Tokyo to New Delhi—*Negotiating the Nonnegotiable* began with the realization that emotionally charged conflicts may feel nonnegotiable, but can be resolved. And it was born of the conviction that no one need suffer the agony that Veronica endured.

The Method

I have developed a practical method to bridge the toughest emotional divides. This method leverages a unique feature of conflict that has been consistently overlooked: the space between sides. We typically view conflict as a binary concept—*me* versus *you*, *us* versus *them*—and focus on satisfying our independent interests. But conflict literally exists *between* us—in our relationship—and in that space live complicated emotional dynamics that thwart cooperation. Learning how to transform an emotionally charged conflict into an opportunity for mutual benefit requires that you learn how to effectively navigate this space.

My goal has been to decode the space between disputants and to design processes to help them work through intransigent emotions, divisive dynamics, and clashing beliefs. The result is the method that I call Relational Identity Theory, which features practical steps that produce dynamic effects, much as the few simple actions necessary to light a pile of wood produce the dynamic effect of fire.

The single greatest barrier to conflict resolution is what I call the Tribes Effect, a divisive mindset that casts you and the other side as inevitable adversaries. As long as you are trapped in this mindset, you will be trapped in conflict. The way out is to counteract the five hidden forces that draw you toward this outlook—the Five Lures of the Tribal Mind—and to cultivate positive relations via the process of *integrative dynamics*. In the course of doing so, you will confront unavoidable tensions—*relational dialectics*—that threaten to make your conflict feel like a no-win proposition. This book will show you how to find your way past these apparently nonnegotiable obstacles.

To arrive at this method, I have conducted laboratory experiments, reviewed thousands of research articles, consulted for political and business leadership, advised struggling families and couples, and interviewed hundreds of experts ranging from political negotiators to citizen activists, heads of state to business executives. I also founded and direct the Harvard International Negotiation Program, which serves as a research and educational base for investigating the emotional and identity-based roots of conflict resolution.

These experiences have taught me a lot, and in *Negotiating the Nonnegotiable* I share these insights with you. While this book is designed to help you resolve your most fraught disagreements, it is also my attempt to honor my word. I wish to honor Veronica, the other twenty-three youths from our workshop, and all those people around the world, on whatever side of a given conflict, who suffer in the name of identity. I believe there is a better way. I believe there *must* be.

This book is a testament to that vision.

Daniel L. Shapiro
CAMBRIDGE, MASSACHUSETTS

Section 1

———

The Tribes Effect

The Hidden Power of Identity

The world exploded at Davos. It happened several years ago at the World Economic Forum's annual summit in the snow-capped mountains of Switzerland. I had convened a meeting of forty-five world leaders in a small room tucked away from the eyes and ears of the reporting press. These leaders had negotiated some of the world's most challenging conflicts, but none were prepared for what would happen next—a negotiation of the strangest kind that would reach beyond the halls of that summit to the epicenter of all our lives.

It all started innocently enough. As the leaders streamed into the room, a young staffer handed each of them a colored scarf and escorted them to one of six tables. I watched as the CEO of a *Fortune* 50 company made his way to his seat, followed by a deputy head of state, who greeted the CEO with a diplomatic nod. A prominent university president settled next to a security expert, while at a neighboring table an artist chatted with a professor. Soft music played in the background, and the mood was light.

As the clock struck one, the music quieted and I stepped to the center of the room. "Welcome," I said a bit nervously, taking stock of this esteemed group, who looked at me in anticipation. "It is an honor to be here with all of you today."

As the word "tribes" appeared on a screen behind me, I launched into the session. "Our world is becoming more and more of a tribal world. As global interdependence and advances in technology intertwine, we have more opportunity to connect with more people. Yet this very thread of connection—this emerging global community—also threatens fundamental aspects of who we are. It is only natural, then, that we tend to withdraw to the security and continuity of tribes."

The group appeared intrigued. I continued. "We all belong to multiple tribes. A tribe is any group to which we see ourselves as similar in kind, whether based on religion or ethnicity or even our place of work. We feel a kinlike connection to the tribe; we emotionally invest in it. This means a religious community or nation can feel like a tribe. A family can be so tightly knit that it feels like a tribe. Even multinational corporations can take on the feel of a tribe. Tribes are all around us.

"Today we'll be exploring the power of tribes. You and the others at your table will have the opportunity to get to know one another—by forming a tribe of your own at your table. You'll have fifty minutes to answer a small set of challenging questions to define the key qualities of your tribe. Please answer all these questions through consensus, not voting. And be sure to remain true to your own belief system."

The instructions seemed acceptable to everyone—until I passed out the worksheet containing the questions. The professor's hand darted into the air. "You want us to answer *these* questions through consensus? In fifty minutes? Come on!"

He was justifiably aggravated, as the participants were being asked to answer such morally divisive questions as "Does your tribe believe in capital punishment?," "Does your tribe believe in abortion?," and "What are the three most important values of your tribe?"

"I've facilitated this exercise dozens of times," I assured the professor, "and everyone is always somehow able to finish. So just give it your best shot, and be sure to have a response to each question by the end of the allotted time." He nodded begrudgingly, and the participants set to work. One tribe spent nearly thirty minutes defining and prioritizing its tribal values, while another got stuck on whether capital punishment should be legal. A tribe in a far corner laughed and joked like friends at a bar while a neighboring table became deeply absorbed in the task.

At the fifty-minute mark, the room went pitch-black. Ominous music began to play—a pipe organ droned a haunting scale of notes. "What's going on?" whispered an eighty-five-year-old venture capitalist. His head swung around as he heard a loud knock on a side door, then a loud bang.

Everyone in the room went still, unsure what to expect. In barged a wide-eyed alien with pale green skin and flylike black eyes. It weaved through the tables, passing the gaping venture capitalist, and slowed to rake the professor's hair with its long green tentacles. "You measly earthlings," the alien growled. "I have come to destroy the Earth!

"I will give you one opportunity to save this world from complete destruction," taunted the alien. "You must choose one of these six tribes as *the* tribe for everyone here. All of you must take on the attributes of that one tribe. You cannot change any of that tribe's attributes. And if you cannot come to full agreement by the end of three rounds of negotiation," the alien snarled, "the world will be destrrroyyyyyed!" The creature then raised its arms wide, shrieked with laughter, and left the room.

The lights came back on, and everyone looked around, bewildered. There were a few chuckles, and then the participants sprang into action, huddling at their tables to define their strategy for the upcoming negotiations.

Six barstools stood in the middle of the room, one for a delegate from each tribe. I announced the advent of round one, and the tribes sent their representatives to negotiate. This round was fairly amicable. The six tribes familiarized themselves with one another's key characteristics.

After a few minutes, the CEO of a Dubai-based company said, "We must start by talking about our negotiation process. *How* are we going to make our decision here?" It was a good, rational question, the kind that virtually any negotiation consultant would advise should be raised. But the CEO was drowned out by a magazine editor from the Happy Tribe, who, feeling pressure to advocate for his own group, complained, "Why is no one listening to *our* tribe?"

"You'll get your chance," replied a representative from the Cosmopolitan Tribe. But round one ended before the magazine editor could say another word.

In round two, the emotional temperature of the room intensified. These leaders were determined to save the world. The charismatic delegate for the Rainbow Tribe, a sharply dressed business executive, proclaimed, "We believe in all colors, all genders, all ethnicities. Come to our tribe! We will accept you all!" He spread his arms in a welcoming gesture, and two tribes immediately joined with him. A venture capitalist crossed his arms, glared at the Rainbow Tribe delegate, and complained, "If we are all equal, why don't you join *our* tribe?"

In round three, a frenzy overtook the room. The delegates for this round included five men and one woman, all of whom argued about whether humanitarianism or compassion represented a more important core value. The men yelled over one another and over the woman, who became so enraged that she stood on her stool, her face flushed, and pointed her finger and shouted, "This is just another example of male competitive behavior! You all come to *my* tribe!" Only one tribe agreed to join hers.

Moments later the world exploded.

The Fundamental Force of Conflict

It is tempting to write off the dynamic of the Tribes Exercise as unique to the leaders at Davos, but *their instincts are essentially no different from yours or mine.* Over the past two decades, I have facilitated the exercise dozens of times with students of law, business, psychology, and politics, and key political and business leaders in Europe, the Middle East, North America, Australia, and Asia. The world has exploded all but a handful of times. This tribal dynamic appears so compelling that participants lose sight of their goal of saving the world for the sake of an identity crafted in a mere fifty minutes.

My international research has led me to conclude that the Tribes Exercise evokes emotional dynamics intrinsic to real-world conflict. Think how easily the world explodes in the lives of divorcing couples, competing business units, and rival factions. And as our world faces shared crises around security, climate change, and world trade, tribal entrenchment increasingly puts the entire human race at risk.

But it is hard to notice these dynamics when caught in them. After the Tribes Exercise in Davos, an internationally recognized rabbi admitted with great shame, "My parents and I were nearly victims of the Holocaust. I vowed, 'Never again.' But here I am, responding to the constraints of this exercise without as much as a word of protest until it's too late." An academic observed,

"I set out to either show unifying leadership or to become a demagogue, breaking the rules of the game. But I failed to do either, and let down history and humanity."

Key Dimensions of Conflict Resolution

This book provides crucial advice to resolve emotionally charged conflicts. The world could have been saved at Davos if the leaders had addressed the key dimensions of conflict resolution: rationality, emotions, and identity.* While scholars often treat these dimensions as independent, neuroscience suggests they interrelate. Only by addressing all three can we hope to arrive at a satisfying resolution to an emotionally charged conflict.

Homo economicus

The first dimension of conflict resolution regards people as rational actors, subscribing to the *Homo economicus* model of human behavior. This model contends that your main motivation is to get your interests met as efficiently as possible. If you can satisfy the interests of the other party while meeting your own, all the better. The defining feature of this paradigm is a search for an agreement that maximizes mutual gains, or at least satisfies your interests without worsening those of your counterpart.

Despite this model's straightforward appeal, the explosion at Davos reveals its limits. The global leaders taking part in the Tribes Exercise had all the tools of rationality at their disposal, along with an unusual collective portfolio of experience leading in times of crisis. They tried to use reason to their favor, as when the CEO of the Dubai-based company urged the tribes to define a process of negotiation. They also had powerful incentives to both save the world and avoid the public humiliation of a failed

---

*I define "conflict resolution" as the process of creating harmony from discord. This means that conflict resolution encompasses everything from international mediation to an apologetic hug for your spouse. The word "resolve" comes from the Latin words *re* and *solvere*. To solve is to loosen, much as a solvent dissolves another substance. "To resolve" connotes a melting away, an untangling, an untying. This is precisely what I believe needs to happen in an emotionally charged conflict. We need to loosen the toxic ties, to melt them away, paving the way for the natural ties of harmony that I believe underlie the human character.

effort. But however high the odds were in favor of these leaders saving the world through rational means, the world ultimately exploded in front of their very eyes—indeed as a result of their very words and deeds.

Homo emoticus

A new generation of research suggests a second dimension to conflict resolution: emotions. You are not merely a rational decision maker; beyond reason lies the emotional domain, which animates your actions and thoughts. You are, in other words, a being one might call *Homo emoticus*. According to this model, emotions can facilitate conflict resolution—provided that you listen to what they are telling you. Just as hunger alerts you to the necessity of food, emotions alert you to unmet psychological needs. For example, frustration tells you an obstacle is in your way; guilt pulls you to rectify a wrongdoing. Emotions are messengers, signaling whether a situation is unfolding in your favor. It is up to you to make use of those signals to adjust your course as needed.

But emotions also can hinder conflict resolution. At Davos the leaders made emotional appeals to attract others to their tribe, but these efforts failed. Anger, pride, and resentment amplified tribal differences to the point that negotiations ended in deadlock. After the world exploded, I asked the group, "How many of you think that someone else in this exercise acted irrationally?" Nearly every hand rose. A deputy head of state summed up the emergent theme of the group's experience: "We live in a tribal world. If we cannot deal with emotions constructively, we are doomed."

Homo identicus

To understand why the world exploded at Davos and why it can explode in your own life, you must look beyond reason, beyond even emotion, to the realm of *identity*. This third dimension of human behavior is represented in a model of human behavior I call *Homo identicus*, which is rooted in the principle that human beings seek meaning in their existence.

An emotionally charged conflict gets its "charge" because it implicates fundamental aspects of your identity: who you are, what you hold as important, and how you conceive of meaning in your life. In other words, it threatens *you*.

While emotionally charged conflicts often hinge on such values-laden differences as religion, politics, or family loyalty, human beings can attach strongly to any issue, imbuing it with deep importance. Again, consider the lesson of Davos: It took only fifty minutes for these leaders to attach so intensely to a newly formulated identity that they sacrificed the world in defense of it. Consider how much more difficult it is in the real world to negotiate cooperatively when long-standing beliefs and values come under threat. How, for example, should a multinational corporation address the culture clash among its Chinese, German, South African, and American employees, each based in their own home country and each trying to reconcile the company's culture with local customs? How should a Kenyan mediator at the United Nations most productively assist in a political conflict in Jerusalem between neighboring Islamic and Jewish communities? Such conflicts are virtually impossible to resolve without taking into account awareness of identity.

Homo identicus entails not just your individual identity but the *space between* you and the other side. What is the nature of your relationship? If a husband and wife argue incessantly, the space between them may feel tense; friends quickly notice and ask, "Is something going on between them?" This space can become cold and clogged or warm and welcoming, and the emotional dynamics involved can pull you and the other side apart or bring you together. In a galaxy, the space between two flickering stars is not *nothing*: It contains a gravitational pull that shapes their relationship. Similarly, the emotional space between you and another party defines your relationship as friends or enemies, lovers or traitors.

Unlocking the Power of Identity

This book reveals a powerful method to navigate the complex landscape of identity. You can know *facts* with certainty, but you can never fully know yourself. The closest you can get is through reflection. The more you reflect, the more you know. So as you read this book, think about the role of identity in your toughest conflicts. You will come to see hidden forces fueling destructive relations, as well as new possibilities for resolution.

At Davos, the leaders stumbled through this process. After the world exploded, they fell silent. I asked, "How are you feeling?" They all looked depressed, save one: the professor. He stood, his face red, and pointed his finger at me. "This is *your* fault!" he shouted. "You set us up to have the world explode—with all your questions we had to answer, with the short time frame you enforced." He shook his head, repeating, "This is all *your* fault." He sat down, crossed his arms, and glared at me.

I had expected that someone in the group might blame me in the event that the world exploded. I was an easy target—in many ways a fair target—but the professor's anger was more intense than I had anticipated. All eyes turned toward me.

"You're right," I said. "I did anything and everything in my power to structure this exercise so that the world *would* explode. I gave you virtually impossible questions to agree upon. I gave you limited time to negotiate. I had the alien force you to choose one tribe over the others. So yes, you're right."

The professor's face softened as I acknowledged my responsibility. His arms uncrossed.

"But," I continued, slowing the pace of my words, "at the end of the day, *you* had a choice. You could have come to agreement. You could have questioned me and resisted the rules. You could have. But you didn't. You . . . had . . . a choice."

The professor nodded, his cheeks flushed. I had revealed the truth he did not want to face: He and the other leaders had possessed full power to save the world, but had failed to do so. They had locked themselves into a narrow definition of identity and let the world go down in flames. The conflict had never been immutable, even if it had felt that way.

The Dual Nature of Identity

In Lewis Carroll's whimsical *Alice's Adventures in Wonderland*, charming young Alice encounters an enigmatic, hookah-smoking caterpillar, who asks her a seemingly simple question: "Who are *YOU?*"

Alice hesitantly replies, "I—I hardly know, Sir, just at present—at least I know who I *was* when I got up this morning, but I think I must have been changed several times since then."

Alice stumbles around tricky questions of identity. Who is she, how did she become who she is, and how does she even know she is who she *thinks* she is? Her musing that she must have changed several times since the morning indicates her conviction that identity is fluid. But what troubles poor Alice is that, despite this belief, she *feels* a consistency in her lived experience. She knows she has changed but feels the same.

This paradox cuts right to the heart of conflict resolution. If identity is absolutely fixed, then the only way to resolve a conflict is to compromise your own identity or persuade the other side to compromise theirs. Conflict thus becomes a win-lose proposition. Yet if your identity is entirely fluid, you have no assurance that either party will honor an agreement. How can you be held accountable for your actions of yesterday if you are a changed person today?

A Way Out

Alice gets us out of this conundrum with an insight that proves essential for conflict resolution: Some aspects of her identity change—while others remain the same. Her identity is both fluid *and* fixed.

In a conflict, however, it is easy to lose sight of this fact. When your identity is threatened, you hunker down in self-defense and conceive of it as a single, immutable whole. I call this the *fixed-identity fallacy*—and because of it, you demand the other party acquiesce to *your* perspectives, *your* sense of right and wrong, *your* values. If the other side holds this same egoistic assumption, both of you get stuck in an ever-escalating impasse, until your conflict feels intractable.

But this is an illusion. To assume from the outset that your conflict is insoluble is to bury the possibility of reconciliation deep in the ground. While an emotionally charged conflict *is* hard to resolve, it is much more useful to direct attention toward those aspects of identity that you *can* affect rather than those that appear immutable. In fact, virtually all parts of your identity have a degree of fluidity, though some are much easier to change than others.

This chapter lays the groundwork for the remainder of the book, providing you with foundational tools to overcome the fixed-identity fallacy. Despite the pervasive impact of identity, disputants seldom know what it is or how to address it. Thus this chapter presents a framework to help you discover and leverage the most deeply significant aspects of identity underpinning your conflict.

What Is Identity?

Your identity comprises *the full spectrum of persistent and fleeting characteristics that define you.* These characteristics integrate to make you *one*: a unified whole that includes your body and mind, your neurological apparatus and position in society, your unconscious processes and conscious thoughts, and your enduring sense of existence as well as your passing observations.

Though these characteristics define you, you also define them. You are as much the *object* of analysis as the *subject* doing the analysis. This reciprocal relationship is vividly illustrated by M. C. Escher's sketch *Drawing Hands*, which depicts the hands of an artist drawing themselves. When I asked my then-six-year-old son, Zachary, for his thoughts on this picture, he said, "He's *making* himself!" When it comes to identity, you make yourself too.

In recognition of this self-referential quality, some negotiation scholars have proposed that your identity is "the story you tell yourself about yourself." This definition is insightful but incomplete. You are a story not just told, but also felt. You are the embodiment of that story and also the person telling it. Pioneering psychologist William James called the story you tell yourself the

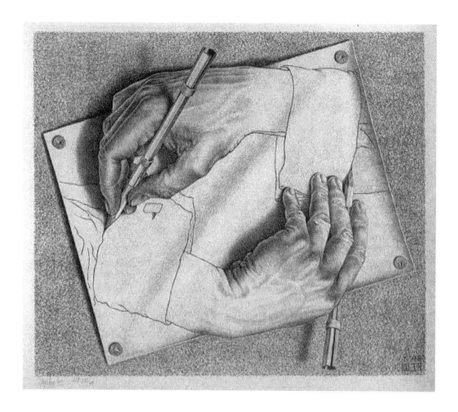

me and your embodied experience the *I*. Everything you experience in a conflict—a wave of shame, an urge to escape, an impulse to yell—will not only be lived and felt by you, but also narrated to you, by you, in real time.

Two facets of identity are critical for resolving an emotionally charged conflict: core identity and relational identity. In the following sections, I describe these two aspects and illuminate how you can leverage them to resolve conflict.

Core Identity: The Biography of Your Being

Your core identity is *the spectrum of characteristics that define you as an individual or as a group.* It includes everything from your body, personality, and occupation to your spiritual beliefs and cultural practices. The world would spin into chaos if no one had a core identity. Nations would have no constitutions or flags; businesses would have no brands; and people would have no names or personalities. Your core identity is the platform from which you synthesize your experiences into a coherent sense of self with both continuity and clear ideals. Should you feel confused about your core identity—unsure of who you are or what you stand for—decisions of all kinds become problematic.

The multiplicity of identity. Your core identity includes your personal preferences and personality traits as well as your identification with social groups. Do you see yourself as American, Japanese, Lebanese, Hispanic, Protestant, Muslim, Jewish, Hindi, or atheist? As a student, parent, executive, liberal, or conservative? Because you belong to multiple groups, you have multiple social identities. A person may be Chinese American, Protestant, a teacher, and conservative.

In a conflict, you must decide which of your social identities to prioritize. You may feel competing loyalties based on your faith, ethnicity, political convictions, and national citizenship. Perhaps your religious identity feels most important to you, but you emphasize your national identity to fit in with your neighbors. Even in casual conversation with a friend, you must decide whether to discuss politics, religion, or work responsibilities, with each decision shaping the contours of your identity.

Just as you identify yourself as a member of specific groups, others pigeonhole you. If you are the only Chinese American executive at your company's meeting on cultural diversity, colleagues may make you feel very aware of that identity, whereas it may fall out of your awareness while you meet with a good friend at a café. But you are not powerless to social labeling—a lesson that Professor Henri Tajfel, founder of social identity theory, learned during World War II. He was a Polish Jew who studied in France and joined the French army during the war. A year into his service, the German army captured him and tossed him into various German prisoner-of-war camps for five years. The Germans repeatedly interrogated him: Are you a Jew? Where are you from? He revealed his Jewish identity, confident that the authorities would discover this information. But he realized that this identity was not entirely fixed. He decided to live under the pretense as a *French* Jew. Had the Germans discovered his social identity as a *Polish* Jew, he would have met certain death.

The most meaningful aspects of your core identity are what I call the Five Pillars of Identity: beliefs, rituals, allegiances, values, and emotionally meaningful experiences. These pillars provide you with a structure to assess what is at stake in an emotionally charged conflict. A threat to *any* of these pillars gives rise to an existential crisis, because meaningful aspects of your core identity feel endangered.

The primary function of identity is not merely to stay alive or pass along your genes, but to *find meaning in life*. It is the Five Pillars that bring significance to existence. Just as the brain, heart, and lungs are central to physical survival, the Five Pillars are central to the vitality of identity. They help explain why the world explodes again and again in the Tribes Exercise: Participants care less about preserving the world than they do about safeguarding what they see as their tribe's significance.

The sooner you realize which of your own pillars feel threatened, the more readily you can address those vulnerabilities and refocus on resolving your conflict. The Five Pillars of Identity form the acronym BRAVE.

The Five Pillars of Identity

1. **Beliefs** are your convictions, principles, and morals.

2. **Rituals** include your meaningful customs and ceremonial acts, whether holidays, rites of passage, regular prayer, or evening dinner with the family.

3. **Allegiances** are the deep loyalties you feel toward a family member, friend, authority figure, nation, tribe, ancestor, or any other person, place, or thing, whether real or mythical.

4. **Values** represent your ideals, which can be explicit ("Our nation values liberty and justice") or embodied in a memorable narrative ("I remember hearing about how grandfather fought day and night for this land").

5. **Emotionally meaningful experiences** are intense events, positive or negative, that define a part of your identity. They comprise everything from the day you got married to the hour your first child was born, the moment your parent slapped you to the memory of mass violence conducted against your group.

When you experience an emotionally charged conflict, run through the Five Pillars of Identity to detect which may feel endangered. Is a core belief at stake? Is the other side threatening a family or religious allegiance? After assessing your own pillars, imagine which might be at stake in the other side. Neither you nor your counterpart is likely to commit to an agreement that threatens a personally important pillar.

Core identity is not completely fixed. My ten-year-old, Noah, competed in a recent soccer match, scoring seven points for his team while the opposition scored none. So with only one minute left in the game, the coaches decided to switch him to the other team. Noah scored two goals for his opponents and ended up "losing" the game two to seven. He felt frustrated the whole evening, for in the course of seconds, his allegiance had shifted from one team to the other.

But Noah's core identity had not undergone a complete makeover. He was at summer camp and felt no strong attachment to either team. Had this been the World Cup and had he been switched to the opposing team, he would have struggled tremendously to redefine his allegiance. Core identity has *some* fluidity, but the deepest pillars of identity are extremely entrenched.

A group's core identity also can change. A company can redefine its guiding values but remain the "same" company, just as a political party can modify its essential beliefs and remain the "same" political party. In fact, groups are constantly negotiating the boundaries of their identities, deciding who is "in," who is "out," and even what it means to be "in." It is as though there were a circle representing the group, and members negotiate what values, beliefs, and rituals belong within that circle. Political, religious, and social groups often keep their traditional social labels despite redefining the fundamental meanings of those labels.

While your core identity is often resistant to change, another facet of identity is more malleable and provides a powerful pathway for resolving even the most emotionally charged conflicts.

Relational Identity: The Hidden Source of Leverage

Your relational identity is *the spectrum of characteristics that define your relationship with a particular person or group.* When interacting with your spouse, do you feel distant or close, constrained or free to be as you really are? While your core identity seeks meaning in existence, your relational identity seeks meaning in *coexistence.* It changes constantly as you negotiate the nature of a relationship, which means that you have tremendous power to shape it.

To illustrate the concept of relational identity, look at the image below. Before reading on, decide which square is darker, A or B.

Edward H. Adelson

The answer: They are the same. Despite the perception that square A is darker than square B, they are in fact identical. (If you remain in doubt, cover everything but squares A and B.) The optical illusion is a result of the fact that you perceive not the objective reality of the boxes but each box relative to the other.

This same perceptual dynamic holds true for differences of identity.

You have a core identity that remains distinct, yet what matters in reconciling a conflict is not just your core identity but also your relational identity—how you perceive who you are in relation to others, and how they perceive their relation to you.

Consider Davos. In the Tribes Exercise, the tribes began their negotiation as colleagues eager to save the world from destruction. But each tribe's affiliation to other tribes quickly collapsed—and *mounting tensions had virtually nothing to do with differences in each tribe's core identity*. The Happy Tribe's perceived rejection in round one led them to attempt to dominate subsequent rounds. The Rainbow Tribe's delegate attracted two other tribes to unite with his in a tight coalition. The central question that preoccupied each tribe was "To whom do we feel connected—and by whom do we feel rejected?"

No quantitative measure can tell you the precise degree of your connection to the other side. The best gauge is to be aware of how you *feel* in any given relationship. But while the characteristics defining core identity are typically concrete ("I am a psychologist and value authenticity"), those defining relational identity are much more abstract ("I feel like our relationship is withering away").

Though relational identity may seem a bit amorphous, it actually involves two concrete dimensions: affiliation and autonomy. Becoming aware of them and understanding how they function can help you to build cooperative relations in a conflict.

Affiliation: How Close or Distant Do You Feel to the Other?

Affiliation denotes your emotional connection with a person or group. Stable, constructive connections tend to produce positive emotions and a desire to cooperate, even in times of war. When I interviewed Lieutenant General H. R. McMaster, who at the time was a colonel in the Third Armored Cavalry Regiment in Tal Afar, Iraq, he reported that the most successful efforts to stabilize parts of Iraq were based largely on the ability of U.S. troops to build affiliation with the Iraqi people. He in fact had introduced a training program in which soldiers obtained desired information only after first sitting down with residents, drinking tea with them, and asking culturally respectful questions. These seemingly simple tokens

of affiliation had a great impact on the extent to which each side supported the other, shared information, and worked toward mutual security.

The flip side of affiliation is rejection. If the manager gathers your
peers for an important internal meeting but does not invite you—despite
your being an authority on the subject—you are likely to feel resentment.
You may wonder what you did to lose your position in the inner circle and
fear that everyone has turned against you. The pain of rejection is equally
acute outside the workplace. If all your relatives receive an invitation to a
family holiday party and you do not, you may feel emotional distress.

Neuroscientists have discovered that the anguish of social rejection
registers in the anterior cingulate cortex, the same part of the brain that
processes physical pain. Your brain responds to rejection much as it does
to a punch in the gut: Once hit, you resist cooperating, even if doing so
goes against your rational interests, and attempts to resolve your conflict
become far more difficult.

Autonomy: How Free Are You to Be Who You Want to Be?

"Autonomy" refers to your ability to exercise your will—to think, feel, do,
and be as you would like without undue imposition from others. I recently
witnessed a couple in a café get into a fight. "Calm down!" the husband
hissed. The wife glared back and snapped, "Don't tell *me* to calm down! *You*
calm down!" Whatever the original issue had been, this pair's conflict now
devolved into a battle over autonomy. Neither wanted to be told what to do.
The moment you feel someone stepping upon your autonomy, resentment
boils up—and you hanker to bite back.

The concept of autonomy helps explain why something even as basic as a
country's name can be grounds for serious international conflict. Tensions
erupted during the breakup of Yugoslavia when one of its six republics declared
itself an independent state under the name "Republic of Macedonia." This set
off a host of troubles with neighboring Greece, where a northern region of the
country had long been called Macedonia. This region is home to about three
million citizens who claim Macedonian ancestry and exclusive use of the
name "Macedonia."

As a Greek leader explained the conflict, "We feel our neighbors are usurping our cultural heritage by erecting statues in their main squares of Alexander the Great and the like. These are historic *Greek* icons. They are trying to steal our culture, our soul." For his part, a top leader from the neighboring republic argued, "We have the right to determine our own name and destiny. Isn't that the right of every state? We are not imposing upon Greeks. Just the opposite. Our culture celebrates all cultures. We are a community of communities. Mother Teresa lived here in Skopje, only one hundred feet from a church, mosque, and synagogue. We celebrate our diverse heritage."

Understood in terms of relational identity, one side is saying, "By erecting statues of Alexander the Great in your main squares and claiming the Macedonian name, you are challenging our autonomy!" The other side insists, "By demanding we change our name and celebration of diversity, you are infringing upon *our* autonomy!" Note that the core of the conflict is not substance alone but a struggle for *autonomy* over such factors as geographic boundaries, history, culture, and sovereignty.

Whether in the Macedonian name dispute or in everyday life, there are differences of opinion about how much autonomy is appropriate or to be expected, just as there are variations in how much affiliation is acceptable. The race car driver wants to drive one hundred miles per hour on local roads because he loves to feel the rush of speed; families who live in the area want slow and cautious driving. A girl wants to wear a headdress to school; administrators demand everyone wear a standard uniform. The very same laws, policies, and norms formulated to hold the fabric of society together can also tear it apart at the seams, generating what Freud called the discontent of civilization.

The Tribes Exercise again provides a case in point. Several years after my experience at Davos, I facilitated the exercise in Cairo, Egypt, for a group of business executives and political leaders. Six delegates sat in the center of the room to negotiate which tribe they should embrace, well aware that indecision would lead to world destruction. In the second of three rounds, a business executive named Mohammed said, "There's *no way* we are going to have time to listen to everyone's tribal beliefs and come to a consensual decision. Let's draw a tribe randomly from a hat and all join that tribe." Fadi, another business executive, nodded in agreement. Mohammed tore a sheet of paper into six pieces and wrote the name of each tribe on one of them, then put the slips into a coffee mug and drew one out. By chance, it was his tribe. He and Fadi felt satisfied and returned to their seats. They had saved the world . . . or so they thought.

I turned to the other negotiators, still sitting in the middle of the room, and asked, "Do you all agree to go with Mohammed's tribe?"

They shook their heads. "No!" said one.

"What do you mean, you do not accept my tribe?" Mohammed exclaimed. "This was a fair process!"

"You rigged the process!" shouted another delegate.

"No I didn't!" he yelled back, taking out the slips of paper and showing them to the group.

"It doesn't matter!" insisted a political leader. "Who gave *you* the right to decide the process?"

This group was now spiraling out of control, and for the remainder of rounds two and three they argued. But there was no debate about any of the tribes' belief systems, their core identities. Nor was there any discussion about what should serve as a good process for deciding how to save the world. What they argued over was whether Fadi and Mohammed had the right to impose the process. The group turned against these two men, whose unilateral decision infringed upon the other tribes' sense of autonomy to such an extent that they resisted agreement. The world exploded in Cairo.

The Bottom Line: Making One from Two

In a conflict, the core relational challenge is to figure out how to satisfy your desire to be simultaneously one *with* the other party (affiliation) and one *apart from* the other party (autonomy). Fundamentally, how can you coexist as both two ones and one set of two?

Both autonomy and affiliation are intrinsic to any relationship, and your ability to keep them in equilibrium is paramount to harmonious relations. Children, for example, try to fit into their families *and* find their own independent voices as they mature. A romantic couple tries to balance the desire to cultivate their relationship while preserving some "alone time." In a merger, senior management seeks to create a singular organizational corpus as individual departments struggle to maintain cultural and political autonomy.

Even more broadly, international organizations such as the United Nations work to advance a global ethos of peace and at the same time to respect the unique values of member states.

At a deeper level, the ability to *transcend* the tension of autonomy and affiliation represents life's central ethical challenge—a point that Confucius understood well. It is told that he conceived of heaven, earth, and humankind as parts of a singular universe, a Great Whole. He observed that as we live our lives, we have the opportunity to pass through deepening spheres of existence. The shallowest is to live in the natural world, governed only by instinct. Once we discover our ego, we realize we have the autonomy to enhance our place in the world; we can self-actualize. Eventually we come to perceive not only our own ego, but also the greater social order; we enter the moral sphere of existence and feel obliged to serve humanity. Finally, we realize that social order itself is but a part of the Great Whole, which transcends autonomy and affiliation in pursuit of the good of all.

In Sum

It is no wonder that Alice felt so confused in explaining who she was to the hookah-smoking caterpillar. Identity is a complicated matter. It is both fixed and fluid, psychological and sociological, conscious and unconscious. Just as Wonderland disoriented Alice's sense of self, an emotionally charged conflict can disrupt your own sense of identity. By better understanding how each side's core identity may be at stake, you can overcome the fixed-identity fallacy and uncover fundamental sources of discontent, as well as hidden wishes and fears. And by reshaping your relational identity as cooperative, you build closer ties of connection.

But even so, identity can prove more of a liability than an asset—unless you know how to guard against dynamic forces that can overwhelm it in a conflict. The remainder of this book presents a concrete method to tackle this challenge.

3

A Way Forward

Only those who attempt the absurd will achieve the impossible.
I think it's in my basement . . . let me go upstairs and check.

—M. C. ESCHER

Mindset matters. If you believe that a conflict is negotiable, you open yourself to opportunities for connecting with the other side and finding creative pathways to resolution. But threats to identity often elicit a divisive mindset that transforms disagreement from a workable problem into a seemingly insurmountable one. I call this mindset the Tribes Effect, and to avoid succumbing to it, this chapter alerts you to its main characteristics and the emotional forces that lure you toward it. By looking out for these dynamics, you can steer clear of them, embrace a cooperative state of mind, and bring about fundamental change without fundamentally changing.

Beware of the Tribes Effect

A threat to identity can elicit the Tribes Effect, an adversarial mindset that pits your identity against that of the other side: It is *me versus you, us versus them.* This mindset most likely evolved to help groups protect their bloodlines from outside threat. Today it can just as easily be activated in a two-person conflict, whether between siblings, spouses, or diplomats.

The Tribes Effect spurs you to make a blanket devaluation of the other's perspective simply because it is *theirs.* It is thus more than a fleeting fight-or-flight response. As a *mindset,* it can hold you hostage to polarized feelings for hours, days, or years; through learning, modeling, and storytelling, it can even be passed down through generations, relentlessly resistant to change.

The Tribes Effect aims to protect your identity from harm—but it tends to backfire. As you tighten your psychological borders and enter a self-protective state, your prospects for collaboration diminish. Fear drives you to prioritize short-term self-interest over long-term cooperation. As a result, if both you and the other side embrace this mindset, you create two self-reinforcing systems bound to clash ad infinitum. You collude in reinforcing the conflict you aim to resolve. This is the core paradox of the Tribes Effect.

How Do You Know When You Are in It?

The Tribes Effect is fundamentally an adversarial, self-righteous, closed mindset.

(1) **Adversarial.** The Tribes Effect causes us to view our relationship with the other side through an adversarial lens, magnifying differences between us and minimizing similarities. Even if we feel close to the other person, the Tribes Effect instigates a kind of relational amnesia, in which we forget all the good things about our relationship and recall only the bad. At Davos, for example, the leaders walked into our workshop as colleagues with innumerable commonalities, but quickly became adversaries and stuck to a divisive disposition. Philosopher Martin Buber describes this as a transformation from an "I-thou" to an "I-it" relationship. The other is no longer a fellow human but a savage *it*.

(2) **Self-righteous.** The Tribes Effect breeds the self-serving conviction that our perspective is not only right but also morally superior. Legitimacy stands on our side, and we prepare a rationale to defend it. Even when a warring group commits an act as violent as a massacre, "the butchers often have a clear conscience and are amazed to hear themselves described as criminals." Indeed, in the Tribes Exercise I often observe each group contemptuously blaming the others: "How could you choose your tribe over global survival?" Tribes rarely acknowledge their own critical role in bringing about the world's demise. Self-righteousness is easy to recognize in others, but less obvious in our own behavior.

(3) **Closed.** The Tribes Effect molds our identity into a fixed entity. In this closed system, we come to characterize ourselves and the other side as

immutable. Rather than listening to the other side to learn about their concerns, we critique their perspective and condemn their character. But we dare not criticize our own perspective, for we fear being disloyal to our own identity.

What Triggers the Tribes Effect?

When our identity feels threatened, we tend to react with a rigid set of behaviors that neuroscientists call a *threat response*. This response can be simple, such as instinctually retreating when we see a snake slither before us, or more complex, such as the Tribes Effect itself, which aims to protect not only our body, but our mind and spirit.

The Tribes Effect triggers when a *meaningful* aspect of our identity feels threatened. This means that even a seemingly small disagreement can elicit a strong emotional reaction, a dynamic that Freud termed the *narcissism of minor differences*. The more alike we are—whether siblings, neighbors, or religious brethren—the more we will compare ourselves with one another and feel threatened by minor differences. At Davos, for example, delegates argued over whether "humanitarianism" or "compassion" represented a more important core value. While an outsider might perceive this distinction as insubstantial, insiders viewed it as an existential threat. Backing down to another tribe would have deflated their own tribe's significance.

This same dynamic leads marital couples to fume chronically over "trivial" differences, just as it leads brother to turn his back on brother during civil war. Humanity's infinite commonalities pale in comparison to a singular difference that takes on outsized importance. In short, the trivial can become more than a matter of trivial concern.

While a *threat* to identity triggers the Tribes Effect, *respect* of identity produces harmonious relations. We feel the freedom to be who we want to be and enjoy our emotional connection with others. But when our sense of autonomy and affiliation feels endangered, protective emotional forces swoop in, and self-protection trumps collaboration.

Counteract the Five Lures of Your Tribal Mind

Overcoming the Tribes Effect requires a strategy much like that adopted by the Greek hero Odysseus. As he navigated his ship home after ten long years of fighting in the Trojan War, he met the goddess Circe, who warned him of a danger he would face on his journey: beautiful Sirens with enchanting voices who bewitched sailors, compelling them to steer toward the Sirens' island, where their ships would crash against the shoreline's sharp rocks and leave "heaps of bodies." Before he set sail, Odysseus ordered his crew to put wax in their ears and tie him to the mast. If he begged to be released, they were to refuse his orders and bind him even tighter. With this plan in place, Odysseus and his men sailed safely past the Sirens.

The Tribes Effect, like the Sirens, draws you toward it. The more deeply you are enveloped in its emotional folds, the more difficult it becomes to resist its pull. In an emotionally charged conflict, this attraction originates in a powerful set of emotional dynamics, which I call the Five Lures of the Tribal Mind. The chart below provides an overview of them.

The Five Lures of the Tribal Mind

1. **Vertigo** is a warped state of consciousness in which a relationship consumes your emotional energies.

2. **Repetition compulsion** is a self-defeating pattern of behavior you feel driven to repeat.

3. **Taboos** are social prohibitions that hinder cooperative relations.

4. **Assault on the sacred** is an attack on the most meaningful pillars of your identity.

5. **Identity politics** is the manipulation of your identity for another's political benefit.

The lures are *emotional forces* that shape your relations as adversarial, drawing you toward the Tribes Effect or pulling you deeper into it. They saturate your consciousness with self-righteous feelings, banish distressing sentiments to the unconscious, and promote oppositional behavior. They also tend to affect your relations at different points in the course of a conflict. Some, such as identity politics, frequently incite conflict; others, such as taboos, appear during the conflict itself; still others, such as vertigo, arise as a psychological consequence of conflict.

Though the lures aim to shelter your identity from the perils of blame, change, and exploitation, their impact is typically counterproductive. Like the Tribes Effect itself, they reinforce a self-protective mindset that diminishes the prospects for collaboration. The chart on this page depicts these dynamics through what I call the Relational Matrix. It illustrates how the Five Lures pull

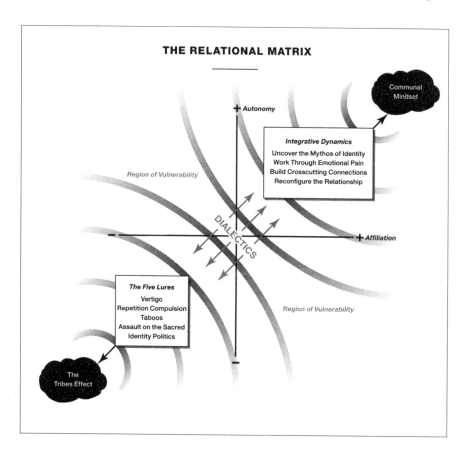

THE RELATIONAL MATRIX

Autonomy

Integrative Dynamics
Uncover the Mythos of Identity
Work Through Emotional Pain
Build Crosscutting Connections
Reconfigure the Relationship

Communal Mindset

Region of Vulnerability

DIALECTICS

Affiliation

The Five Lures
Vertigo
Repetition Compulsion
Taboos
Assault on the Sacred
Identity Politics

Region of Vulnerability

The Tribes Effect

you toward the Tribes Effect while another set of forces—integrative dynamics—pull you toward a more productive mindset. Unless you steer carefully past the lures, they will draw you toward the Tribes Effect, leaving you to the same fate as the sailors who could not resist the song of the Sirens.

In Sum

I recently rewatched *Star Wars* with my kids and found myself captivated by a key theme of the movie—one that speaks directly to the issues at play in emotionally charged conflicts. Jedi master Obi-Wan Kenobi describes the "Force" as an energy field created by all living things that binds the galaxy together. The Force has a dark side, which feeds upon hatred, anger, and fear, and a light side, fueled by compassion. These two energies are in constant tension, forever drawing citizens of the galaxy toward them.

When your own identity feels threatened, you have a choice in how to respond. The Tribes Effect tempts you toward the dark side, polarizing relations in a divisive dynamic, whereas a communal mindset draws you toward the light side, seeking to bring you closer through integrative dynamics. In the next section of the book we will examine how to counter the Five Lures of the Tribal Mind, the dynamics that draw you toward the dark side of conflict. Although the lures often operate outside your conscious awareness, you can free yourself from their power over you. Chapters 4 through 8 show you how to achieve this, and subsequent chapters provide advice to help you proactively foster integrative dynamics that lead you toward the light.

The Five Lures of the Tribal Mind

4

Vertigo

During my first year in college, an eccentric English professor shared an argument he had experienced with his wife at the mall over the purchase of an expensive floral bedspread.

"It would fit perfectly in our bedroom!" his wife exclaimed.

"We already have a bedspread," the professor said.

"Have you seen how ragged that thing is?" she asked.

"I sleep with it every night. It's fine!"

"Ugh!" she replied. "Does *everything* have to be a battle with you?"

"Here we go again," he sighed. "Every time we get into a fight, it's *my* fault."

"All I want to do is buy a bedspread!" she complained. "Can't you support me for once?"

The professor wondered, *Why does she have to be so controlling?* He looked his wife in the eye and said coolly, "I can't imagine a purchase in the world *worse* than this bedspread!"

With that, the situation escalated dramatically. "I don't know why I ever married you in the first place!" she fired back.

Just as the professor was about to storm off, he noticed a crowd of onlookers watching their argument. Embarrassed, he glanced at his watch and had another surprise: Twenty minutes had passed, when he thought that the argument had lasted for no more than a few. He told his wife the time, and their anger turned to concern: They were now late to meet friends for lunch. They hurried to the restaurant, shaking their heads in bewilderment: How had debating the merits of a floral bedspread turned into a public screaming match?

The Disorienting World of Vertigo

The psychological force drawing the professor and his wife toward the Tribes Effect is something I call vertigo: *a warped state of consciousness in which a relationship consumes your emotional energies.* As the couple slipped into vertigo, a hypnosislike state overcame them; each fixated on the other's angry words, determined not to resolve the argument but to win it.

The word "vertigo" derives from the Latin *vertere,* meaning "to turn." You may know the term from Alfred Hitchcock's film *Vertigo,* which depicted it as dizziness brought on by a fear of heights. Modern medicine differentiates a variety of disorders in which people experience a spinning sensation. I have borrowed the term to describe the unique condition in which one feels trapped within a dizzying state of adversarial relations. The argument between the professor and his wife started benignly enough. But as egos were bruised, each spouse passed an emotional threshold and fell into the spiraling state of vertigo.

Picture vertigo as a tornado surrounding you and the other side. Its swirling walls prevent you from seeing anything beyond the boundaries of your conflicted relationship, just as the professor and his wife saw nothing beyond the frenzy of their squabble. Strong gusts of wind blow at you and the other side, heightening the intensity of your emotional experience and turning anger to rage, sadness to despair. Standing at the center of this tornado, you can see the sky above, a vivid image of your greatest fears for the future, while the uprooted ground beneath you reveals your painful past. This tornado can keep you trapped in the Tribes Effect for hours, days, or even generations.

In this chapter I explore vertigo's lure, why it can be so damaging, and how you can break free of it.

Obstacles

Several factors make it especially difficult to overcome vertigo:

1. Vertigo Afflicts You Outside Your Awareness

Vertigo is a particularly powerful force in that it can trick you into believing that it is not actually influencing your behavior. You become so caught up in its whirling emotions that you do not even notice that they are inciting you to fight. You continue to feel rational and levelheaded; it is the world around you that seems to be spinning out of control, not the world within you.

Under the influence of vertigo, a seemingly innocuous situation can easily turn into a much more intense one. A squabble about a bedspread devolves into one person asking himself, *Is my spouse going to control me like this forever?* as the other sifts through a catalog of past pains: *Must everything be a battle with you?*

Even if vertigo seems to abate, it can persist over time, varying in intensity, and after a while, you may stop noticing it altogether. Although it fades into the background, however, it can continue to subtly poison your relationships and cloud the emotional space between you and the other party.

2. Vertigo Diminishes Your Capacity to Self-Reflect

As a human being you have the ability not only to think and feel but also to *reflect* on those thoughts and feelings. Because vertigo consumes your emotional energies, it severely diminishes your capacity for self-reflection, forcing you to rely on habitual patterns of behavior and predetermined notions about the other side. Three striking consequences result.

You mindlessly reenact a conflict script. The professor's wife did not view the argument in the mall as an isolated incident—she saw it as yet another example of her husband's turning a simple conversation into a fight. As a result, she reflexively responded with a habitual reaction, restating the same frustrations she had expressed time and again.

It is all too easy to slip into a counterproductive conflict script. In training military officers in negotiation, I have found that they have a keen understanding of this tendency. One high-ranking army officer told me how, after confronting death on a daily basis during his nine-month tour in Iraq, he returned home and early one evening heard his parents arguing over which film to watch. Unable to believe that they were arguing over a movie, he stormed into the room, shouting, "Who the #$%& cares which movie we see?" and then stomped away. After fuming for five minutes, almost in a daze, he calmed down and apologized to his parents. He later realized that after living for such a long time side by side with death, engaging in combat and watching his comrades perish, he had grown so accustomed to a constant state of vertigo that his reaction to an even relatively innocuous conflict had become extreme. The conflict script had become so embedded in his mind that it now replayed with unwelcome ease.

You suffer diminished capacity for self-conscious emotions. Another unfortunate consequence of vertigo is that it reduces your ability to experience self-conscious emotions like guilt or shame. The soldier in the anecdote above, for example, did not experience such pangs when angrily confronting his parents. Self-conscious emotions typically result when there is a discrepancy between how you think others feel about you and how you *want* them to feel about you. Because the soldier relied on prescripted behavior, however, he was inattentive to the present moment and unable to monitor the morality of his behavior. Once vertigo receded, he was left asking himself, *What came over me? Am I* really *that type of person?*

You stereotype the other party. Not only does vertigo diminish your ability to reflect on your own behavior, but it also reduces your ability to see *others* clearly. Professors Susan Fiske and Steven Neuberg have found that everyone automatically engages in stereotyping: Whether you realize it or not, you categorize people based on age, gender, ethnicity, and other readily apparent factors. In a nonthreatening environment, you can reexamine these assumptions and determine how true they are likely to be, but when you are in a state of vertigo, you exert only minimal energy to evaluate the accuracy of your stereotypic perceptions.

As the professor and his wife argued, they came to view each other as oversimplified caricatures. She was the profligate, controlling wife; he, the combative, cheap husband. They ignored all their years of accumulated knowledge about each other's quirks, habits, values, wishes, and fears—

indeed, they overlooked the very love they shared. And rather than seeking to discover each other's *rational* intentions, they sought to confirm the other's *irrationality* by any means necessary, even if it meant shouting in a crowded department store. Stereotyping reinforced their self-righteous perspectives.

The term "stereotype" derives from the Greek words *stereos*, or "rigid," and *tupos*, or "impression." A stereotype reduces the grand symphony of a person's character to a single note. If you cling to a negative impression of the other side—if you reduce a person to a one-dimensional picture, refusing to appreciate his or her nuances or to question your own assumptions—you consign yourself to the swirl of vertigo.

Stereotyping has been explored in further research by Fiske and Neuberg, who have shown that after you categorize someone, you look for confirmatory evidence to support your view and disregard any inconsistent information that would challenge it. The professor's wife searched through her data bank of memories for an example of her husband's cheapness, identified a few solid examples, and used them to confirm her judgment. Meanwhile, the professor employed the same mental process to find evidence of his wife's overspending. The countless occasions on which the professor was *not* cheap and his wife did *not* overspend went ignored; because these examples did not support the rigid view to which each party had committed, they were dismissed automatically.

3. Vertigo Constricts Your Perception of Time and Space

In a very literal sense, vertigo warps your sense of time and place. Your focus narrows to exclude all else but the situation immediately before you—without your realizing that this is happening. The professor and his wife were so consumed by their conflict that they failed to notice either the onlookers who had gathered or the lengthy passage of time. Vertigo affects your state of consciousness to such an extent that while your world spins upside down, you still believe you are right side up.

Time warps. Vertigo has a dual impact on your sense of time, similar to the experience of a first-time skydiver. As she jumps out of the plane, time dilates in the thrill of the moment. At first, seconds pass very slowly, and she notices every sound and image. But as she keeps falling, she acclimates to the sensation. She still feels frightened, but her consciousness shifts from a state of hypervigilance to a trancelike state of thrill. Time constricts: She now feels it passing faster than her watch suggests. When she reaches the ground, she wonders, *Is it over already?*

In the course of vertigo, the initial threat of conflict slows your sense of time, and you become highly attentive to the other side's every word, action, and feeling. But as you adjust to vertigo, your sense of time speeds up so that hours feel like minutes. In this trancelike state of mind, you are effectively operating on autopilot and begin to draw on old conflict scripts to guide your behavior. In the language of William James, your sense of consciousness (the *I*) steers your experience while your core identity (the *me*) huddles in the background replaying these scripts. Once you break free of vertigo by actions such as finalizing a divorce, reconciling with a colleague, or reconnecting with a relative, it can feel surprising to discover just how much time has passed.

Space warps. When you are in a state of vertigo, the emotional space between you and the other party feels constricted, condensed. The professor and his wife filled the emotional space between them with anger, despair, and loneliness, adding more and more grievances to the point that they could no longer bear it. The unfortunate result? The wife's stinging assertion that she could no longer recall why she married her husband.

Because vertigo is a state of mind, onlookers will view such behavior as irrational; they are unable to appreciate the strength of the emotions that are consuming the opposing sides. I have worked in war zones and regularly hear people who do not live in such conflicted regions ask, "Why can't they just get along?" But those in the grip of vertigo are simply unaware that they are in the thick of such powerful emotions. This is the paradox of vertigo: It affects your perception of time and space without your realizing it.

If you become involved in an emotionally charged conflict between other people, *you* are likely to unconsciously absorb some of *their* emotions. You enter the emotional swirl of their tornadolike vertigo. Think of the emotional burden children suffer growing up in a home with constantly fighting parents. Or envision the challenge that mediators face in trying to keep calm as disputants hurl insults at each other. Even at the international level it is easy to absorb the emotions of vertigo. In the 1990s during the war in Yugoslavia, I worked with Serbian, Croatian, and Bosnian refugees in a town on the outskirts of Serbia and rapidly became accustomed to the vertigo-driven tension in the region. When I called my mother, who had been in the United States regularly watching news reports about the fighting, she expressed concern for my safety. "Stop worrying, Mom," I assured her. "Everything's fine." I indeed believed that was the case, but I did not realize I was effectively a fish in water until after my work was completed. Traveling by train from Serbia to Budapest, I felt a weight lifting from my shoulders and an easing in my chest and arms as the train crossed the border. My muscles relaxed, and I entered an odd state of calm. I recognized that while in Serbia, I had been in a region gripped by vertigo, and I was unaware how much I had been affected by it until I left.

4. Vertigo Fixates You on the Negative

Perhaps the greatest challenge vertigo presents is that it binds your attention to *negative memories*, recollections that provide you with "evidence" that you are right and good while the other side is wrong and bad. Overcoming vertigo means overcoming this fixation. It can be an extraordinarily challenging proposition, however, because vertigo amplifies negative memories of the past *and* future.

Past pain haunts you. During Northern Ireland's bloody conflict, a pilot once joked to passengers upon landing in that country: "Welcome to Belfast. Please turn your watch back three hundred years." As he understood, the region's struggle was the result of long-standing grievances that endured into the present. The wounds of the nation were still felt with an intensity that time had done nothing to diminish.

Professor Vamık Volkan of the University of Virginia has developed a compelling theory about this phenomenon, observing that many groups define their current identity in part through a "chosen trauma"—a painful, unresolved injury from the past. Think of the importance of the Holocaust to Jews; Nakba, the forced exodus, to Palestinians; European colonization to Africans; or Jesus' crucifixion to Christians.

If a traumatized group does not sufficiently work through its feelings of shame, humiliation, and helplessness, the emotional pain can be passed down for many years. Volkan calls this the *transgenerational transmission of trauma*. Feelings and thoughts from the past become linked to the present through a *time collapse*, leaving the group feeling victimized *now* for what happened *then*, in the distant past. As scholar Michael Ignatieff writes, "Reporters in the Balkan wars often observed that when they were told atrocity stories, they were occasionally uncertain whether these stories had occurred yesterday or in 1941, 1841, or 1441."

Vertigo is often the source of this projection of past trauma upon the present. When it takes hold of an entire group, it awakens dormant traumas and deeply entrenched pain, which makes reconciliation extremely difficult. Even in an interpersonal conflict, vertigo can stimulate a time collapse and complicate resolution. At the mall, the professor's wife summoned past grievances into present circumstances, fueling resentment over slights that dated back decades.

Memories of a feared future consume you. How can you have memories of the future? Aren't memories an artifact of past experience? Not always. In an emotionally charged conflict, you tend to imagine worst-case scenarios about what the other side might do to you in the future, such as to humiliate or attack you. If such an imagined scenario possesses sufficient emotional charge, it can imprint in your memory, until over time you may forget that it is something you invented. Consequently, your brain houses a freestanding memory as a frightening eventuality, and you experience the remembered narrative as though it actually occurred. Your feared future becomes a de facto past, and this "reality" pulls you toward the Tribes Effect. Now you have "proof" that the other side cannot be trusted.

Psychologically, a chosen trauma from the past is no different from a memory of a feared future; they have the same effect, because both involve incorporating an emotionally significant scenario into a current conflict. An ethnic group might conceivably go to war based upon a chosen trauma from five hundred years ago or one they fear will occur five hundred years from now. Strikingly, no member of the group actually experienced either event. But to them it is a story that evokes an emotional response powerful enough to motivate a call to arms.

Vertigo creates an echo chamber of negative sentiment. Because you immerse yourself in a closed system of noxious memories, trivial issues can magnify in importance. In the Tribes Exercise, for example, the world commonly explodes because a tribe feels excluded. When the planet's very survival is at stake, concerns about exclusion should not be such a significant matter. But within the distorted realm of vertigo, exclusion is a potent threat to the tribe's identity. The argument over the bedspread is equally trivial, but from the distorted vantage point of vertigo, the professor's identity felt battered, heightening the issue's resonance.

Breaking Free of Vertigo

If the essential problem of vertigo is that it narrows your range of thoughts, feelings, and actions, it follows that breaking free of it requires a strategy for expanding your state of consciousness. Doing so involves several steps, which are summarized in the chart that follows.

Obstacle	Strategy
1. Vertigo afflicts you outside your awareness.	1. Be aware of the symptoms of vertigo.
2. Vertigo diminishes your ability to self-reflect.	2. Jolt your relationship out of its trancelike state.
3. Vertigo constricts your perception of time and space.	3. Expand your field of vision.
4. Vertigo fixates you on negative memories.	4. Externalize the negative.

Step 1: Be Aware of the Symptoms of Vertigo

While in graduate school, a good friend and I drove from Boston to New York, talking on the way about everything from world peace to our kindergarten sweethearts. We became so engrossed in our conversation that, despite having precise directions, we missed our highway exit—and failed to realize we had done so for ten minutes. Vertigo operates in a similar manner. Because it diminishes your capacity to self-reflect, present reality slips out of conscious awareness. Regaining that awareness is critical and involves three stages:

First, learn to identify the symptoms of vertigo. Three stand out:

Are you consumed by the conflict? Take note if you find yourself thinking about the conflict more than virtually anything else in your life. You might be obsessing over the wrongs committed by the other party or be feeling hypersensitive to the other party's criticism of you.

Do you view the other as an adversary? Be alert to the danger of viewing the conflict as an emotional battle rather than a difference of opinions.

Are you fixated on the negative? Notice if the conflict triggers you to mull over painful events from the past or feared events in the future.

Second, stop. The moment you become aware that you are slipping into vertigo, take a breath. Then take another. Slow down. Wait until you regain perspective before continuing the discussion.

Third, name it. The simple act of naming vertigo can profoundly reduce its power over you. By giving it a label, you turn your abstract swirl of emotions into a discrete "it" to discuss and surmount, reactivating your capacity for self-reflection. When my wife and I recently got into an argument that threatened to lose its bearings, she said, "I feel like we're slipping into vertigo. Do we really want to spend the afternoon arguing?" Merely recognizing the onset of vertigo helped us resist its allure. We agreed to discuss the issue at hand for a few more minutes and, should we not reach a resolution, to take a break, which would keep us from getting lost in the muddled space between us.

Step 2: Jolt Your Relationship Out of Its Trancelike State

Sometimes the only thing that will break you out of a trancelike state of consciousness is a jolt—an abrupt shake-up that reorients your perception of your relationship with the other party. The following are some methods to achieve that.

Remember your purpose. Vertigo thrusts you into a frenzy of emotions, making it easy to get lost in defensive feelings rather than to address the concrete issues at the heart of the conflict. One powerful way to jolt the relationship is ask yourself, *What is my purpose in this conflict?* Is it to scoff at the other party or to figure out better ways to get along? As your discussion unfolds, emphasize shared aspirations. A divorcing couple, for example, might benefit from reminding themselves that their joint purpose is to ensure their child's physical, mental, and spiritual well-being.

Use the power of surprise. A second strategy to jolt your relationship is to draw on the power of surprise. Imagine what might have happened if, during that ugly scene in the mall, the professor had cast aside his conflict script and startled his wife out of her anger. Suppose, for example, that after she snapped that she was no longer even sure why they had ever gotten married, he had responded, "In my case, because I loved you. And I love you now. Should we go back and look at the bedspread?" His wife's anger might well have begun to deflate in response to his solicitude. Soon they would have felt their sense of perspective returning, along with their ability to think rationally and generously. They might even have laughed about the absurdity of it all: Was a bedspread really enough to tear them apart like this?

The well-placed jolt can be equally effective in international relations. Consider the famous visit of Egypt's President Sadat to Israel. Until 1977, no Arab leader had ever made an appearance in the Jewish state. Israel and Egypt had fought four wars, and Israel maintained control over the Sinai Peninsula, a region of Egypt it had captured in the 1967 conflict. Israelis felt little hope that peace could ever exist between the two nations. Then, in an act that surprised the world, President Sadat landed at Ben Gurion Airport and spent thirty-six hours in Israel, addressing the Knesset and meeting with key leaders. Sadat's visit jolted the Israeli public into seeing Egyptians not as adversaries but as partners, leading to a peace agreement between the two countries.

An unexpected apology may be the most powerful jolt of all. As the couple argued in the mall, the professor could have taken a deep breath, paused, and told his wife, "I've said a lot of mean things to you just now. I'm sorry. I spoke without thinking." That admission would have been likely to stop her in her tracks, surprised at this sudden turn of events. If she felt her husband's apology was a sincere expression of remorse, the space between them would have opened for constructive conversation.

Summon a legitimate authority. In a café near Harvard several years ago, I saw firsthand how tapping into the power of authority can snap one out of vertigo. I was sitting at a table enjoying a hot chocolate on a late-winter evening, hunched over my laptop while writing an article, when I noticed two of the servers pushing each other. At first I thought it was a jovial exchange, until one of the men took a swing at the other and they began trading blows. My heart raced as this typically peaceful place was transformed into a boxing ring.

How do I stop this? I thought. Step in and break it up? Alert the manager? Yell something inane, yet distracting? Years later I can still recall that my impulse, however bizarre, was to shout, "Look, it's Jerry Seinfeld walking into the café!" Seinfeld was television's most popular star at the time, and my intention was to jolt these combatants out of their vertigo. But I said nothing.

Meanwhile, the servers continued pounding each other in full view of us patrons. Not knowing what else to do, I finally yelled, "Stop!" and attempted to put myself between them. But the would-be raging bulls ignored me, swinging punches around me.

Moments later two police officers entered the café, and, as if by magic, both the servers froze. The mere sight of officers in uniform immediately reminded them of a thing or two about the law and the consequences that come from breaking it. They looked at the police officers with palpable fear, and that fear was more than enough to break them out of vertigo. The officers questioned the servers about the incident, and within three minutes the erstwhile opponents were shaking hands.

To escape vertigo, call in a mutually respected authority figure: a spiritual adviser, mediator, lawyer, therapist, or family head. Consider the case of middle-aged siblings who found themselves in conflict after their wealthy, widowed mother died, leaving behind an imprecise will. It was a recipe for tribal disaster: Who should get Mom's ring? The paintings in the dining room? Their childhood home? When these siblings met with a mediator, he saw that they were already deeply embroiled in a classic case of vertigo, so he invoked the only authority figure available: their mother. "If she were here," he asked them, "what would *she* want?" Their mother had cherished family cohesion, and once these siblings were made to remember that, they wanted to honor their mother's values. The mediator returned to that question frequently, pulling them out of vertigo every time it was on the brink of recurring.

Change the subject. A former head of state once shared with me his own secret for dealing with diplomatic crises: "Don't change people's minds. Change the subject." That is the fourth strategy to jolt your relationship out of vertigo.

Imagine the year is 1996, and you are a high-level U.S. official in the Middle East. Deadly violence erupts after Israelis open a tourist tunnel in the Old City in Jerusalem. Palestinians allege that the act undermines Arab control of the sacred Al-Aqsa Mosque and their claims to East Jerusalem as their future capital. What would you advise be done to prevent further acts of violence?

Ambassador Dennis Ross, then the State Department's director of Middle East affairs, faced this very situation. He saw signs of vertigo and realized that "things [were] spiraling out of control." The parties involved were reacting not only to present circumstances but also to chosen traumas and feared futures, which served to reinforce their labeling of each other as adversaries. As Ross noted, "We need something to give them the space to think, to step back," so he orchestrated a summit in the United States between Palestinian President Yasir Arafat and Israeli Prime Minister Benjamin Netanyahu. The meeting shifted attention away from retaliatory violence, directing it instead toward the possibility of mutual agreement. The vertigo afflicting both sides had been deftly subdued.

Step 3: Expand Your Field of Vision

Vertigo generates emotional claustrophobia; it clogs your relations with negative emotions that narrow your sense of space and time. In order to escape vertigo, you need to expand both of those senses.

Broaden Your Sense of Space

Consider revising your physical and psychological orientation to the other side to promote cooperative relations.

Alter your physical environment. The design of a negotiating room has a substantial impact on how matters progress within it. Negotiating in a sterile white office is a very different experience from conducting a discussion in a living room. Even in international relations, some key negotiations have taken place in the homes of global leaders, with kids running around; these humanizing factors have helped to keep vertigo at bay. Discussing issues in informal settings helps you feel unconstrained by the narrow confines of tribal loyalties. The smaller details of the environment are equally important. Are you and the other side sitting at opposite ends of the table or side by side, indicating that you are both facing the same problem?

I recall running one fascinating iteration of the Tribes Exercise for a set of international leaders, including global CEOs, security experts, and health authorities. After the six tribes defined their unique tribal attributes, they returned to the plenary room and took their seats in separate, condensed circles. As usual, the alien arrived and gave its ominous warning. But what happened next was unusual. One by one, a representative from each tribe walked to the front of the room and presented his or her tribe's values, turning the negotiation process into a competitive political campaign among six tribes, each vying for the "votes" of the other tribes. Vertigo quickly struck. The tribes could have jolted themselves out of vertigo by seating themselves in one big circle to negotiate their differences or by arranging a smaller seating area in which agents from each tribe could confer. Both arrangements would have helped to increase cooperation. But instead they chose this unusual structure, which, unsurprisingly, destined their world to explode.

Look at the conflict from a new vantage point. In vertigo, the issues at hand can take on such gravity that backing down from your position feels like a crushing defeat. You can counter this by examining your situation from a broader vantage point.

Imagine taking a spaceship to the moon, looking down at the Earth, and realizing just how small your conflict is in the grand scheme of things. Frank White, a colleague at Harvard, studied the psychology of astronauts and discovered that after they return to Earth, they share a profound cognitive shift in their view of human relations: To them, all the world's troubles seem secondary to the goal of embracing the Earth as a whole. He calls this expansive perspective the *overview effect*. Even if you never make it into space, you can still benefit from this exercise in perspective.

You also can change your vantage point in more modest ways. Imagine your conflict is a twelve-story building, and both parties are on the top floor. Up there the situation is intense, gut-wrenching, an emotional whirlwind. Now imagine telling the other party in your conflict to wait there on the twelfth floor for a few minutes. You enter the elevator. As you travel downward, floor by floor, you take a deep breath and feel the calm that arrives as you exhale. You begin to perceive the other party's feelings of vulnerability and can better appreciate your own. By the time you reach the ground floor, you more clearly understand each side's contribution to the conflict. Now press the button to return to the twelfth floor and finish your conversation.

Reorient Your Sense of Time

A final way to expand your field of vision is to broaden the way you approach time.

Slow down. Because vertigo causes a chain of reactive emotions, it may be helpful to slow the tempo of the conversation and just listen—not to register incoming attacks, but to detect underlying emotions. You might also slow communication: Wait a few hours before responding to the e-mail that angered you. Speak more slowly, reminding yourself to take a moment before responding. Or, if you are involved in an extended conversation, take breaks periodically to maintain some distance between the conflict and your emotions.

Fast-forward. In our mall example, the professor might have said to his wife, "Pretend it's ten years from now, and we're looking back on this fight about the bedspread. What advice do you think those older, wiser versions of ourselves would give us?"

I drew on this fast-forwarding technique several years ago when designing and co-facilitating a private negotiation workshop for Israeli and Palestinian negotiators. Rather than asking them to discuss ways to break their impasse—which would have quickly brought them into a state of vertigo—I challenged them to imagine what a peaceful state of coexistence between them would look like twenty years in the future, from an economic, social, and political perspective. That question transformed a potential battleground into a collaborative brainstorming session. Envisioning a specific future made that future more tangible than the abstract fears brought on by vertigo. That session planted the seeds for a major peace initiative.

Rewind. When my wife and I get into a conflict, vertigo regularly tempts us to turn a short-lived argument into a long-term fiasco. On those occasions, I get myself to remember our relationship at its happiest: the first time I flirted with her, the day we got married on Block Island, the feeling of laughing at the ridiculous jokes of our three boys. These memories open up space in my mind to decide whether I want to walk down the path toward vertigo—and I almost always choose not to.

I say "almost always" for two reasons: First, I am human, and sometimes the pull of vertigo is too strong for me to resist. Second, vertigo, when properly controlled, does sometimes have its merits. For example, you might think to yourself, *I'm in vertigo now, but it feels good to express myself.* However valuable that may be at a given moment, I recommend that you set a specific time limit at which to end it: *Let me look at my clock, and in ten minutes I'll propose that we take a break.* While such deliberateness of purpose may sound unnatural, it helps you establish an important mechanism to break through vertigo's hold on your sense of time.

Step 4: Externalize the Negative

You need a strategy to combat vertigo's obsessive focus on the negative—one that enables you to reveal distressing emotions without reveling in them. But how do you formulate one?

Name the Dynamic

Oscar Wilde once remarked that "man is least himself when he talks in his own person; give him a mask and he will tell the truth." In a conflict, talking directly about distressing emotions can feel combative, especially if you see your pain as a result of the other's words or behavior. You need a technique to allow you to talk about emotional obstacles without specifically talking about emotions—in other words, to help you have a direct conversation in an indirect fashion. You need to *externalize the negative*—that is, to use symbolic communication to discuss the emotional forces weighing down your relationship.

Rather than reacting to conflictual dynamics at play in a conversation and heading straight toward vertigo, you can identify those dynamics and strategize aloud about how best to deal with them. By objectifying your subjective experience, you give a name and concrete reality to the intangible forces driving your conflict.

A Case Study: Zachary and the Dark Side

As my youngest child, Liam, transitioned from infant to toddler, my middle child, then-six-year-old Zachary, struggled to find his place in the sibling hierarchy. He began to act out, directing a stream of aggression toward both his older and younger brothers. Rather than punish Zachary for expressing what I knew to be genuine emotional discontent, I attempted to help him externalize his emotional experience so he could better deal with it. One Saturday morning, I sat down with him on the couch.

"Mommy and I notice all the ways you are respectful of your brothers," I told him. "We also have noticed that in the past few days you've been pushing Noah and little Liam. It's not the typical Zachary we know. What should we call the feeling that makes you want to push your brothers? Is there a cartoon character you know that can describe the feeling? Or a color? Or something else?"

He thought awhile and then, having just read a book on *Star Wars*, he blurted, "The dark side!"

"Great!" I said. "And what should you do if you feel it starting to take control of you?"

"Take out a lightsaber . . . and fight it off!"

"Good idea. And how are you going to do that?"

He smiled, pretending to wave a lightsaber. "Like this!" he said with a grin, before running off to play outside with his brothers. I looked out the window to watch them, and only moments later I saw Zachary again push his younger brother.

I walked into the backyard and asked, "Zachary, what just happened?"

"Nothing," he said guiltily.

"Did you push Liam?"

"Yes," he admitted.

"Did the dark side get you?"

Referring to his emotions this way let me address the problem without making him feel attacked or chastised.

"Yes," he replied quietly.

"Will you try harder to fight against it?" I asked.

"Yes," he said with a shy smile.

Later that day Zachary ran over to me. "Daddy, guess what!" he said. "The dark side wanted me to push Liam, but I used my self-control!"

He was proud of himself, and I was proud of him. What could have been a punitive situation turned into a learning opportunity that ultimately benefited not only Zachary, but our entire family.

Externalizing the negative is a useful technique in a broad range of conflict situations. The process is fourfold: First, envision a typical scene from your conflict, such as Zachary's fight with his brothers. Second, recall the dominant feelings that pulled you toward adversarial relations. There is no need to pinpoint precise emotions—just recollect the general sentiment that swept over you. In Zachary's case, an aggressive impulse overcame him. Third, choose a metaphor to describe that feeling, as Zachary did with "the dark side." Finally, imagine that dynamic sitting on a chair nearby, and strategize your relationship with it. Consider what triggers it to appear, and decide how you are going to grapple with it. Zachary realized that his dark side emerged when his brothers excluded him, and he decided that he would use his self-control to resist it. His strategy worked. The dark side became a tangible force outside himself that he could now struggle with and ultimately defeat.

In Sum

Vertigo helps us understand why quarreling spouses end up in a screaming match and colleagues quickly turn against each other in a heated dispute. This emotional condition so dramatically impacts our psyche that even the most trivial issue can mushroom into a serious conflict. But by becoming aware of the symptoms of vertigo, you can guard against it. And should you find yourself in its hold, remember to jolt yourself back to a more collaborative mindset, and you will find dealing with an emotionally charged conflict to be infinitely easier.

Of course, your troubles are not over, for four other lures are equally vying for control of your tribal mind.

Repetition Compulsion

We are, all of us, creatures of the repetition compulsion.

—DANIEL SHAPIRO,
NEGOTIATING THE NONNEGOTIABLE

We are, all of us, creatures of the repetition compulsion.

—DANIEL SHAPIRO,
NEGOTIATING THE NONNEGOTIABLE

In the movie *Modern Times*, Charlie Chaplin shuffles into his broken-down shanty and, as he closes the front door, a plank swings down and wallops him on the head. The same scene repeats daily: Chaplin shuffles inside, shuts the door, and sustains a blow. Then, one bright day, Chaplin walks in and the plank stays put. He looks up, flustered, then reopens the door and slams it shut. The plank crashes down on him. *Now* he can go about his business.

Chaplin's experience illustrates one of the most powerful forces that drives people to conflict: the repetition compulsion. This force compels the reenactment of the same behavioral patterns time and again. The issues themselves may change—perhaps you disagree with your spouse over finances today and divisions of household chores tomorrow—but the underlying dynamic remains maddeningly static. At the international level, the repetition compulsion leads rival ethnopolitical groups to engage in a never-ending series of clashes as the world looks on and laments, "They'll never change."

Perhaps more disturbing, the repetition compulsion unconsciously spurs you to re-create the *conditions* that produce a recurring conflict. It effectively turns you into a self-saboteur, implanting in you an irresistible urge to reenact past pains and convincing you that, just like Chaplin, you need that plank to strike you on the head yet again.

But why are we prone to such behavior? And more important, how can we rid ourselves of this compulsion?

In this chapter, we'll explore both the nature of the repetition compulsion as it relates to conflict resolution—drawing on insights from psychoanalysis, neuroscience, cognitive-behavioral treatment, social cognition, ethology, and relational theory—and a four-step method designed to help you free yourself from it.

The Anatomy of the Repetition Compulsion

Repetition is a fundamental aspect of human life. You wake up at the same time each morning, eat the same types of food, and laugh at the same kinds of jokes. Some repetitive behaviors are helpful—but others, like the repetition compulsion, can do harm.

Sigmund Freud initially presumed that human beings are fundamentally driven by the *pleasure principle*, which leads them to seek pleasure while avoiding pain. This theory made sense—until Freud encountered a series of paradoxes. Why, he wondered, do some people repeatedly engage in relationships that result in "unpleasure"? Is it a mere accident that each of an individual's friends eventually betrays him? That his protégés all angrily abandon him? That his romantic relationships always begin with a bang but fizzle out at the three-month mark? Freud conceived of the repetition compulsion as a way of explaining this "demonic force" that is "more primitive, more elementary, more instinctual than the pleasure principle which it overrides."

I view the repetition compulsion as a *dysfunctional pattern of behavior that you feel driven to repeat.* It is a more complex form of a habit, which springs to life when a stimulus produces a desired response. (For example, you crave caffeine, so you mindlessly walk to a café and order a latte. The stimulus produces the response you wished for—and soon you develop a serious espresso habit.) The repetition compulsion goes deeper, luring you to repeat that which you would rather not. You unwittingly place yourself in a self-defeating situation, unconsciously repeating an age-old pattern of behavior while assuming that it is a product of present circumstance.

To break free of the repetition compulsion, it is important to first understand how it distorts your perceptions during a conflict.

First, you suffer an emotional wound. When your identity feels violated—whether by aggression, abuse, or a catastrophic change in circumstance—the experience leaves a painful emotional wound. Consider the experience of my friend Jen. When she was seven, her father left home and never returned. His abandonment affected her deeply and gave rise to a lasting emotional scar. When she was growing up, she would play outdoors with friends but look incessantly toward the top of the street, hoping to see her father's car approaching. It never came.

Second, you exile painful emotions to your unconscious. You lock those emotions in a cell within the back corridors of your mind, hoping never to see them again. When I first met Jen, she was thirty years old, but her father's abandonment remained the most painful event of her life. She had never sought therapy, however, and rarely discussed her childhood with friends, instead confining her sadness, shame, and rage within that chamber in her unconscious, pretending those emotions did not exist.

Third, you scan hypervigilantly for any stimuli that may produce a similar emotional wound. Though Jen repressed her emotions, they refused to stay sequestered in her unconscious. They pounded the walls, banged the ceiling, and shouted incessantly. Whenever she unconsciously detected a conflict situation in her life that was even modestly suggestive of abandonment, she drew on the only experience she knew. Despite evidence to the contrary, she held firm to the belief that her husband would eventually betray her, her boss would fire her, and her best friend would end their relationship. In situation after situation, Jen cast herself as a victim of desertion. The pain of her childhood wound regularly resurfaced, turning even unrelated conflicts into painfully familiar scenarios.

Fourth, you unconsciously attempt to alleviate your painful feelings. While the most effective way to address painful emotions is to unearth them and work through them head-on, facing them can be frightening. The repetition compulsion offers an alternative route—it attempts to help you master them without dealing directly with them.

But it has limited effectiveness, because it restricts your behavioral repertoire. On the one hand, the repetition compulsion may encourage you to unconsciously "act out" painful emotions, repeating the very conditions that hurt you initially in the hope that *this time* you will "master" your age-old trauma. Whenever Jen's husband traveled on a business trip, she felt deeply abandoned, and when he would return home, she would pick fights with uncharacteristic intensity, with the secret hope that *this time* she would be able to achieve command of her situation. But of course the more she yelled, the more distanced her husband felt, leaving her repeatedly promoting the very abandonment she so deeply feared.

On the other hand, you may avoid situations in which your repressed emotions will emerge. For example, Jen remained alert to any context in which someone might abandon her. When she believed she had identified such a prospect, she would take preemptive action, distancing herself before the other party could do the same to her. The result of her premature withdrawal was predictable: Her friends felt rejected—and abandoned her. Once again Jen recreated the very circumstances of abandonment she was attempting to master.

While the repetition compulsion can cause you ongoing grief due to its self-defeating nature, it is in some respects well intentioned and a necessary part of the healing process. It prompts you to wonder, *Do I really need to endure this pain again?* And ultimately it is that very question that will help you finally halt the repetition compulsion.

Possible Narrative to Employ	Anxiety				
	Jealousy				
	Abandonment	X	X	X	X
		Fight with Husband	Fight with Friends	Fight with Mother	Fight with Colleague
		Circumstance			

Barriers to Breaking Free

You may find yourself at the mercy of the repetition compulsion, struggling against a seemingly invincible foe. Several characteristics of the repetition compulsion make it seem nearly impossible to defeat.

1. The Repetition Compulsion Happens Automatically

Because the repetition compulsion operates outside awareness, you tend to replay the same old conflict—but are unaware you are doing so. Those with whom you interact, meanwhile, are replaying their own repetition compulsions. Together you create a cycle of discord founded as much on each of your independent fears as on objective fact.

After Jen got married, she and her husband, Mark, sought to address some concerns in their marriage. They argued over everything from the best time to eat dinner to how family finances should be managed. In one of their typical conflicts, Mark might open up a credit card statement, turn to Jen, and say, "We need to be more careful about finances." She would view this as an accusation, an invasion of her autonomy, and respond, "Agreed—and you can start by cutting down on all those technology toys that *you* buy!" Now Mark and Jen would both be angry, unwittingly slipping into a pattern they knew all too well.

2. The Repetition Compulsion Feels Education-Resistant

While awareness of *vertigo* helps you see past it, awareness that you are entangled in the *repetition compulsion* does little to help you break free of it. Jen and Mark were well aware of their tendency to fall into recurring two-hour fights, but even acknowledging this directly did nothing to discourage their repeating them. When Jen sensed an impending battle, she would sometimes plead for them to change course.

"Wait!" she would say. "This is spinning out of control. Do you really want to dive back into our typical fight?"

Mark's eyes would narrow: "Why are you putting the blame on *me?*"

"I'm just trying to help us, Mark!" Jen would insist. *"You're* the one who started it!"

"What do you mean *I* started it?"

The compelling lure of the repetition compulsion outweighed both spouses' knowledge of its futility. They were well aware that they were in its clutches, but felt helpless to overcome it.

3. The Repetition Compulsion Takes Control of Your Feelings

The repetition compulsion pulls you away from the emotional realities of your present conflict, instead causing you to reenact a past pattern of behavior *with the complete conviction that your present conflict is determined only by present circumstances.* You no longer differentiate past memories from present reality, resulting in a broken "feeling system" that cannot maintain full emotional presence. While you do feel present in the moment, you are in fact living out the past.

The moment your identity feels threatened, your anxiety rises—and the repetition compulsion steps in to reduce that unease. It acts as a puppeteer, controlling your emotional experience and rendering you effectively passive. You experience feelings as things that happen to you, entities beyond your control, as though you were "drawn to some fatal flame." This was certainly true for Jen and Mark, who tried several times to talk things out calmly, to listen to each other and problem solve rather than succumb to their usual hostility. But even when they did succeed in resolving a conflict amicably, they admitted to feeling a nagging craving to return to their old ways, as though they had unfinished emotional business to complete. The repetition compulsion beckoned them to revert to their familiar patterns.

4. The Repetition Compulsion Feels Ingrained

One of the biggest misconceptions regarding the repetition compulsion is that such self-defeating reactions can simply be "unlearned." The problem is that this behavior feels ingrained, part and parcel of what makes you

you. How can you unlearn that which in part defines you? When Mark tried in good faith to help Jen let go of her fears of abandonment, she snapped back, "I am who I am—and am not going to change! Why can't you just accept me for who I am?".

Breaking Free

If you cannot unlearn the repetition compulsion, are you destined to repeat it forever? No. To regain control of your emotional fate, you can adopt a four-step strategy that addresses each of the repetition compulsion's key difficulties.

Strategy for Breaking the Repetition Compulsion

1. Catch the repetition compulsion at the earliest possible moment.
2. Resist the pull to repeat the same patterns.
3. Reclaim power over your feelings.
4. Add a new routine to your repertoire.

---

1. Catch the Repetition Compulsion at the Earliest Possible Moment: The TCI Method

Just as the police are better able to catch a bank robber if they have a mug shot, you will be more effective at halting the repetition compulsion with a picture of your typical pattern of conflict.

Start by identifying a relationship that repeatedly comes under strain from conflict. Do you bicker time and again with your spouse, your kids, or a colleague? Conflict is inevitable—you can expect to have differences with other people—so look specifically for patterns of recurrent mayhem, situations in which you repeatedly avoid, confront, accuse, blame, or otherwise sabotage straightforward resolution. If you keep finding yourself having the same sort of disagreements with the same unsatisfying results, the repetition compulsion is likely at play.

Once you identify this recurring conflict, map out the key pattern that you tend to repeat, including the trigger, cycle of discord, and impact ("the TCI method"). Awareness of this pattern empowers you to stop its repetition. The chart on page 59 provides a guide to get you started.

(a) Trigger

To determine your conflict's trigger, ask yourself what particular behaviors or events instigated the tension. Were you not invited to a family member's wedding? Did your business partner back out of an agreement? Was your political organization excluded from a regional economic conference? Conflict is often seen as the confluence of great forces, but even a small bout can serve as a potent trigger. In Mark and Jen's case, their toughest disagreements tended to occur when Mark returned from a business trip, having left Jen home alone for days and feeling deeply abandoned.

(b) Cycle of discord

A trigger throws you into what I call the cycle of discord, which causes you to reenact a counterproductive pattern of conflict. Examine that pattern: Who confronts whom? Why? Who first attempts to resolve the conflict? When? How does the conflict end? Your cycle of discord tends to stay the same; the way you fight with your spouse or boss is unlikely to change from day to day. That means it is predictable, and because it is predictable, you can learn to recognize it. If you learn to recognize it, you can work to change it.

The cycle of discord functions like a volatile chemical chain: One action begets another, and another, and so on, leading to an explosive outcome. But because this chain follows a regular sequence, you can interpose a new action at any point and affect the entire cycle. Likewise, in a conflict, small shifts at any stage of the disagreement can mean the difference between a constructive dialogue and an explosive fight.

To map the cycle of discord, chart the gist of what typically happens after your conflict is triggered by asking three questions: (1) Who says or does what? (2) How does the other person respond? (3) Why? Keep asking these questions until you get a full picture of the cycle of discord. You might even try to observe the cycle while in the throes of it, noticing your unfolding pattern of behaviors and feelings; immediately afterward, record what you discovered.

After you map your cycle of discord, name it. As with vertigo, giving the dynamic a label enables you to externalize and confront it. Mark and Jen named theirs the "Trip Fit," a nod to the typical trigger of their conflict: Mark returning from a business trip.

(c) Impact

To understand the impact of your conflict, examine its effect on your relationship and on your ability to get things done. You might be surprised by the toll the conflict takes on your life.

A few years ago, I consulted for a regional company at which productivity had suffered a recent decline. In interviewing executives across the organization, a theme emerged: Conflict regularly arose because employees felt hypercriticized, devalued, and subservient. The cost of this toxic culture to the firm was tremendous: Executives sought jobs elsewhere, worked halfheartedly, and felt unenthusiastic about coming to the office. Upon being briefed on these findings, company leadership initiated an organization-wide negotiation training to improve camaraderie and empower employees at all levels. The results were striking. An intensive multiyear program positively transformed the corporate culture, improved the way employees dealt with conflict, and boosted the bottom line. None of this would have happened if not for the initial evaluation documenting the detrimental impact of conflict on the company.

Keep Your Map in Mind

Now that you have a map of your repetition compulsion, be diligent in using it, staying conscious of your triggers, cycle of discord, and typical consequences. One simple tool to help you do so is to become sensitized to what neuroscientist Antonio Damasio calls "somatic markers"—the waves of unease that occur when a given situation is perceived to be similar to a previous threatening one. Monitor these feelings—they are your body's way of informing you of potential danger. That discomfort you sense may be a hint that you are on the cusp of reenacting the repetition compulsion.

2. Resist the Pull to Repeat the Same Patterns

The repetition compulsion's driving force is what I call the *lure of the compulsion,* the core urge pulling you to repeat your pattern of behavior. To

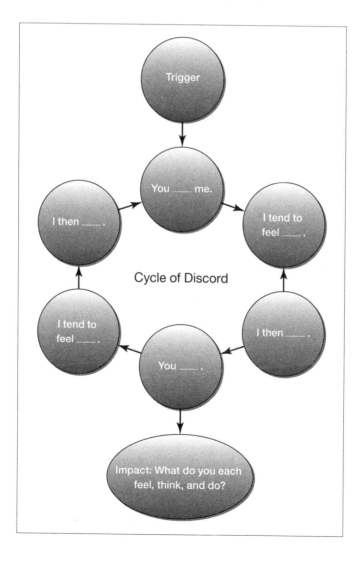

Trigger

You ___ me.

I then ___.

I tend to feel ___.

Cycle of Discord

I tend to feel ___.

I then ___.

You ___.

Impact: What do you each feel, think, and do?

break free of the repetition compulsion, you need to be aware of the lure of the compulsion and acknowledge its power—without giving in to it.

Look for the Lure of the Compulsion

The cycle of discord typically commences when you feel mistreated with respect to a deeply sensitive personal issue, such as rejection, abandonment, helplessness, or emasculation. These issues are "deep" because they extend beyond the particular surface concerns of the conflict in question. Whether the issue at hand is borders or budgets, even the smallest slight can trigger a big reaction.

To discover the lure of the compulsion, notice a dysfunctional behavior you repeatedly reenact in a conflict—excessive anger, fear, avoidance—and try to understand the underlying reasons for your reaction. Professor Paul Russell likens this process to learning how to ski. Imagine heading down a steep hill and stumbling at the same spot each time. Your instructor pelts you with questions in an effort to solve the problem: "You keep leaning on your right ankle—was your left ever injured? Is there something about that spot that makes you anxious?" Russell suggests that while your struggle may at first seem arbitrary, at some point it "ceases to be simply a lingering pocket of difficulty and becomes a systematic dysfunction pointing to trauma. Sooner or later, if the individual wants to ski, or live life, the hill forces the issue."

Ask yourself the same sort of questions that the skiing instructor poses. Do you enact a recurrently dysfunctional pattern in your conflicts—failing to listen, avoiding connection, or sabotaging cooperation? At the moment when this pattern occurs, is something threatening your identity? Are you frightened of something specific? Pay close attention to issues that give rise to strong emotions, which suggest the lure of the compulsion may be close at hand. Consult the chart on page 61 for common issues that consume attention during conflict.

Be particularly alert for hidden issues that may be difficult to acknowledge. Mark, for example, realized that in his fights with Jen he often felt emasculated. Jen was tough and decisive, making him feel weak and small, which led to his compensating by shouting forcefully, out of character, to demonstrate his "masculinity." Afterward, he analyzed his behavior objectively and came to understand that the real purpose of his behavior was to avoid the shame of feeling weak.

Acknowledge the Lure of the Compulsion—Without Succumbing to It

Once you identify a deeply sensitive issue compelling you toward conflict, imagine that issue sitting on the table in front of you. Accept it as something real, a tangible object. When you recognize it in a subsequent conflict, allow yourself to feel its full emotional force pulling you. Instead of succumbing to it, though, observe the emotions it is stimulating within you—whether anxiety, fear, anger, or shame. Your emotions are exactly that: just emotions. You have power to respond to them however you like.

Mark learned this firsthand. When arguing with Jen, he felt the urge to be tough and yell like a "real man." He examined his feelings of shame, embarrassment, and resentment, witnessed them with compassion, and accepted their power. He was surprised at how strong the lure of the compulsion really was, but rather than reacting with aggression, he evaluated this inner experience without judgment and gained control over it. He did not succumb.

The Lure of the Compulsion

Do You Repeatedly Fear Being . . .

• Abandoned	• Insignificant
• Alienated	• Patronized
• Dependent	• Powerless
• Emasculated	• Rejected
• Empty	• Subordinate
• Enmeshed	• Used
• Helpless	• Weak
• Inferior	• Worthless

The lure of the compulsion is a deeply sensitive issue that repeatedly permeates your conflict.

3. Reclaim Power over Your Feelings

To respond authentically to current circumstances rather than deploying a pre-established script, you need to clarify the emotional contours of your conflict, sideline feelings unrelated to the issue at hand, and work to heal old wounds.

Clarify the Emotional Contours of Your Current Conflict

While some of your emotions will undoubtedly be stirred by the circumstances of your current conflict, others will likely be a product of the repetition compulsion. To detect the latter, ask yourself three powerful questions:

1. *Are these issues mine, or are they yours?* Distinguish the ones that drive each of you to conflict.

2. *Is this now, or is this then?* Attune to past wounds affecting your present experience.

3. *Did I do this, or did you?* Notice what you each contributed to the conflict—and whether any blame may be misplaced.

Sideline Extraneous Feelings

Once you clarify the contours of your current conflict, separate extraneous feelings—those based on past pain. Imagine your conflict as a soccer game, and allow only two teams onto the field: you and the other side. If players from your past reappear—rejection, abandonment, inferiority—send them back to the bench. They are not part of your current conflict. They can watch the game, but they cannot participate.

Should these emotions persist, confront them directly: *You are not part of this conflict! I know you are worried that I may be rejected again, and I appreciate your concern. But right now you're on the bench.* Remain resolute. Then, after your conflict is resolved, decide whether or not to delve into the extraneous feelings.

Jen acknowledged her tendency to feel abandoned when Mark traveled and vowed to get control over her fear of abandonment. Every time Mark came home from a trip, she and Mark knew that they had to work hard to avoid launching back into a cycle of discord. Jen took ownership of her emotions, separating past pain (her father's abandonment) from her sense of loss during her husband's business trips. She admitted feeling the lure of the compulsion pulling her to react angrily to Mark's weeklong "abandonment" of her and their kids. But rather than acting out, she addressed her anger directly and simply: *Mark's trip helps to support our family,* she told herself. *It's different from my father leaving.* With time, patience, and a lot of work, her repetition compulsion faded.

Work Through Emotional Wounds

Jen had figured out an effective way to manage her emotional wound: She became aware of her feelings of abandonment and set them aside in her conflicts with Mark, thereby breaking the hold of the repetition compulsion. But the pain of the wound itself endured, as she still held deep resentment toward her father. To conquer that pain and fully reclaim power over her emotions, she needed to work through her emotional injury.

This process takes commitment and courage. It can be done with the support of a good friend or healing professional, or even through such creative activities as writing in a diary, painting, or playing music. If you feel ready to delve into your pain in an effort toward releasing it, here are a few basic steps that will offer a useful place to start.

First, identify a deeply sensitive issue that repeatedly triggers strong emotions, such as fear of rejection, abandonment, or inferiority. Revisit the chart on page 61 to help you pinpoint a lure of the compulsion that regularly drives you to conflict.

Second, trace the origins of that issue. Where might your sensitivity to rejection or subordination have originated? Begin by thinking back to your childhood. When did you find yourself feeling that way? Of course, not all sensitivities develop in early life. If your ex-spouse was unfaithful, for example, you may find yourself consistently dealing with issues of loyalty in your close relationships. Emotionally sensitive issues can often take root at the group level as well. The Holocaust left an indelible mark of hypersensitivity on the Jewish experience of security.

Third, explore painful feelings that accompany the wound. For Jen, a host of painful emotions were connected with her fear of abandonment. She sat down with a trusted friend and engaged in the painful process of trying to understand and accept those emotions. Entering this emotional space felt scary to her. So she gave herself permission to enter that scary place and exit whenever she wanted. Next she sat with her fear of abandonment, named the dominant emotions that arose, and articulated the message that each emotion conveyed to her. She delved into her feelings of anger, self-doubt, and fear of intimacy, ultimately asking in an ashamed voice, "Am I worthy of love?" She had contained these dark emotions for more than two decades, but now she was reclaiming control over them.

Fourth, release the pain. This requires both a conscious decision and conscious effort. Once your pain has been "heard," you can let it go; it has said what it needs to say. Jen realized she could decide whether to hold on to the emotional burden of abandonment—and chose to release it. The process was emotionally wrenching but purifying.

Fifth, turn your wound into a source of strength. The scars of Jen's abandonment will remain with her forever, even though she has released the pain of her childhood memories. Rather than seeing herself as a victim of those circumstances, however, she has reframed her perspective, vowing to be a beacon of love to her own family and friends and to never abandon a friend or relative in need.

4. Add a New Routine to Your Repertoire

While you cannot unlearn self-defeating behaviors, are you destined to repeat them? No. Neuroscience tells us that you can add new routines to your repertoire. Imagine driving home from work along your habitual route. Though your brain draws on firmly established neural pathways, you can create new ones. The more often you drive a new route, the more you strengthen the neural pathways associated with that route. Soon the "new" route becomes your default. Similarly, in a conflict you can devise a new behavioral routine to supplant your old self-defeating one. Soon you will find that your newer, healthier route is the one to which you naturally gravitate.

While you cannot change the other's behavior, modifying your own routine can productively affect the relationship. To devise a new routine, recall your typical pattern of conflict, which you mapped out in the chart on page 59. Now conceive a constructive alternative to this behavioral repertoire, considering what steps you might take to do the following.

- **Preempt the trigger.** When you know what sets you off, you are better equipped to halt it. If you and your spouse frequently fight over finances, you might agree to discuss money matters only with a financial adviser present, or commit to uphold a monthly budget.
- **Replace a behavior in the cycle of discord.** Review your cycle of discord and choose one behavior to alter. For example, imagine a typical cycle of discord between you and a colleague over project plans. She criticizes you, you criticize her, she criticizes you again, and you withdraw. One alternative approach would involve you empathizing with her situation after her initial attack.
- **Replace the entire cycle of discord.** Envision a constructive cycle of dialogue to replace your current one. The two founding partners of a technology start-up company heeded this advice. As investments in their company increased, the intensity of their arguments escalated. Realizing that their deteriorating relations might jeopardize their company, they sat down and articulated an alternative process to deal with their differences. Rather than engage in a cycle of attack and counterattack, they agreed to share perspectives and search for common ground, an approach that proved much more effective for their company and their relationship.

Guard Against Relapse

The decision to change your fundamental patterns of behavior requires a reconceptualization of your identity—a task that can be extremely difficult. I remember watching my loving grandmother, whom I called Nan, struggle to quit smoking. As the years wore on, the habit took its toll. Even with an oxygen tank helping her to breathe and lung cancer spreading, she would still sneak an occasional cigarette. The habit cost her her life.

While addiction certainly was a contributing element to my grandmother's behavior, I believe identity was her core obstacle. She identified herself as a smoker—I saw her that way too—and she could not envision herself otherwise; it had been part of who she was for nearly fifty years.

Revise Your Self-Image

Breaking free of the repetition compulsion requires you to envision a new self-image and visualize yourself enacting it. You might even choose a role model and channel that person's qualities in your next conflict. What will it feel like to act as that person? What might you say if the other side offends you? What can you do to generate their goodwill? Rehearse your response in your mind again and again until it becomes second nature.

Devise a Plan to Guard Against Relapse

William James wrote, "Accumulate all the possible circumstances which shall reinforce the right motives; put yourself assiduously in conditions that encourage the new way; make engagements incompatible with the old; take a public pledge, if the case allows; in short, envelop your resolution with every aid you know." Perhaps the most powerful way to live up to James's exhortation is to enlist help in guarding against the repetition compulsion's return. Jen, for example, knew that while she was ultimately responsible for pulling herself out of its hold, the combined effort of Mark's assisting her in achieving that goal was ultimately more effective than Jen's attempting it alone.

Guard Against the Unguarded Moment

Before engaging with the other side, reflect on what they might say or do that could trigger you to repeat a destructive pattern of behavior. Then consider the most important question: What might you say or do to avoid the repetition compulsion?

When I mediate a heated dispute, I establish norms to prevent the disputants from returning to the repetition compulsion: "The goal of our session is to help you come to a better understanding of each other's perspectives and to explore ways to reconcile your differences. I recognize you are in a rut—and it's easy to fall back into your same old conflict dynamics. So our goal today is to have a different conversation, a more productive one in which you listen to learn rather than to defend." During the mediation, I listen carefully to ensure that each disputant treats the other with respect. If either party offends the other, I immediately interrupt to remind both parties of our norms—and redirect discussion toward constructive dialogue.

There are times, however, when you are likely to let down your guard and no mediator is there to rescue you. With a little bit of forethought, you often can anticipate these situations and make a plan to prevent them. For example, during vacations with extended family, my wife and I used to engage repeatedly in an emotionally draining pattern of conflict, in which we felt angry over some perceived offense, then felt embarrassed and ashamed that our relationship was not "perfect," at which point we would pretend our connection was fine, which merely exacerbated our tension. Once we realized this pattern, we made a plan to guard against it, agreeing to talk privately each evening to vent any frustrations and emotionally reconnect, in effect keeping the repetition compulsion at bay.

In Sum

The repetition compulsion is a pattern born of fear—the fear of opening a Pandora's box of emotions that are so painful, so difficult to bear, that they have effectively been locked away. But while the repetition compulsion allows you to temporarily delay reckoning with these raw feelings, it soon tempts you to relive them, to engage in the same destructive behaviors again and again. It affords you no room to feel anything other than the same familiar emotions or to respond with anything other than the same customary script. Fear numbs you, and the repetition compulsion compromises your ability to change.

But the situation is not hopeless.

Every fear is a wish in disguise. For all its destructiveness, the repetition compulsion carries a message of hope. It represents your desire to liberate yourself from past pain and provides you with the seeds of change. If you can reimagine the core desire driving you to repeat—the desire for connection instead of abandonment, love instead of indifference—you are on the path toward breaking the compulsion's spell forever.

$$\boxed{6}$$

Taboos

Think of something you feel you absolutely cannot express to a family member: a deep resentment, a long-standing grudge, a pang of envy. Now imagine the two of you embroiled in a conflict, with this unspeakable thing, nearly impossible to vocalize, at the very heart of your discord. How do you solve a conflict you cannot discuss?

Welcome to the challenge of the third Lure of the Tribal Mind: *taboos*. In this chapter we examine what they are, why they frustrate your efforts to resolve conflict, and how you can successfully navigate them. Taboos serve important social functions, but if you are not careful, they can lure you toward the Tribes Effect.

The Marrakesh Incident

During the World Economic Forum's regional summit in Marrakesh, Morocco, some years ago, I appeared on the BBC's *The World Debate* in an episode titled "Are the Right People Talking?" The episode was designed to educate its seventy million viewers about the Israeli-Palestinian conflict by featuring a debate between Israeli and Palestinian business and political leaders. I was asked to serve as a challenger to the issues raised.

The debate took place in a large outdoor tent, the audience composed of well over one hundred political leaders, CEOs, and directors of nongovernmental organizations. Onstage a blunt-speaking Bahraini businessman sat beside steely-eyed Mohammed Dahlan, former security minister for the Palestinian Authority. There was supposed to be an Israeli onstage as well, but a few days earlier the king of Morocco had refused to meet with Israel's president, and so the Israeli government boycotted the summit in reprisal. This put the BBC in a bind. It had publicized the debate as a fair and balanced representation of both sides' views, and now one side was unrepresented.

Fortunately, the network was able to enlist a former Israeli ambassador to the United Nations to appear via satellite from Jerusalem. The room hushed as the show began.

"Welcome to Marrakesh!" said the host, Nik Gowing. "Can face-to-face meetings between the main leaders in the Middle East ever achieve lasting security and peace right across the region and beyond? The momentum for high-level negotiations seems to be faltering. Gloom and distrust between the two parties seem to be growing again. So peace in the Middle East: Are the right people talking?"

The audience applauded.

Gowing walked toward the side of the stage, where I was seated. "I'm joined here by Professor Daniel Shapiro," he said by way of introduction and then asked me, "You analyze why negotiations work and why they fail. You provide advice to groups and governments around the world. Dan Shapiro, what kinds of people or personalities offer the chances for negotiations to succeed?"

I argued for the importance of negotiation and the need for opposing parties to listen to each other's concerns, then took a deep breath, relieved. I had hit the key points I wanted to make.

Then Gowing approached Dahlan, asking him, "So are the right people talking?"

When Dahlan began to respond in Arabic, Gowing interrupted him and said, "Could you please speak in English?"

"No," Dahlan replied.

"I thought we had agreed that you would speak in English," Gowing said, clearly frustrated.

"No," answered Dahlan, with equal frustration. "We didn't."

Gowing fiddled with his earpiece, apparently receiving a message from the producer, confirming, I assumed, that Dahlan had *absolutely* agreed to speak English. The show did not have a translator on hand. As the audience whispered and rustled and the tape kept rolling, the producer joined Gowing onstage for a quick huddle.

Suddenly I realized that this show was not just *about* the Israeli-

Palestinian conflict: We were effectively in the *midst* of it, and taboos had taken center stage. The king of Morocco had felt that meeting with the Israeli president was taboo, because doing so could suggest that he was normalizing relations with Israel. The Israeli president, for his part, had regarded it as taboo to join a summit after that public rejection. And Mr. Dahlan saw straying from his identity-based roots as taboo: He wanted to represent the Palestinian people by proudly upholding his native tongue and identity, and it was clear he was not going to back down. Ultimately Mr. Dahlan refused to compromise, and Dr. Husam Zomlot, from the Palestinian Authority, replaced him. The program had to be refilmed from the beginning.

The BBC fiasco raises several important questions. What exactly are taboos—and why do they matter? Why do we stumble over them? And how should we accommodate them to promote constructive dialogue?

What Are Taboos?

Taboos are social prohibitions—actions, feelings, or thoughts that a community deems unacceptable. The word "taboo" was introduced into the English language in 1777, when British explorer James Cook sailed the HMS *Resolution* across the Pacific to what were then known as the Friendly Islands and are now known as Tonga. Cook discovered that the island's inhabitants used the word *tabu* to refer to all that was forbidden, and the term soon found its way into English parlance—perhaps because it handily describes a dynamic familiar to people in just about every culture.

Every taboo has three components—a prohibition, a punishment for breaking it, and protective significance.

Prohibition

A taboo identifies certain feelings, thoughts, or actions as being off-limits, creating a boundary between what is acceptable and what is forbidden within a community to which you belong, whether your family, your workplace, or broader society. For example, premarital sex is acceptable in some cultures but taboo in others. A taboo is thus a social construction and is prohibitive only to the extent that we tacitly agree on its restriction. Curse words hold no inherent power: If you were to say an English obscenity calmly to someone who speaks no English, he would stare at you just as blankly as if you had said the word "chair." We attach prohibitive meanings to words, thoughts, and actions—which means we can also attach *new* meanings to them.

Punishment

Every taboo comes with punishment for violation. The more intense the punishment, the more likely you are to feel pressure to comply with the taboo. You either hang together or get hanged. Typical penalties for breaking a taboo:

Don't talk about that issue . . . *or I will walk out the door.*
Don't negotiate with those people . . . *or we will ostracize you from our community.*
Don't eat that type of food . . . *or you will break a religious covenant.*
Don't touch that dead body . . . *or you will contaminate your body and soul.*

Protection

Taboos act as unwritten social rules guarding you from saying or doing things that offend values deemed important by society, or by the powerful members within it. Some taboos protect you from committing sacrilege. For example, in the Jewish religion it is taboo to drop the Torah, with one tradition commanding the violator and those who witness the act to fast for forty days. Other taboos shield you from dangers both moral and practical—the taboo against adultery helps maintain a stable social and familial order and also reduces the spread of sexually transmitted disease. Still others may protect your identity from criticism, as when rules of politeness inhibit people from disparaging one another's views.

Taboos bear a close functional resemblance to the repetition compulsion: Both are imperfect systems designed to defend your identity from harm. The repetition compulsion uses *psychological* mechanisms such as repression to protect you from undesirable thoughts, feelings, and behavior, whereas taboos use *social* mechanisms such as ostracism to protect you from unacceptable thoughts, feelings, and behaviors. And just as attempts to break the repetition compulsion are met with *psychological* resistance, attempts to break a taboo are often met with *social* resistance. In Marrakesh, as BBC host Nik Gowing requested that Dahlan speak English, Dahlan refused; the harder Gowing pushed, the more strongly Dahlan resisted.

Why Do We Stumble over Taboos?

Several obstacles often make it difficult to deal with taboos.

1. We Are Unaware of a Taboo

Sometimes we inadvertently stumble into taboo territory, accidentally offending a person's values. Several years ago, while conducting a negotiation workshop in the Middle East, a teaching assistant and I role-played a negotiation for a group of high-ranking attendees. Typically I find that participants enjoy role play, as it energizes the room. But that day something was off, and there was a mysterious but noticeable tension in the room. During a break, a government official approached me and asked if we could speak privately. "We love your workshop," he told me, "but during the role play you crossed your right leg, exposing the sole of your shoe to the participants on the left side of the room, including a member of the royal family." I had unwittingly breached a taboo, having forgotten that in Arab culture showing the sole of your shoe is viewed as a serious insult. I had meant no offense, but that had not prevented me from causing it.

2. We Fear Discussing the Taboo Issue

Taboos make difficult conversations even more difficult. To break a taboo can feel frightening—but to avoid breaking it keeps you mired in a conflict. Your mother's favoritism toward your sibling drives you mad, but you cannot envision broaching such an impossibly fraught subject with her. Your colleague, who happens to be the boss's nephew, fails once again to prepare his portion of a presentation, but the thought of discussing the problem with your boss makes you shudder. Taboos can lock you in a no-win situation.

In fact, merely *thinking* about breaking a taboo can be distressing, as a compelling set of studies by Wharton professor Philip Tetlock demonstrates. Tetlock and his colleagues asked participants to judge the permissibility of certain activities, such as selling human organs to people at the bottom of the transplant list. For those participants who felt the activity was morally objectionable, the mere thought of violating that taboo was deeply unsettling. The longer the participants contemplated the taboo-breaching proposal, the greater their sense of moral unease.

Taboos are fundamentally conservative: They preserve the status quo. If you break a law, you risk being punished, but that punishment is typically in proportion to the seriousness of the crime. If you break a taboo, you risk being *disproportionately* punished. Because taboos protect a community's values and norms, the stakes involved are especially high, and excessive punishment is a deterrent designed to prevent the most unacceptable of offenses. In Hawthorne's *The Scarlet Letter*, Hester Prynne commits adultery and is sentenced to wear a scarlet *A* on her dress for the rest of her life, a public acknowledgment of her transgression. The message is clear: Violate a taboo and risk endangering your physical, social, and spiritual standing within the community.

3. We Have No Framework

Most people have no systematic framework for how to treat a taboo issue. Should such a prohibition be ignored or respected? Sam, an executive attending a negotiation workshop of mine, faced this very dilemma. He confided that he was a strict Catholic and bisexual and had spent years researching theological texts in an attempt to reconcile these two facets of his identity. He had concluded that they could coexist without contradiction. He had never raised the matter of his sexuality with his parents but knew that they would strongly disapprove, viewing it as an offense against God. Sam felt guilty, ashamed, angry, and torn: How should he approach this confrontation with the taboo? He lacked a practical system for doing so.

How to Navigate Taboos

The stumbling blocks described above are formidable, but overcoming them *is* possible. Doing so requires you to become aware of taboos, to establish a safe zone to discuss them, and to decide systematically how to treat them. The following chart summarizes the stumbling blocks and strategies involved.

Stumbling Block	Strategy
1. We are unaware of a taboo.	1. Become aware of taboos.
2. We fear discussing the taboo.	2. Establish a safe zone.
3. We have no framework to decide how to treat a taboo issue.	3. Make an action plan: the ACT System.

Step 1: Become Aware of Taboos

Several years ago I visited a couple at their newly purchased home; I was joined by a friend named Terri, a real estate enthusiast, who asked our hosts, "So how much did you pay for this house?" The couple looked at each other and said, "We don't discuss those kinds of things." Terri had unwittingly hit upon a taboo subject—financial privacy—and was punished for her error with an awkward silence and never again invited to their home.

Breaking taboos yields predictable results: The offended party is likely to express some variation of "Now you've gone too far" or "That's crossing the line." Taboos protect important parts of identity, and violating them provokes a strong emotional reaction. If you stay aware of taboos, however, you can avoid violating at least *some* of them.

Recognize Taboo Issues

In my family it is taboo to hug my father. He is a loving person, but shuns physical affection. Every family has its own unique parameters that establish certain behaviors as unacceptable. *Don't talk about grandpa's wartime past. Don't talk about mom's bout with depression. Don't talk kindly about the other side of the family.* Similarly, every culture has taboos that limit or silence certain behaviors. In any conflict it is critical to become aware of relevant taboos that might impede constructive resolution.

To recognize taboos in your own life, imagine that you have been commissioned to write a secret guide about what you cannot say or do in your own conflictual relationships. What are the "rules"? What subjects are off-limits? Whom can't you talk to? When? Where? Even the expression of specific emotions can be taboo: Is it acceptable to show anger or sadness in your relationship? What emotions must you repress to preserve good relations?

Be particularly sensitive to a few specific types of taboos:

(1) **Taboos on personal expression.** These taboos prohibit you from revealing information that a community to which you belong deems too intimate. When I was a teenager, my friends and I saw it as taboo to share the secrets of our romantic lives with adults. Yet when my grandfather fell ill with cancer and had an estimated one month to live, I met privately with him while he lay in bed and told him my deepest secrets. He went on to fight the cancer and live another three healthy years, to my deep happiness, but all my teenage secrets soon became the subject of family gossip.

(2) **Taboos on blasphemy.** These prohibit disrespect to that which you revere. You can criticize the behavior of people within your own tribe, but others outside your tribe can make no such criticism. My wife can criticize our children's behavior, but I will take offense if a neighbor makes the same observations. Taboos protect what we hold sacred. In Islam, for example, there is a taboo against desecrating the Koran, a blasphemous act punishable by imprisonment or even death.

(3) Taboos on association. These taboos prohibit associating with any person, place, thing, or idea deemed dirty, diseased, or morally polluted; we distance ourselves from them to protect the sacred purity of our beliefs. This makes direct negotiation with certain adversaries extremely difficult, for each side fears getting too close—and ultimately becoming morally contaminated. Breaking a taboo on association meets with heavy punishment, as basketball superstar Dennis Rodman learned. Despite strained relations between the United States and North Korea, he befriended passionate basketball fan Kim Jong-un, supreme leader of North Korea. Though their friendship opened unorthodox channels for international negotiation, Western media chastised Rodman for his relationship, which broke a Western taboo on association.

Become Aware of Taboos Constraining the Other Side's Behavior

Before you judge another party's actions as irrational, consider how taboos may be limiting their ability to express their identity. A case in point comes from Žitište, Serbia, a small village devastated by war, flooding, and landslides. In 2007, locals rallied around a proposal to erect a statue in the village square, ultimately deciding to honor the iconic film character Rocky Balboa, his boxing-gloved hands raised high in triumph. A country still rebuilding after both the ravages of war and a United States–led NATO bombing campaign chose an image that originated in Hollywood as an object of civic reverence—a decision that on its face is hard to comprehend.

But when viewed in the context of local taboos, the Rocky statue takes on deeper meaning. The citizens of Žitište faced a prohibition on honoring a soldier—a more typical subject of a memorial—in a conflict that was anything but clear-cut. The town also faced the difficulty of honoring any single ethnic leader or group; choosing one over another would lead to resentment among rival constituencies.

So the people of Žitište worked *around* the taboo, arriving at a compromise that did not violate either of the thorny issues at hand. "We thought long and hard about what would represent our image," one citizen wrote. "Rocky Balboa . . . is a character who never gives up." The moral: Taboos limit our freedom, but through creative means we can escape their hold.

Step 2: Establish a Safe Zone

Exploring taboo issues requires feeling secure enough to think the unthink-able, to discuss the undiscussable—to dare to question beliefs and conven-tions that feel unassailable. Begin by picturing the relational space between you and another party as an enclosed region of land on a map. Most of the region is safe for both of you to explore—it is a safe zone of topics to freely and comfortably discuss. But scattered across that region are enclaves of extremely sensitive issues. These taboo territories are heavily guarded and strewn with emotional land mines. Anyone who might try to breach their borders risks getting hurt. This was the reality facing the leaders in the Mar-rakesh incident, who each came to the boundary of taboo territory—and decided not to cross the line. To resolve an emotionally charged conflict, you need to move sensitive topics from taboo territory to a safe zone—a temporary social space in which taboos can be examined without fear of punishment or moral compromise.

Here are guidelines to help you establish a safe environment for dis-cussing taboo issues:

(1) Clarify Your Purpose

Define what you want to achieve in your discussion. Do you hope to air unspoken grievances, better understand points of contention, or divulge your pain? Keep your purpose firmly in mind to anchor you should ver-tigo arise.

(2) Establish the Bounds of Conversation

Explicitly discuss what issues you each are open to discussing. "Might we talk sometime about the incident from last May?" Or "I find it hard to talk about our company's dysfunction without being able to consider some of the leaders involved. Might it be okay for us to privately discuss that?" Come to a mutual agreement. If you raise a taboo issue without shared consent, the other side may see the taboo issue as a threat and blame you for broaching it.

Discuss the bounds of confidentiality. What material can you share with your boss or best friend? If you are talking with your spouse about an act of betrayal, for example, you might agree that your conversation is completely confidential, to be shared with no one, save perhaps a therapist. If you are negotiating a peace treaty and want to discuss a taboo issue, you might agree that each party can share the content of discussion with its respective government, but without personal attribution.

(3) Explore Taboo Issues Without Commitment

Agree to *explore* taboo issues—but not to make any binding commitments about how to deal with them. Because taboo issues are so sensitive, this guideline allows you to discuss them without fear of violating them. Political negotiators regularly put this guideline into practice. Years ago in Oslo, Norway, a group of academics and marginal political representatives—all unofficial negotiators—secretly hammered out the Oslo Accords on the basis of *deniability*: Though these negotiators informed their respective governments of their progress, the governments themselves were not directly participating and therefore could deny direct involvement should the negotiations fail.

(4) Build In a Process of Moral Reaffirmation

Whether or not you decide to break a taboo, the mere act of exploring it can feel like a moral transgression. You may become guilty and ashamed for even *thinking* about breaking a prohibition. So a safe zone must include a process to help you reaffirm your values and clear your conscience. For example, you can write down the values you most deeply cherish, confirm your commitment to those values, and remind yourself about how the taboo discussion has served those values. Alternatively, take tangible action to purify your conscience: After discussing a spouse's drinking problem, for example, donate time or funds to support research on addiction.

Step 3: Make an Action Plan—Using the ACT System

Once you have created a safe zone in which to speak, you can use the "ACT" system to evaluate whether to accept the taboo, chisel it away slowly, or tear it down in short order.

Accept the Taboo?

Consider the costs and benefits of preserving the taboo rather than breaking it. Accepting a taboo can take work, but it does not mean you must commit to doing so forever. A husband may accept that it is taboo to discuss his wife's infidelity now, but acknowledge that this implicit agreement may change with time. Or he may decide to accept the restrictions regarding the taboo in some circles but not others—for example, declining to discuss the topic with his wife, but confiding in a close friend.

While acceptance of a taboo may impede open communication, it does have one chief benefit: It can promote harmony. Several years ago, I led a negotiation training session at Harvard for top Chinese business executives. Over lunch, the CEO of a multinational company discussed the importance in China of saving face and cultivating *guanxi*, the personal connection that exists between people.

"How do you negotiate particularly sensitive issues, then?" I asked him.

He smiled, thought for a moment, and replied, "In Chinese culture, harmony is essential. We may put even a critical conflict under the carpet to be dealt with later."

"But won't that just intensify the conflict?" I asked.

"On some level. But resolving the conflict is secondary. Resolution is more of a Western concept. Chinese culture emphasizes the preservation of relationships."

Chisel Away the Taboo?

Chiseling away at a taboo requires steady, open communication. When I facilitate dialogue between disputing ethnic groups, for example, I am conscious of taboos inhibiting conversation, which can result in a tense silence or guarded dialogue. To advance the expression of the unsaid, I may say to the group, "We've discussed a variety of important topics today. I wonder if, before we close, we might each share something we thought of saying but didn't." To break the ice, I add: "I've felt that we've been skirting some of the real issues, but I don't want to be the one who presses you to say things." Another technique I sometimes use is to have the group reflect on their emotions: "Before we end for the day, imagine yourself heading home tonight: What will be your dominant feeling about our session today? Anything you wish you had said but didn't?"

Chiseling away at taboos is a gradual process. A striking example involves the dismantling of restricted communication between the United States and the Soviet Union. During the era in which I grew up, the Cold War between these two powers was still very much in effect, and the idea of an American interacting with someone from a communist country was nearly inconceivable. I still remember my tough-as-nails seventh-grade gym teacher calling any trouble-rousing student a communist. So imagine my surprise when, a few years later, my family decided to host an exchange student from Hungary—*communist* Hungary.

Any number of obstacles stood in the way of Andy's coming to the United States, and it took a solid year of red tape and bureaucratic holdups before he arrived. But the impact of his presence on me and on my friends was deep. The more I got to know him, the more senseless the taboos between East and West felt. Andy loved the blues, the Beastie Boys, and staying up late to eat bowl after bowl of Cheerios—the same things I loved. He and I had a good time playing guitar together and talking about girls. It did not take me long to understand that whatever taboos existed between us, we were fundamentally both human beings. The fact that Andy spent the year in the United States broke a societal taboo, but also chiseled away at one that existed in my mind. I learned, little by little, that interacting with everyday people living in a different political or cultural system was a key step toward peaceful relations and did not merit prohibition.

In the heated political world of government relations, this lesson can quickly get lost. So what should be done to improve relations? How, for example, might two governments with rising adversarial sentiment and

no formal relations reduce the risk of confrontation in the face of a prohibition on cross-country communication?

Consider out-of-the-box methods to chisel away the taboo. Business
leaders can work on joint economic development projects. University students can collaborate on negotiation skills training over the Internet or in
a neutral third country. Doctors can come together to tackle the global
spread of disease. And environmentalists may cooperate on reducing pol-
lution. Such efforts may sound unconventional during a conflict—and
indeed they are, for they draw people into the taboo territory and, accordingly, put them at risk of social disapproval from family, friends, media,
and society writ large. But such efforts also hold the potential to open new
pathways for reconciliation.

Chiseling away taboos is an activity well known to a small but
important segment of the population: comedians, who are largely exempt
from prohibitions on communication. Comedians are given latitude to
publicly examine, comment upon, and criticize accepted norms and practices, whether through incendiary comments on politics or bracing views
on religion. In giving voice to difficult truths, comedians have an ability to
drive public discourse in ways unavailable to nonperformers, vocalizing
the illogical nature of many taboos and stripping them, if only for the
duration of the joke, of some of their power. Should we too hold a damaging taboo up to the light, we can begin to deflate it.

A case in point involves the spread of HIV and AIDS in Africa, where
many people infected with the virus felt the stigma of disease so acutely
they hid their diagnosis to preserve their connections to their families,
friends, partners, and communities. Because of this taboo, the virus spread
uncontrollably. Ultimately health professionals, community activists, and
other organizations took on the role of taboo breaker, voicing the importance of safe-sex practices. Had more people spoken up—spoken *out*—
sooner, the infection rate might not have been so high.

To chisel away large-scale taboos, it is critical to convince the gatekeepers, people who control access to pathways to change. For example, in Aris-
tophanes' classic comedy *Lysistrata*, the titular character, frustrated at the
protracted Peloponnesian War, implores the women of Greece to withhold

sex from their men until the conflict ends. Even after the women's strike begins, the Athenian and Spartan negotiators continue to argue over the terms of a peace agreement. But when Lysistrata introduces the negotiators to the beautiful goddess of peace, their desire overrides their obstinacy and they quickly conclude a pact.

Lysistrata's strategy—to influence those who can affect change—is highly useful in conflict resolution. For example, if two departments in your organization are embroiled in a heated dispute, figure out whose views most greatly influence each department's attitudes. Enlist these gatekeepers in a process of reconciliation, and you will find that chiseling away a taboo will come much more easily within reach.

Tear Down the Taboo?

This is the most direct approach to breaching the walls of a taboo, and it requires a great deal of courage. It involves deploying a kind of social wrecking ball, bringing about rapid change but potentially incurring the wrath of those who prefer to maintain the status quo.

Nelson Mandela spent his life tearing down taboos. In 1948 the ruling regime of South Africa, the National Party, enforced a system of racial segregation known as apartheid, which severely diminished the legal rights of blacks. Mandela protested the policy, at first committing to nonviolent dissent but later organizing attacks on government targets. He was arrested, convicted of sabotage, and sentenced to life in prison. After twenty-seven years in captivity, he returned to lead South Africa through a nonviolent transition to the multiracial government.

Mandela recognized that the greatest challenge in this transition was, as antiapartheid activist Tokyo Sexwale predicted, "not so much about liberating blacks from bondage, but . . . liberating white people from fear." Mandela had the courage to tear down taboos about mixing the races, creating a model for the multiracial society he so clearly envisioned. Upon election as the first black president of South Africa, Mandela did the unthinkable: He invited to lunch Mrs. P. W. Botha, wife of the former white president of South Africa, along with the widows of other apartheid leaders, embracing those who had perpetuated an ugly system for decades. This was one step in his introduction of a new national norm based on the African philosophy of *ubuntu*, which emphasizes the interconnection of all human beings.

Applying the ACT System

Before your conflict escalates, take the time to complete the Taboo Analysis Chart, a simple tool to evaluate whether to accept, chisel away, or tear down a taboo. By examining the costs and benefits of these approaches, you can come to a thoughtful decision about what to do. Be sure to also observe your emotional reaction to each approach, noticing which *feels* right to pursue.

Another useful technique to assess the costs and benefits is to imagine you broke the taboo yesterday. What exactly did you say and do, and how did others respond? Now imagine you broke the taboo five years ago. Is your life still miserable from that event? This simple mental exercise can help you evaluate the impact of your decision.

After you've evaluated your own situation, revisit the Taboo Analysis Chart, but now from the other party's perspective. If the other party clings to a taboo that aggravates the conflict, consider the ways in which it benefits them to preserve the taboo, as well as what they may see as the costs of breaking it. Mandela recognized that many whites held a taboo against interacting with blacks. He chiseled away at the other's taboo—to powerful effect.

Should you unintentionally break a taboo, however, take personal responsibility and repair relations as soon as possible. During the Middle East workshop at which I accidentally exposed the sole of my shoe, I returned to the room, acknowledged that some participants might have been offended by my actions, and then explained that my offense was unintentional. I offered a sincere apology, and there was a noticeable shift in the mood. The group I knew to be enthusiastic became enthusiastic once again. At the end of the day the member of the royal family approached me and said, "You're much too sensitive." But in his tone I noted appreciation that I had taken responsibility for breaking the taboo.

Taboo Analysis Chart

	Benefits	Costs
Accept the taboo	1. Who might benefit from preserving the taboo? Why?	2. What are the costs if the taboo is preserved?
Chisel at the taboo	1. Who might benefit from slowly chiseling away at the taboo? Why?	2. What are the costs if the taboo is slowly broken down?
Tear down the taboo	1. Who might benefit from tearing down the taboo? Why?	2. What are the costs if the taboo is torn down?

Taking Back Power: Creating Taboos to Curb Harmful Behavior

Thus far, this chapter has discussed taboos as problematic factors that are detrimental to conflict resolution. They can, however, also serve a constructive purpose, acting as social prohibitions against destructive behavior. If the heads of two major companies get into a disagreement, they have a wide range of possible options for resolving their conflict: They can talk their differences out, insult each other, file a lawsuit—or one of them can even knife the other to death. This last option, of course, seems nearly inconceivable, as it is immoral and by its very nature taboo. The social prohibition against stabbing in the corporate context makes such acts extremely infrequent.

We have the power to create "constructive taboos"—rituals that forestall aggressive behavior. The utility of constructive taboos became clear to me in the course of a conversation with a couple in which the husband was a die-hard Republican and the wife a rock-solid Democrat. They clearly loved each other, but I was curious how they actually *lived* with each other. As it turned out, they had a simple policy. "Every Tuesday night we talk politics," the wife explained. "The rest of the week the subject is taboo." They created a functional prohibition that preserved their relationship and made space for each partner's values to be respected.

Like that couple, you can follow four simple steps to create a constructive taboo:

(1) Identify a behavior that inflames conflict, such as discussing politics or rehashing a toxic interdepartmental rivalry.

(2) Define when and where the behavior is unacceptable. Should political discussion be off-limits on weekdays or holidays? Is it permissible to share anxieties during the election season?

(3) Implement the taboo. The wife might decide to independently implement the taboo, telling her husband, "I refuse to talk to you about politics on any day but Tuesdays." Whether or not he agrees, she can uphold the restriction. Alternatively, the couple could jointly implement the taboo. A third option is for an authority figure to institute the taboo, such as if the couple's parents demand that the couple refrain from discussing politics.

(4) Clarify the social punishment for breaking the taboo. The couple in the example above established the taboo with the understanding that whoever broke it would bear the shameful brunt of spousal anger for prioritizing self-interest over the peaceful conduct of their relationship.

Economist Kenneth Boulding noted that taboos define activities "which could physically be done but which are beyond our psychological barrier." If, for example, your community experiences a rash of street violence, you might join with your neighbors to make violence taboo, perhaps by launching a grassroots antiviolence campaign including local youth, religious leaders, parents, government officials, and community leaders. This same approach can be used to combat radicalized violence—such as school shootings or extreme acts of ethnopolitical violence—by mobilizing gatekeepers who can institutionalize legitimate taboos against these behaviors.

Putting It All Together

In the sunny resort town of Sharm El-Sheikh, Egypt, I facilitated a workshop called "Building Peace, Breaking Taboos." Its purpose was to help regional leadership wrestle with political taboos constraining progress in the Israeli-Palestinian negotiations. Co-led by Tony Blair, former prime minister of the United Kingdom and the United Nations' Middle East Quartet special envoy at the time, the session included participants ranging from high-level negotiators and government leaders to royalty and religious figures.

To create a safe zone, I established the rules of our workshop, including confidentiality and mutual respect. In the tense context of the conflict, I knew that productive conversation would be possible only if participants felt safe enough to voice their honest opinions. I also emphasized that our workshop was *exploratory*, providing everyone a chance to think outside the constraints of the conflict. No one would be asked to commit to any action discussed in the workshop. This freed the participants to engage in energized conversation.

Mr. Blair took the floor to discuss his involvement in negotiating the Good Friday peace agreement that helped to resolve the Northern Ireland conflict. He explained that effective negotiations could not have taken place within an environment of violence and counterattack. Both sides needed "breathing space"—a safe zone that, once established, opened up possibilities that Blair said he had "never imagined possible."

The remainder of the workshop was a working session. At the center of the room, I had placed a circular table cordoned off by a red velvet rope. This was taboo territory. On that table sat ten envelopes, each containing a slip of paper on which a specific taboo in the Israeli-Palestinian conflict had been written: Jerusalem's status, the right of refugee return, control of holy sites, and the very use of the names "Israel" and "Palestine."

I divided participants into small working groups, and a representative from each randomly selected an envelope, brought it back to his or her table, and read aloud the taboo topic for which the group was to complete a Taboo Analysis Chart. The symbolism involved in this process was important: I wanted participants to tangibly experience removing the taboo from the dangerous taboo territory and bringing it into the safe zone of our workshop, where they could explore ideas at minimal personal risk of contamination or punishment.

One hour later the groups shared their key findings. As Tony Blair later noted, "The Taboos Session at Sharm El-Sheikh raised important questions around the fears each party holds about broaching taboo issues. It is only by raising awareness of these issues and tackling them head on that we can hope to make progress on challenges such as the Middle East." A *New York Times* writer discussed the session afterward with one of the high-level delegates, who reportedly had walked into the session feeling nearly hopeless about the negotiation process but left it optimistic, fortified with new insights on how to deal constructively with the taboo issues standing at the heart of stalemate and peace.

I had designed the workshop to conclude with an act of moral reaffirmation. Each working group had a choice: They could insert the description of their taboo back into the envelope and return it to the taboo territory—or take the taboo with them when they left the workshop, a symbolic gesture demonstrating that they would continue to consider breaking it. Several groups returned their envelopes to the table at the center of the room, a low-cost action that confirmed their values and thwarted feelings of moral transgression.

Despite any precautions you may take, no safe zone is 100 percent safe. In one of the Sharm El-Sheikh workshop's groups, two men established a quick rapport, discussing their taboo topic with great animation. I noticed that one of the men suddenly looked surprised, gathered his belongings, and bolted for the door. "Is everything okay?" I asked, running over to intervene. The gentleman, a prominent Lebanese businessman, responded, "I didn't realize whom I was talking to until just now." The man with whom he had been speaking was in fact a former Israeli politician and peace negotiator. "I have no issue with the Israelis," the Lebanese businessman explained. "I just can't risk the photo." Lebanese law forbade contact with Israelis, so if a photograph had been taken of the two men, the implications for the businessman's career and family could have been grave. While he did not personally identify with the taboo, he feared breaking it and suffering the consequences. Even in the reputed safe zone of our workshop, taboos held tremendous sway.

In Sum

Taboos have a bad reputation—and deservedly so, considering the role they play in creating conflict. But we have also seen how they serve an important function in preserving that which we hold dear. They put us in a bind during emotionally charged conflicts—but they also bind us together, providing us with a primer on proper behavior, as well as a sense of order and together-ness. And when crafted with care and mutually adopted, taboos can even *solve* conflict.

Assault on the Sacred

"Why are you here?" King Solomon asked cousins Magda and Anya, who stood before him with worried eyes.

"Your Majesty," said Magda, "I have a newborn baby boy. Three days after he was born, Anya gave birth to a son of her own. The other night Anya fell asleep with her baby by her side, rolled on top of him, and he died. When she awoke and saw what she had done, she crept into my room and exchanged her dead boy for my living one."

"Liar!" said Anya.

"You're the liar!" responded Magda, and accusations flew back and forth between the two women.

"Enough!" the king shouted. "Bring me a sword. I shall divide the boy in two and give half to each woman."

Anya looked at the king in a panic. "Please, Your Majesty, give the child to her," she tearfully pleaded. "Just don't kill him."

"Let the boy be neither mine nor hers. Slice him," said Magda.

The king paused, looking between the two women. "Give Anya the boy," he pronounced. "She is the rightful mother, for none would want her own son slain."

This biblical story, adapted from "The Judgment of King Solomon," forcefully illustrates the immense challenge inherent in negotiating issues that are sacred. Anya and Magda were both mothers, but the king's threatened assault on the sacred revealed the distinction between them. Had theirs been a property dispute, they could have simply divided the land in question, with each claiming a partial victory. But when negotiating the sacred—in this case, the child—there is no easy split. The sacred is indivisible, and the king used this fact to identify the true mother.

Welcome to the World of the Sacred

When your deepest beliefs feel threatened, you may find yourself mired in the fourth lure of your tribal mind, an *assault on the sacred*. This is an attack on the most meaningful pillars of your identity: any matters so deeply significant that they feel sacrosanct, exempt from debate. Spouses passionately disagree over which values to instill in their children. Employees reject a colleague who criticizes core institutional values. International negotiators deadlock over who should control sacred land.

An assault on what you hold as sacred triggers a powerful emotional reaction that to the outsider may seem an overreaction, irrational. But that is not the case from your own vantage point. The central purpose of identity is to help you make meaning of your experience in the world—and the sacred represents your deepest form of meaning. An assault on the sacred cuts you to the quick, shaking the most sensitive pillars of your identity and raising fears that it will not withstand the blow.

What Is the Sacred?

I define the sacred as *that which we perceive to be imbued with divine significance*. The "divine" need not refer to a specifically religious entity. While the object of one's veneration can be a deity, prophet, or holy text, it also can be a family member, beloved place, or cherished event. Just as a religious person holds hallowed scripture as sacred, a nationalist views his country's flag as a sacred object never to be defaced, and a widow holds sacred her departed spouse's ashes.

We revere as divine whatever we view as imbued with infinite, intrinsic, and inviolable significance.

Infinite

My love for my children, and their worth to me, is boundless. But love that is nonquantifiable presents problems in conflict resolution. When negotiators are forced to quantify the sacred, the act feels both morally offensive and practically impossible. After a deadly act of terrorism, how should a government distribute compensation to the families of the victims? Should the amount vary by recipient, based on such criteria as the victim's age and income? Asking such questions is discomfiting, and making the resulting decisions is enormously difficult.

Intrinsic

The divine holds intrinsic significance. It is not just that I feel my children are sacred; from my perspective they *are* sacred in their very being. Their infinite value resides in them, not in my belief about them. We perceive the significance of the divine to be an innate feature of the object of our reverence.

Inviolable

Because every aspect of the divine possesses infinite worth, to insult one part of a sacred entity is to insult its entirety. It is immaterial whether someone burns ten pages from the Bible or Koran or crosses out a single word; the offense is sacrilegious. To dismiss an assault on the sacred as "minor" neglects the fact that any offense committed against a revered object, however slight, can feel enormous to the offended party.

People Differ in Their Convictions About the Sacred

My holy book may be your storybook. While you may find some moral value in the story, I revere the book as sacred. You may step on the book accidentally and be unfazed, while I would feel deep shame and guilt should I do the same. Where the sacred is concerned, we believe with our entire heart that our truth is *the* truth.

Should I commit an assault on what you hold sacred, I violate the ultimate taboo—respect for your deepest truths—and conflict quickly can erupt. I have trespassed into your sacred space, into what is "set apart and forbidden." Failing to treat that space with due reverence can result in anything from the dissolution of a family to the declaration of a fatwa.

Salman Rushdie experienced this firsthand upon the publication of his novel *The Satanic Verses*. Many Muslim communities deemed the title and content of the book a direct offense to the tenets of Islam, whereas Rushdie argued that he had the literary freedom to write fiction without limits. The fallout of this clash was intense and far-reaching. Rushdie received thousands of death threats, the novel was banned in many countries, and protests erupted around the world. A few months after the book's initial publication, Ayatollah Khomeini, then supreme leader of Iran, issued a fatwa: "I am informing all brave Muslims of the world that the author of *The Satanic Verses*, a text written, edited, and published against Islam, the Prophet of Islam, and the Qur'an, along with all the editors and publishers aware of its contents, are condemned to death. I call on all valiant Muslims wherever they may be in the world to kill them without delay, so that no one will dare insult the sacred beliefs of Muslims henceforth. Whoever is killed in this cause will be a martyr, Allah Willing."

Rushdie and his wife went into hiding for years, and sporadic episodes of violence marred any hope for resolution of the issue. The fatwa was lifted a decade later, though Rushdie remained uncompromising with his stance on literary freedom. Undoubtedly many opponents of Rushdie's book also maintained their position, thus leaving unanswered the challenge of how to reconcile disparate perspectives on the sacred. Is it even possible?

Obstacles to Negotiating the Sacred

The best strategy for dealing with an assault on the sacred is prevention. Rather than falling victim to a conflict over the sacred, take proactive action to "negotiate the sacred"—to collaboratively address differing views on meaningful issues. A few obstacles make this task particularly difficult.

1. We Are Unaware of the Sacred

We may offend someone's sacred concerns without even realizing it. A businesswoman recently forgot to respond to an important e-mail from a key client, who called her up and yelled at her. The businesswoman apologized and explained that her teenage son had just suffered a concussion. The client had not known about this situation and now expressed remorse.

2. We Conflate the Sacred and the Secular

Imagine you are hosting a dinner party, and when one of the guests arrives, he smiles, gives you a hug, and hands you thirty dollars. "I didn't have time to stop at the store," he explains, "but this is how much I planned to spend on a bottle of wine."

Your friend's gesture is, at heart, well intentioned; he wants to demonstrate his gratitude for your generous invitation. His gesture is also rational; he is offering you not only the total amount of money he would have spent on wine but also a choice as to how you would prefer to spend the money, rather than giving you a bottle you might not like. But the wad of bills he presses into your hands leaves you cold as you think, *It's not the money, it's the thought that counts*. But as your guest goes on to recount his busy day, how overwhelming his week has been with his wife out of town and his youngest kid sick with the flu, you begin to realize that, even in the face of this temporary chaos in his life, he was sincerely *determined* to bring you some manner of gift. So why does the situation feel so awkward?

In a small way, this situation demonstrates the means by which the sacred and the secular can come into conflict. The thought that one puts into an act of kindness—bringing a hostess gift, for example—is in itself a sacred gesture, but because the proffering of cash is a feature of the secular world, handing over thirty dollars as an offering at a dinner party confuses these two worlds in a disconcerting way.

On a larger scale, blurring these two realms can lead to moral outrage—as Salman Rushdie learned. Two years after the Ayatollah issued a fatwa, Rushdie wrote an essay titled "Is Nothing Sacred?" in which he argued that "literature is the one place in any society where, within the secrecy of our own heads, we can hear *voices talking about everything in every possible way*." Rushdie viewed literature as a "privileged arena" for exploring the bounds of the sacred. For the Ayatollah, this was blasphemy.

3. We Fail to Give Due Respect to the Sacred

When people are in conflict over something sacred, each side tends to resist expressing respect for the other's sacred beliefs out of fear that doing so will imperil their own identity. As a result, neither side appreciates what the other deems sacred, leading everyone to feel devalued.

4. We Refuse to Compromise on Sacred Issues

A conflict over the sacred can feel impossible to overcome—and for good reason. The sacred invokes absolutes, and absolute differences appear absolutely irreconcilable. It can feel intolerable to compromise our beliefs for the sake of resolution.

Imagine telling a Hasidic Israeli Jew that you have the answer to the conflict over Jerusalem: Simply divide the Western Wall in half. Similarly, envision suggesting to a devout Muslim living in East Jerusalem that all this conflict could be avoided if his people just relinquished the Al-Aqsa Mosque. Such unrealistic propositions would undoubtedly cause offense, because they fail to adequately respect these two holy sites and the peoples who revere them. The sacred has such power over all of us that compromise feels unbearable to address these conflicts.

Obstacle	Strategy
1. We are unaware of the sacred.	1. Sensitize to the sacred.
2. We conflate the sacred and the secular.	2. Disentangle the sacred from the secular.
3. We fail to give due respect to the sacred.	3. Acknowledge what each side holds sacred.
4. We refuse to compromise on sacred issues.	4. Problem solve within each side's sphere of identity.

A Strategy for Negotiating the Sacred

To effectively address conflicts invoking the sacred requires overcoming the obstacles described above—each of which has a corresponding strategy to make that possible.

1. Sensitize to the Sacred

An assault on the sacred is often easy to identify, as was the case with Rushdie's novel. If someone issues a fatwa sentencing you to death, it is a safe bet that the sacred is at stake. To negotiate collaboratively, however, you must work to *avoid* an assault on the sacred. This necessitates becoming aware of what each party holds sacred so you can respect those boundaries.

The best way to determine what is sacred is to reflect on the Five Pillars of Identity introduced in chapter 2: beliefs, rituals, allegiances, values, and emotionally meaningful experiences. Start by reviewing the chart on page 97 and considering which pillars feel sacred for you in the conflict. For example, do you feel a threat to a spiritual belief, to a close friend to whom you hold allegiance, or to a ritual that your family has practiced for generations?

Then take the perspective of the other party and envision which of their most sacred pillars may feel endangered. When you meet with them, you might ask: "What feels most at stake for you in this conflict?" While it is difficult to discuss a taboo issue (precisely because it is taboo), the sacred is a subject that people tend to be willing to discuss once rapport is established.

Listen for the issues that most impassion the other party. A friend of mine is open to personal feedback on almost any issue—you can disparage her intellect, personality, or style of dress—but should you criticize her two children, who hold sacred significance in her life, prepare for a storm of wrath.

Also take notice of convictions to which the other side holds steadfast. Sacred beliefs and values are core elements of our identity and extremely resistant to change; they feel self-evident and indisputable to us. A fervent military proponent may debate the merits of war with an equally impassioned pacifist, but both are likely to stick to their own beliefs no matter how strong either side's case may be.

Learn about the deeper stories the other side tells about who they are, where they came from, and where they are going. For example, as you come to understand their ethnic heritage, you may glean insight into meaningful values they have acquired from this affiliation—such as to work hard, to maintain faith in the divine, or to trust only kin. Also listen for transcendent ideals that call them to action in their organization, ethnic group, or nation. What beliefs and values do they aspire to leave as their legacy within their organization or on this earth?

Heighten your awareness of the physical spaces that the other side regards as sacrosanct. Though the sacred is limitless, human beings sanctify spaces by consecrating a physical location such as a mosque, church, or synagogue. Even schools and hospitals can be sanctified in this manner. Because these *sanctuaries of identity* serve as physical manifestations of our sacred beliefs, their desecration stirs moral outrage. For example, arson is unacceptable, but should the building involved be a spiritual temple, the emotional impact on a community can be devastating.

The sacred is similarly embodied in *cathedrals in time*, or specific periods set aside for sanctified activities. As we learn about the other side's sacred time—holidays, days of remembrance, times of prayer—we gain insight into the rituals and values that define who they are. Those who observe the Sabbath, for example, are expected to rest, relax, and free their minds from the concerns of everyday life. Disrespecting a cathedral in time is another example of an assault on the sacred. Should your family respect the ritual of a nightly dinner together, your teenager's unexpected absence may feel like an assault on the sacred, a display of disregard to sanctified family time.

Do You Feel a Threat To . . .

1. **Sacred beliefs**—vital cultural, religious, or social convictions?

2. **Sacred rituals**—meaningful activities or spiritual practices?

3. **Sacred allegiances**—intense loyalty to close friends, family members, or political allies?

4. **Sacred values**—deeply held ideals or principles?

5. **Sacred experiences**—emotionally meaningful experiences that integrally define your identity?

2. Disentangle the Sacred from the Secular

Recently a relative of mine, Clare, faced a serious dilemma. A brilliant lawyer, she has dedicated her life to providing legal services pro bono to struggling Native American families—a commitment that keeps her perpetually on the verge of bankruptcy. She lives in a small suburban community, where she owns one hundred acres of wooded land. An energy company has been drilling for natural gas wells in the area and offered her close to $100,000 to access the gas on her property, plus a percentage of any gas brought to market. This proposal would provide her with much-needed income but violate her deep convictions—and those of the very people she was helping—regarding the sacredness of the earth. What should she do?

Distinguish the important from the sacred. To begin with, Clare had to evaluate the value of the land to her, searching within to clarify her feelings. Was the land important, pseudosacred, sacred, or *sacred* sacred?

If it were merely **important**, she would feel attached to the land but would be able to sacrifice it for financial gain. Therefore, she would be inclined to negotiate a contract with the gas company.

If the land were **pseudosacred**—a term coined by Harvard Business School professor Max Bazerman and his colleagues—it would possess intrinsic value under some conditions. Perhaps she would feel its sacredness while interacting with her Native American friends but privately view the land as a secular concern. In that case she might be persuaded to proceed with the gas-extraction contract.

If the land were **sacred** to her, it would hold intrinsic value, and to allow drilling would betray a core value. Nevertheless, this sacred value would not be beyond the realm of negotiation, because she might realize that sacrifice of the land could serve other sacred values, such as her ability to continue her pro bono work.

Finally, if she regarded the land as **sacred sacred**, it would possess ultimate sanctity. She would feel a profound attachment to it, viewing it as something that could under no circumstances be violated. There would be no conceivable way that she could negotiate a contract with the natural-gas company.

Ultimately, Clare concluded that the land was sacred to her. She was both emotionally and spiritually attached to it and believed it held intrinsic value.

Now Clare worried about what to do with this land she deemed sacred: If she allowed the drilling in exchange for money, she would feel as if she had compromised her integrity. Social psychologist Philip Tetlock calls this a *taboo trade-off,* where we exchange a sacred value for a secular one. Even the mere thought of doing so can generate a sense of shame, for the act of comparison itself violates the sacred value, a phenomenon philosopher Joseph Raz termed "constitutive incommensurability." To compare the sacred (earth) with the secular (money) is itself effectively to commit sacrilege. In fact, the longer Clare entertained the idea of allowing the gas extraction, the more ashamed she felt.

Some decisions inevitably pit sacred values against secular concerns. Governments, for example, must decide how to allocate limited funds to subsidize such expenditures as health-care costs (expenses supporting the sacred value of life) and the improvement of roads and buildings (costs that serve the secular interest in convenience and order). Even within your own family, you must decide how to allocate limited finances without violating your sacred beliefs. Are you going to donate all of your discretionary income to feed the poor, or stop paying your bills and donate that money to advance cancer research?

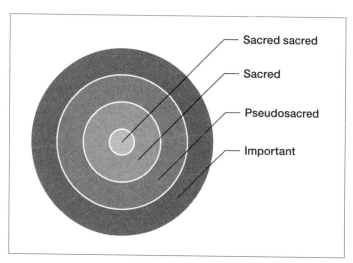

Degrees of sacredness. The further toward the center, the more inviolable the belief.

Consider reframing issues as sacred or secular. If your conflict pits a sacred value against a secular one—an explosive mix—consider recasting either the secular value as sacred or the sacred value as secular.

Clare realized that her dilemma rested not in sacrificing land for cash, but in choosing between two sacred values: protecting her land or helping her impoverished clients. On the one hand, if she refused the contract, she would adhere to her value of protecting the earth—but because all her neighbors had already signed the contract, her land and well water would still remain at risk. On the other hand, if she signed the contract, she could continue her service work and gain legal assurance that any damage to the land would be rectified. Now her conflict involved a clash of sacred values. (Philip Tetlock refers to this type of situation as a *tragic trade-off*, for choosing one sacred value means compromising another.) Ultimately she signed the contract to ensure she could continue serving her clients. Reframing the situation as a conflict over sacred values was not just a rhetorical tactic: It clarified what was truly at stake.

But the danger of pitting sacred values against other sacred values is that the dispute can become hopelessly deadlocked. If a ship is sinking and the lifeboat has room for only one more passenger, should the survivor be your child or that of another person? It is a virtually impossible question, for there exist no ultimate criteria for answering it. Converting a conflict over the sacred into a practical problem offers the potential of solving it. In the lifeboat analogy, the question can be reframed from "Whose child is more valuable?" to "How can we save both children?" By recasting the sacred in secular terms, we can sidestep the problem of trying to determine inherent worth.

3. Acknowledge What Each Side Holds Sacred

Imagine the other side's mind as a museum. Your goal is to acknowledge their sacred artifacts, historical treasures, and mementos of pride or shame. Just as you would never enter a museum and rearrange the paintings, you should not attempt to change what they deem hallowed.

While you may not share the other side's beliefs, you can respect the *reverence* they hold for those beliefs. Imagine a husband and wife arguing over the religion in which they will raise their children. While the husband does not want the children allied to his wife's faith, he can acknowledge her reverence for that faith by saying, "I know we have differences, but I also appreciate how deeply you revere your values and how important it is for you to pass them on to our children." This statement demonstrates that the husband is cognizant of his wife's sacred beliefs, which opens up the conversation to a deeper discussion of her values and how theirs overlap.

You want the other side to feel that you recognize and respect their concerns. Two tactics can help you honor their sacred values while not compromising your own:

Speak the "language of the sacred." Sociologist Émile Durkheim suggested that we cast the sacred in a wholly different world of meaning than the profane. A glass of wine is just that, unless you are a Christian attending Mass, where it symbolizes the blood of Christ. Should we treat the consecrated wine as simply a beverage, we commit an assault on the sacred. Secular language focuses on concrete reality and quantifiable measurements of worth. The language of the sacred, in contrast, converges around themes of symbolic value that exist outside the strictures of cause-and-effect logic. It requires a special vocabulary to ensure optimal respect for its subject. So when you speak to other people about what they hold sacred, consider your choice of words as a demonstration of respect for their beliefs.

To speak secular language:	To speak sacred language:
Focus on "value maximization."	Focus on honoring values.
Direct attention to tangible interests such as money.	Attend to moral, emotional, or spiritual values driving the conflict.
Argue over the terms of the deal.	Discuss narratives of suffering, pride, and connection to the sacred.
Debate what you "owe" each other.	Appreciate the merit in each side's perspective.
Make tangible concessions.	Offer symbolic concessions, such as an apology or action to mitigate offense.
Argue on the basis of secular laws and rules.	Persuade through implicit social rules, spiritual norms, religious edicts, and rituals.
Frame the discussion as an exchange of goods.	Frame the discussion as advancing mutual understanding.
Communicate interests directly.	Draw on metaphor and other indirect methods to illuminate your feelings about the sacred.
Create a contract to build trust.	Take the time to create close personal ties to build trust.
Concentrate on tangible issues (e.g., Should they have nuclear weapons?).	Explore emotional, cultural, and spiritual concerns (e.g., country X wants to maintain cultural pride and national autonomy).

After you have shown that you appreciate the other party's sacred values, they will be more open to honoring yours. Help them understand what you hold as sacred and why. Rather than simply listing your sacred values, present them in the context of a personal narrative: When did these values first take on special meaning for you? What motivates you to hold them sacred: a lifelong belief, a childhood experience, a gut feeling?

Find common ground in the sacred. Should someone desecrate what you deem sacred, they effectively demolish your sense of "symbolic immortality"—the feeling that after you pass away, you will live on through your ideas, beliefs, values, or family. If an adversary destroys the temple or manuscript most holy to your faith, you experience life's ultimate pain.

But symbolic immortality also presents an opportunity for connection. While you and the other side may hold many diverging beliefs, there is also likely to be common ground in the sacred. Recall the example of the husband and wife arguing about which religion in which to raise their children. This couple can find solace in the fact that they both desire a spiritual component in their children's lives.

Consider explicitly acknowledging a relationship, event, or principle that you and the other side hold to be sacred. For example, negotiators meeting to resolve an ethnopolitical dispute may jointly commit to the principle that the future of all their children is sacred. A similar approach was used by President Anwar Sadat, who defined his historic trip to the Al-Aqsa Mosque in Jerusalem and the Israeli Knesset as "truly sacred"; indeed, this framing helped secure political space for him to co-negotiate the Camp David Peace Accords. Even in marriage, couples who deem their affiliation sacred engage in greater collaborative problem solving and less verbal aggression, invest more in their relationship, and reap greater satisfaction from their marriage.

4. Problem Solve Within Each Side's Sphere of Identity

To problem solve sacred issues, you need to understand whether each side construes identity as fixed, fluid, or some combination of the two. I call this conception of the self a *sphere of identity*, and framing your communication within the other side's sphere of identity can boost the effectiveness of negotiation.

Tailor Your Message to Their Sphere of Identity

Several years ago a prominent international lawyer shared a story with me about how he had once arranged to meet with a teenager preparing to execute a suicide mission in the Middle East. The lawyer planned to tell the boy, "If you become a suicide bomber, you might make the newspapers for a day or two. But if you dedicate the next seventy years of your life to improving education, human rights, and economic prosperity here in the region, think about the profound difference you could make." The meeting never took place—and the lawyer never got the chance to make his case.

While the lawyer's argument made rational sense, I felt uneasy about it. I imagined myself as the teenager preparing for my moment of martyrdom, reveling in the thrill of being on a sacred mission, the support of my community, and the encouragement of my mentors, and readying myself for the fanfare that would greet me in heaven. I then pictured myself seated across from an American lawyer who was presenting a rational argument against undertaking my mission. I came to see that the lawyer's approach, while brilliant, was in fact *too* rational: It failed to take into account the boy's sphere of identity—how he saw himself in the world. While the lawyer spoke the language of the secular, the boy was more likely to respond to the language of the sacred. Combating a sacred narrative with a secular argument would almost certainly have proven ineffective.

You, too, will be much better positioned to influence the other party if you can tailor your message to their sphere of identity. I have observed that people typically position their identity within one of four spheres: fundamentalist, constructivist, anattist, or quantumist.

- In a *fundamentalist* mindset, you see your identity as fixed and governed by forces outside your control. Laws of nature or the intention of the divine determines who you are. Consider an everyday example. My wife frequently asks me to wake up early to spend time with her and our children before school; for my part, I ask her to stay up late to spend time with me. She is a morning person while I am a night owl, so our arguments on this matter go in circles until one of us throws his or her hands in the air and says, "I can't change you, and I can't change myself."

- In the *constructivist* frame of mind, identity is an ever-evolving social construction. You create your identity through interactions with others and through introspection. In this perspective the sacred has no divine essence, and an object like a holy book, no inherent holiness. It is the individual who projects meaning upon the book, transforming it from a stack of paper into something imbued with the divine. For the fundamentalist, reality is an absolute that exists outside human influence; for the constructivist, reality is in the eye of the beholder.

- In the *anattist* sphere, you have no permanent identity. You are "thoughts without a thinker," a conscious shell with drifting emotions and thoughts but no essence. This sphere is based upon the Buddhist term *anatta*, which refers to the idea that we exist as a nonself, an illusion of self, a continuously evolving flow of awareness. In the words of psychologist William James, we are *pure ego* living in the experiential world of the *I*. According to the Buddha, *anatta* is founded on the idea that "form is not the self, sensations are not the self, perceptions are not the self, assemblages are not the self, consciousness is not the self." The *anatta* transcends the material world of attachment, experiencing identity as shifting waves within the ocean of life.

- In the *quantumist* framework, identity is a combination of nature and nurture. Fundamental spiritual or biological beliefs set the stage for a panoply of possible selves while social forces construct your unique consciousness. Your identity is both fixed and fluid, and you perceive sacred objects from this same perspective. A holy book contains both intrinsic and constructed significance. You imbue it with sacred meaning and in turn revere it for its now-intrinsic significance.

These four categories do not have strict boundaries, and an individual's sphere may change over time. Negotiating the sacred does not mean you have to categorize precisely the other's sphere of identity, but rather that you must gauge it well enough to frame your message with words that will emotionally resonate within them. As a guideline, if the other side is in a fundamentalist sphere of identity, for example, discuss sacred issues from *within* their context of doctrines and absolutes. If, on the other hand, your counterpart views identity through a quantumist framework, you have greater latitude to discuss both absolutist arguments and creative options to problem solve sacred issues.

In the lawyer's never-realized conversation with the potential suicide bomber, his advice—that the boy had a long life of potential influence ahead of him—was insightful, but did not address the most appropriate sphere of identity. The lawyer assumed the boy was a quantumist, open to creative thinking about how to change course. But imagining the boy as a fundamentalist requires a recasting of the lawyer's message into the language of the sacred. Rather than initially discussing the boy's future, the lawyer could have inquired about his sacred convictions, why he believed in them, and which in particular were most important to him. He could have inquired into the boy's interpretation of Islam and how it was driving him to sacrifice his life. He could have asked what cultural and familial pressures felt so cherished that they were worth dying for. By guiding the conversation into the realm of the sacred and directly connecting the conversation to the boy's fundamental beliefs and values, the lawyer could have invited the boy to explore alternative interpretations of absolutist religious truths, maintaining reverence for his spiritual dogmas while introducing new ways of interpreting them.

Negotiating with people who hold fundamentalist beliefs is hard for a negotiator, but it is also difficult for the fundamentalist. Ironically, their ideological fixation limits *their* autonomy to negotiate with you. Their rigid identity boxes them in, making it imperative to tailor your words to their sphere.

Spheres of Identity: How We View the Nature of Identity

		Fundamentalist	Quantumist
Is identity innate?	*Yes*		
	No	Anattist	Constructivist
		No	*Yes*

Is identity socially created?

Formulate Options to Bridge the Divide

Once you adapt your message to the other's sphere of identity, invent options to bridge the substantive divide. Here are some illustrative ways to do so.

(a) Rely on constructive ambiguity. A pragmatic way to reconcile sacred differences is to come to an agreement that each side can interpret in accordance within its own sphere of identity. Former U.S. Secretary of State Henry Kissinger called this *constructive ambiguity*.

Consider the dilemma of a Hindu friend of mine, Aarti, as she and her Christian fiancé, Joseph, prepared for marriage. An important part of most Hindu marriage ceremonies is to stand in front of a fire to invoke its purifying power. But Aarti's mother learned that in Christianity, fire can symbolize not just the sacred burning bush but also the wrath of God. A fire might make Joseph's family feel uncomfortable, but the absence of fire would diminish the sacred meaning of the ceremony for Aarti's family. To solve their dilemma, Aarti and Joseph decided to take their vows in front of the flame of a candle. The choice was acceptable to Joseph, whose church ritually used candles for religious ceremonies, and it was agreeable to Aarti's family, who welcomed any inclusion of fire. Each family was able to interpret the candle from within the tenets of its respective faith.

(b) Reinterpret the meaning of the sacred. The sacred is often seen as having originated through a higher power, such as a god, who bestows upon mortals divine ordination or grand inspiration. Yet even those in a position to best convey the significance of the sacred—priests, imams, rabbis, and other spiritual leaders—are subject to the pitfalls of being human. In most traditions they are tasked with interpreting dogma, liturgy, and ritual, which means those elucidations remain open to the possibility of reinterpretation.

In a conflict over the sacred, consider exploring alternative interpretations of the sacred, a practice known as *hermeneutics*. I came to appreciate the power of this approach during my advising a negotiation program cofounded by Walid Issa, a Palestinian educator who grew up in the Deheishe refugee camp in Bethlehem. In 1948, his grandfather learned that the Israeli military was approaching his small village of Beit Etab, so the family fled their home. Nearly sixty years later, nineteen-year-old Walid prepared to travel to the United States to attend college. Before he departed, his grandfather told him, "I don't have money to give you, but this is the most valuable thing I own." He handed Walid a rusty metal key, the exact one used to lock his former home in Beit Etab. "I hold it close to my heart," he explained to his grandson. "Don't ever let me down."

Walid was uncertain what to make of this gift, which caused him great anguish. Initially he assumed it meant that his grandfather wanted him to reclaim their ancestral home. But as he looked at the key each day, he came to realize that it represented something very different: It was a symbol urging him to make peace with the Israelis and to honor his grandfather's identity. He looked beyond the physical key itself, burdened with a painful past, to its *spirit*, which opened up possibilities for action. He partnered with an Israeli educator to form Shades, a high-impact negotiation program that trains a new generation of Palestinian and Israeli leaders in government and the private sector.

(c) Give 100 percent to each. I once asked my young son, Noah, "What would you do if two people were fighting over the same thing, and it was so important to each of them that they would never give it up?" He looked at me and, without missing a beat, said, "Share it."

Noah's strategy is often overlooked in situations of conflict, where battles over holy lands and disputed regions routinely result in death and destruction. But his innocent response was a perceptive one: The problem of the sacred is located not within a piece of land or a family heirloom, but in the mind. You cannot bear to share land or a family ring with *them*. You cannot bear to work cooperatively to resolve seemingly irreconcilable differences with *them*. Yet objects, land, and love often *can* be shared. Counteracting an assault on the sacred can bring you to a place of harmony.

How, for example, do you divide sacred land if two countries each assert full rights to it? This was the situation facing President Jamil Mahuad of Ecuador as he negotiated a long-standing border dispute with President Alberto Fujimori of Peru. Each leader claimed the swath of land called Tiwintza as his country's own. Ultimately the two men found a mutually satisfactory solution. Ecuador gained ownership of a piece of the land, particularly the place where its soldiers were buried, while Peru gained sovereignty over it. The heads of the two countries agreed that the disputed territory would become an international park where no economic, political, or military activity occurred without the consent of both governments.

Attend to Both Problem Solving and Identity Affirmation

Despite your best effort to honor the sacred and resolve outstanding issues, you may become so focused on problem solving that sacred concerns feel minimized. At other times, the dialogue may focus so heavily on understanding each other's personal grievances that negotiating progress can come to a virtual standstill.

The *zoom method* is a simple tool to help you manage this dynamic. Imagine viewing your conflict through a camera. You can either zoom in to problem solve specific aspects of the conflict or zoom out to discuss each side's broader identity concerns. Knowing precisely *when* to zoom in or out is a powerful skill. It often makes sense to begin by zooming out, which enables you to examine what is personally at stake for each party in the conflict. Once you have shared your respective narratives, zoom in to problem solve the particulars. If the conversation loses focus or becomes too tense, zoom out again to realign with the broader goals that have brought everyone together. By staying alert to the shifting dynamics of this process, you can ease the emotional tension in discussing sacred issues.

The greatest challenge in negotiating the sacred—and the reason why strong emotions like anger, fear, and shame emerge in the course of doing so—is the uncomfortable reality that resolution requires sacrifice. Coming to an agreement with the other side can often feel like a betrayal of your ideals, your sacred values, your loyalty to the martyrs who fought for your cause. A successful resolution is possible only if you create the emotional and political space to consider sacrificing for the common good, to recognize that the benefits of sacrifice outweigh the costs of continued conflict. As the conversation unfolds, you must zoom in to discuss the pros and cons of sacrifice, then zoom out to validate each side's commitment to their ultimate concern.

In Sum

A conflict over the sacred is one in which the stakes are high and compromise feels inconceivable. In such circumstances it can help to respectfully
acknowledge what each side deems sacred and devise options to bridge
the substantive divide. Ultimately conflict over the sacred has no perfect
outcome. The challenge is to create mutual gains while minimizing sacrifice. Merely gaining awareness of the issues deemed sacred by the other
side is a colossal step forward.

Identity Politics

There is no history of mankind, there are only many histories of all kinds of aspects of human life. And one of these is the history of political power. This is elevated into the history of the world.

—KARL POPPER

Consider what the following three scenarios have in common:

1. The rocky marriage. A friend named Kathy calls me up in tears. Her marriage to Joe is falling to pieces. From a distance, I can see the dynamic at play: While their differences are not insurmountable, their parents unwittingly mobilize them to battle. Every time Kathy calls up her mother for consolation, her response is "You are absolutely right, Kathy. Joe *is* wrong—and as self-centered as ever. I honestly don't know how you live with him." Meanwhile, Joe's mother supports his perspective and dismisses Kathy as "difficult" and "stubborn." The parental support is tearing their marriage apart.

2. The company clash. A multinational company is in the midst of a turf war between the research and marketing divisions. Each fears the other is out to sabotage its productivity and "steal" resources. As preparations begin for next year's budget, each division's leader meets discreetly with the CEO to advocate for her own division as the "soul" of the company and a wiser investment of the company's resources.

3. The turbulent state. Serbian president Slobodan Milošević stands before a huge crowd in Gazimestan, Kosovo, invoking Serbia's defeat in Kosovo six hundred years earlier as a nationalistic call to arms. "Let the memory of Kosovo heroism live forever!" he exclaims. "Long live Serbia! Long live Yugoslavia! Long live peace and brotherhood among peoples!" Many observers credit this speech as the breaking point leading to the Kosovo war.

In each of the previous examples, the fifth of the lures—identity politics—is at play. Identity politics can jeopardize the emotional life of a marriage, the efficiency of an organization, or the security of a region. Unlike the other lures, it is often deliberately used to manipulate and divide people, fueling the Tribes Effect. But armed with the right strategies, you can use identity politics to improve your relationships and reach mutually satisfying outcomes to conflicts.

What Is Identity Politics?

Humans are, by their nature, political animals—an observation made by Aristotle more than two thousand years ago. Your every word and action conveys a message about your political standing in relation to others. You may nestle yourself in good relations with your boss or compliment a friend to strengthen your bond. Simply put, politics is about "who gets what, when, and how."

Identity politics, then, refers to *the process of positioning your identity to advance a political purpose.* You ally with specific individuals or groups within a power structure to better your odds of reaching your goals. But you also may pay a price for associating with one particular group and not another. This whole process occurs within a political space—a social circle in which people interact to make decisions. A government is the most familiar such space, but others include a marriage, friendship, or workplace. Each of these spaces presents opportunity for discord over who gets what—and at what price.

Looking back at the three examples at the beginning of this chapter, we can now see how people positioned their identities to serve some sort of political purpose—and paid the price:

- In the rocky marriage of Kathy and Joe, each mother sought to cocoon her child from emotional distress (*the purpose*), allying herself as a loyal advocate for her child (*positioning*). Each mother delegitimized the other spouse's concerns, strengthening her own child's sense of righteousness but inadvertently fracturing the couple's relations (*the price*).

- In the company example, the research and marketing leaders aspired to gain greater financial resources (*the purpose*) and each met privately with the CEO to argue for her own division's superior importance to the organization (*positioning*). But their actions reinforced their longstanding rift and reduced organizational productivity (*the price*).

- In the Serbia example, Milošević aspired to mobilize support for his vision of a greater Serbia (*the purpose*), rallying Serbian nationalism through his speech on the former battlegrounds in Kosovo (*positioning*). But he also sharpened the lines of division between the region's ethnopolitical groups; the subsequent violence contributed to a massive loss of lives and brought Milošević before the International Criminal Tribunal for the former Yugoslavia, where he was indicted for crimes against humanity (*the price*).

Identity politics unfolds at all levels of daily life. Most of the time it plays out barely noticeably in the background, as when your teenager praises your new haircut (*positioning*) and then asks for a raise in her allowance (*purpose*). But politics can sometimes create uncomfortable situations. A neighbor knocks on your door with homemade cookies (*positioning*), then asks if you can help her son get a job at your company (*purpose*). Even if you fundamentally reject the machinations of identity politics, it is unavoidable. As you head into the conference room for your meeting today, whom will you sit beside? To whose opinions will you pay the most attention? At a purely practical level, your identity can influence the resources to which you have access, and therefore can be your ticket to privilege or paucity. Unless you attune yourself to identity politics, you risk becoming its unwitting pawn.

The Pitfalls of Politics

Beware the many ways one can fall victim to divisive politics. *First*, we may be unaware of the political landscape, which leaves us vulnerable to being exploited. A leader may impose a narrative on us—as Milošević did upon his country—and create feelings of division between us and others. *Second*, we may cling to a *negative identity*, defining who we are as *against* the other side and rejecting anything they propose. In an extreme situation, we lose all semblance of our own identity, identifying ourselves only in terms of opposition to the other side. *Third,* we may feel excluded from the decision-making process, further dividing us from others. *Finally,* we may feel like a pawn trapped within an unfair political system.

The remainder of this chapter offers practical strategies to address each of these pitfalls.

Pitfall	Strategy
1. Ignorance of the political landscape.	1. Map the political landscape.
2. Clinging to a negative identity.	2. Build a positive identity.
3. Reliance on an exclusive decision-making process.	3. Design an inclusive decision-making process.
4. Treated like a political pawn.	4. Protect yourself from being exploited.

1. Map the Political Landscape

People may attempt to use politics against you, but before you can take effective action to protect yourself, you first need to become aware of the particulars of the political landscape. Examine who influences whom, and who has the potential to trigger the Tribes Effect and impede resolution.

Look for Two Levels of Political Influence

Chimpanzees and humans have a great deal in common. On the surface, chimpanzee relations appear to be structured around dominance, with the strongest male at the top of the hierarchy. The eminent primate researcher Frans de Waal, however, observed that alongside this formal structure is a more informal organization of power, which he called "a network of positions of influence." De Waal likens the hierarchical struc-ture to a "ladder" and the informal structure to a "network."

Humans also navigate these same two levels of political influence: ladderlike hierarchies and networklike webs of influence. Maintaining an awareness of both can help you better understand the politics fueling your conflict.

The Ladder: Who's the boss? Most companies are organized such that every employee understands exactly who holds authority over whom: The boss is at the top, and the subordinates, with their varying degrees of power, are beneath. But outside a regimented organization like an office, formal power structures are not always so clear. Several years ago I asked my then-six-year-old son, Noah, to turn off the television and read a book. He looked up at me angrily and asked, "Who's the boss here—you or Mom?" The question was legitimate; Noah was wondering if he might find a loophole in the family power structure that would buy him a few more minutes of TV. Unfortunately for him, my wife and I were *both* the boss in this landscape.

Even when a ladder of influence is not explicitly defined, it can still prove significant. The president of the United States is sometimes referred to as "the most powerful person on earth," in charge of a vast military and economic complex. But when the president flies on Air Force One, who is the most powerful? The pilot. More generally, the world is governed by mul-tiple ladders of influence. If you are trying to influence your CEO's decisions on budget allocation, you may best be served by focusing your efforts on the chief financial officer.

The Network: Who are your allies? Political relations are also influ-enced by your social networks—the web of friends, allies, and acquain-tances with whom you associate and on whom you depend. These connections may be institutionalized, like those created by marriage, fam-ily, or membership in a social organization. Or the ties may be casual, such as those between allies at work or a group of friends.

Positioning yourself wisely can help you advance your political cause. You may cozy up to the boss's spouse; donate money to a university to increase the odds that your child will gain acceptance; or call a well-connected family member for help landing a job. Probably all languages have words akin to "clout." Arabic recognizes the term *wasta*, roughly defined as the use of social connections to influence a decision. In Chinese, *guanxi* refers to personal relations that you can call upon for favors and services. In Spanish, *palanca* suggests you have good connections. In Tanzania, a diplomat described to me the unique concept of *utani*, a Swahili word describing "friendly, joking relations" between rival tribes or villages in which "you can joke about almost anything without insult." Each of these approaches is an example of an informal structure that advances a political objective.

People often assume that formal politics drives informal relations, but generally the opposite is true: The rich are friendly with the rich, the powerful with the powerful, and these informal networks are often a deciding factor in who holds vaunted positions in formal hierarchies.

Your social networks become your tribes—composed of kinlike associates you can count on. You choose your friends freely and know they have your best interests at heart. Consider the case of a recently appointed CEO whose first order of business was to decide whether to sell off part of the company. He sought advice from board members, who outranked him on the ladder of influence. But on whom did he rely for trusted counsel? His smart and faithful administrative assistant.

Stay Actively Aware of the Political Landscape

You have a *continuum of awareness*. At one end are those things of which you are keenly cognizant, such as the angry expression on your spouse's face. At the other end are those things of which you are unaware you are aware. As you read this, for example, in the background may be the ticking of a clock, the humming of a dishwasher, or people talking nearby, but you are not consciously paying attention to these sounds. Where the political landscape is concerned, to be most effective *you must stay aware of your awareness.*

Notice when others seek to shape your identity. In a conflict, identity shapers seek to mold the dominant narrative. This is most apparent in political campaigns, where leaders try to impose an identity narrative on the masses to gain support. The candidate stands on a podium and declares that "we" must now come together and fight "them" on whatever critical issues are in question. Identity shapers turn conflict over resources into a game of identity politics, pressing the masses into a singular identity by any means they can. If they succeed in shaping your identity, they gain the prize they seek: your loyalty.

President Milošević's goal was to get Serbians to embrace a nationalistic identity, thus effectively mobilizing a loyal army to serve his political ambitions. The more forcefully he declared this nationalistic ideology as a sacred part of Serbian destiny, the more successfully he enlisted supporters and silenced dissenters.

Be attentive to circumstances in which you begin to feel caged in a narrative about who you are. In organizations, identity shapers often vie to shape your identity for their own purposes. I once consulted for a senior manager who felt unhappy with his job, despite a recent promotion that raised his pay and earned him more respect. He realized that in his elevated position, he could no longer tell whether his subordinates genuinely wanted to befriend him—or simply played up to him for political gain. This uncomfortable feeling of ambiguity had regularly stirred within him, but he had only recently become conscious of it. Again, when it comes to identity politics, awareness is crucial.

Attune to the other side's political pressures. In a conflict, your negotiating counterpart is rarely a single actor. While an individual may be negotiating at the table with you, he or she has associates *behind the table* who hold vested interests in the outcome. Robert Putnam calls this a "two-level game": Your counterpart's resistance to reconciliation may have nothing to do with *you* (level 1) but everything to do with *their* internal political pressures (level 2). In an international conflict, two leaders may be personally willing to repair damaged political relations, but to do so they must navigate the domestic concerns of policy makers, agencies, interest groups, and their own advisers. In a marital conflict, each spouse may consult with parents to seek perspectives, as Kathy and Joe did. The more each stakeholder attunes to the other's political pressures, the better positioned both will be to devise a viable rapprochement.

To discover the other party's political pressures in the conflict, put yourself in their shoes and imagine whom they might be trying to please.

This mental exercise helped to resolve a difficult conflict between a company and a consultant, Tim, who had never received payment for his services. He submitted an invoice, then another, then a third. Each time, the company's project manager responded with yet another administrative request: "We need a new invoice with these stipulations." "We need a different *kind* of invoice—one that includes reimbursement costs." "We need an invoice *without* reimbursement costs."

Beyond the frustration of not receiving his fee, Tim was infuriated by these e-mails, which seemed to blame *him* for his payment's being delayed. Realizing that a lawsuit would be a major financial and emotional drain, Tim consulted me. We noticed that not all of the e-mails attributed blame to Tim, just those on which the project manager's boss had been copied. It seemed as though the project manager were trying to cover for her own administrative error, hoping to appear responsible to her manager by shifting blame to Tim. After recognizing this political maneuver, I advised Tim to commend the project manager's persistence (at least she had never stopped communicating), and then call the project manager's boss to ask for an expedited payment. Tim had the check within the week.

The same principle—attuning to the other's political pressures—is essential to international reconciliation, as former U.S. Secretary of State James Baker confirmed when the Program on Negotiation at Harvard Law School honored him with its annual Great Negotiator Award. He reminisced about how, after the Soviet Union collapsed, the United States could have declared victory in the Cold War. But Baker and President George H. W. Bush decided that "the one thing we should do is *not gloat*"—despite pressures within their own political party to claim triumph. These two leaders kept their eyes on the prize: building long-term cooperative relations to advance international stability. If the United States were to assert that it had been victorious in the conflict, leaders of the nascent Russian Federation would have faced even more severe political backlash from within, reducing their political power and leaving the United States with a weaker negotiating partner.

Be alert for spoilers. Spoilers are people who try to undermine your efforts to resolve a conflict—and identity politics is a key tool in their arsenal, for conflict suits their political interests more than resolution.

There are *unwitting spoilers*, like the mothers of Kathy and Joe, the disputing marital couple: Both women had good intentions, but their actions destabilized their children's relationship. Then there are *intentional spoilers*—people who are keen on sabotaging agreements, whether a disgruntled employee who slows operations or a political group that attempts to undermine peace talks. Intentional spoilers often keep their efforts secret, for anonymity is their greatest weapon.

The spoiler often supports the negotiation process at first—winning your confidence—but then undercuts it before a peace settlement is reached. In Shakespeare's play *Macbeth*, Lord Banquo warns Macbeth, "To win us to our harm, the instruments of darkness tell us truths, win us with honest trifles, to betray's in deepest consequence."

To recognize spoilers, survey the political landscape for individuals or groups whose identity may feel threatened by reconciliation. Spoilers resist change; they may fear both diminishment of their hierarchical position of power and alienation from influential social circles.

Consider the situation of Amy, a senior manager at a midsized technology company experiencing rapid growth. She noticed that Jack, a senior technician and star employee on staff for twenty years, had recently begun acting erratically. He delayed a project, spread rumors about "inept management," and came to work in an irritable mood. Jack had become a spoiler within the organization—but why? Amy noted that a young hire had recently joined Jack's team, bringing comparable technical skills, and wondered whether Jack viewed the new employee as a political threat.

In a meeting with Amy, Jack confessed, "I'm worried you want to replace me—that I'm getting too old for this company."

Amy, surprised, assured him, "Not at all! We decided to bring the employee on board to *support* you, not replace you. Senior management believes you would be a great mentor." Amy allayed Jack's fears, and he reverted to his usual productive self.

2. Build a Positive Identity

In the course of a conflict, you may become so focused on defeating the other side that you take on a *negative identity*: You define your identity in opposition to theirs. A classic example involves a rebellious preacher's son who so despises his father that he takes up atheism and begins drinking heavily. The same dynamic is characteristic of political ad campaigns, when candidates smear the other's record without sharing anything positive about their own. If you assume a negative identity, you thwart any peaceful resolution, because the moment the conflict is resolved, your negative identity ceases to exist—ironically turning the conflict's resolution from a welcome outcome to an existential blow.

To counteract the temptation to take on a negative identity, consciously build a *positive identity*. This requires you to improve your relationship with the other side—your relational identity—and redefine your core identity in positive terms.

Emphasize the Relentless We

The single most powerful advice for overcoming divisive politics is to persistently emphasize that your conflict is a *shared* challenge. It is not you versus the other side but the two of you attempting to resolve the conflict together. As the Tribes Effect pulls you incessantly toward division, you must fight back with an even more insistent emphasis on the value of cooperation. I call this the *Relentless We*.

Consider the Tribes Exercise. In all of the rare instances when the world has been saved, the common denominator has been not the appeal of rational rhetoric but rather a dogged insistence among the participants that the ultimate goal is a shared one: to save *our* world.

This lesson struck me one day when I answered a knock at my door and encountered an alarmed neighbor. "Did you hear?" she asked, shaken. "There was a terrorist attack at the marathon. We don't know if Melissa is okay." Melissa is a mutual neighbor in our town outside Boston and an avid runner. "No one's heard from her yet."

I hurried inside and turned on the television. Two bombs had exploded near the finish line of the Boston Marathon, killing three people and injuring 250 others. My heart raced. I had nearly taken my boys to the finish line that day, but at the last minute remained at home to catch up on work.

Shortly thereafter, President Obama made an impassioned speech. He could have talked about terrorism and how the United States would renew its war *against* it—constructing a negative identity for us as a nation—but instead he created a positive national identity. "There are no Republicans or Democrats," he said. "We are Americans, united in concern for our fellow citizens." In a situation that threatened to draw an entire nation toward the Tribes Effect, the president resisted, choosing to unite people instead of railing against the yet-unknown perpetrators of the tragedy.

Define Identity in Positive Terms

Positive politics involves clarifying who you *are* rather than who you are not. What are the critical values of your family, marriage, company, organization, or ethnic group? A positive identity bonds people in a shared purpose and value system.

To construct a positive identity, identify your defining values and put them into practice. After the Boston Marathon bombings, for example, President Obama accentuated the values of American unity and concern for fellow citizens. Your goal is to articulate values to which people on all sides of the conflict can relate positively, in the same way that anyone can relate to President Obama's message that after a bombing citizens will be concerned for one another.

During a trip to Northern Ireland several years ago, I met Peter Robinson, the first minister (prime minister) of Northern Ireland, and his leadership team. Although the Good Friday Agreement had brought an end to decades of violence, the subsequent years had seen renewed tension between Protestant and Catholic communities. What might Northern Ireland do to avoid the lure of identity politics? Training political leadership in the tools of negotiation could be useful, I argued, but that alone would not solve the problem.

Meeting with the first minister reinforced my belief that any effort at full-fledged change required restructuring the perceived identity of Northern Ireland in positive terms, an idea I shared with an informal liaison to the political leadership. "The international community associates Northern Ireland with conflict resolution," I explained. "The country represents a success story." He nodded in agreement. "The problem with this," I went on, "is that people *continue* to associate Northern Ireland with conflict. Now that the conflict has been halted, what if you help foster a new image of Northern Ireland that emphasizes its cultural and geographic beauty?"

I wanted to stress that it would be possible to redefine Northern Ireland's identity—not as a formerly conflict-ridden country, but rather as a place with a wealth of attractive attributes. To sustain peace, identity must be painted in the positive.

The first minister, deputy first minister, and ministers from all parties in Northern Ireland's power-sharing government worked impressively together to focus attention on this idea. And the Irish president and the British queen participated in a number of high-profile symbolic acts to draw attention to the strong bonds between the British and Irish identities. Despite these efforts, waves of continued tension in Northern Ireland have highlighted the importance of pursuing a positive identity *over the course of time*, reducing the likelihood that the weight of the past will reignite hostility.

3. Design an Inclusive Decision-Making Process

Even if you work hard to build positive relations, people may feel excluded from the decision-making process and jockey behind the scenes to sabotage agreement. Thus to support cooperative relations, design an inclusive decision-making process that enables everyone to maintain a positive identity while grappling constructively with difficult issues.

Consider as simple a question as where to go on your family vacation. Who decides? Who *decides* who decides? In my family, this issue can quickly ruffle feathers. My wife wants to relax in the Caribbean islands; I prefer the desert sands of the Middle East; the kids want the roller coasters of Disney World; our in-laws urge us to visit them. So Mia and I use the following simple tool to solve our dilemma.

The ECNI Method

This process provides a template for inclusive decision making while also accounting for differences in authority. Begin by considering three key questions: (1) What is the decision to be made? (2) Whom does this decision affect? (3) How much input should each stakeholder have in the decision-making process? If you believe that a stakeholder is likely to be a spoiler, you may even want to exclude them from part or all of the negotiation process—but weigh that against the risk that they may feel rejected and seek retribution.

Now draw three columns on a sheet of paper. In the first column, write the decision to be made. In the second column, list the key stakeholders the decision affects. To complete column three, employ the ECNI method, deciding which stakeholders to

- *exclude* from the decision-making process;
- *consult* before making the decision;
- *negotiate* with to reach a decision; and
- *inform* after a decision has been made.

Mia and I sat down one evening and discussed who should be part of the vacation negotiation and who should merely be consulted or kept informed. The chart on page 124 illustrates the results of our thinking. I **consulted** with my department chair on the date of our trip to ensure there was no major academic meeting scheduled for that time; Mia and I then **consulted** with our parents and kids on their interests; and finally the two of us **negotiated** the location and **informed** everyone: We would head to Block Island in the summer to catch the sun, sand, and hiking trails, and then join the in-laws over the winter holidays at Disney World. We decided to postpone any international travel until all our kids passed the toddler stage. And we agreed that, should any of the stakeholders oppose our suggestions, we would **negotiate** with them. Using the ECNI Method—exclude, consult, negotiate, inform—we streamlined the politics of decision making and enjoyed a great vacation.

What is the decision?	Who is involved?	What is the level of input?
When and where to go on a family vacation	Mia	N
	Dan	N
	Parents	C (on location and date), I
	Kids	C (on location)
	Boss	C (on date) and I (on location)

In terms of the level of input: E = Exclude this person; C = Consult this person; N = Negotiate with this person; I = Inform this person afterward.

In Multiparty Conflicts: Clump

When multiple groups are in conflict, identity politics can inflame divisiveness. There is a serious risk that some parties will feel politically excluded from the decision-making process, turning them into potential spoilers. Even if everyone is well intentioned, the mere challenge of coordinating a negotiation among large numbers of people—each with their own set of interests—can lead to polarization.

The solution is to cluster people in a manageable set of groups, each with its own representative, thus guaranteeing that everyone still can contribute their political input. Imagine, for example, how difficult it would be to reach an agreement on international environmental policies at a summit attended by more than seven thousand delegates from 172 nations, each with their own interests and expectations. This was the challenge facing Ambassador Tommy Koh, chair of the Earth Summit in Rio de Janeiro and recipient of the Great Negotiator Award at the Program on Negotiation at Harvard Law School. Koh knew everyone needed to feel confident that they were an integral part of the decision-making process, so he found creative ways to clump groups together. This enabled a single representative to negotiate on behalf of groups that had a mutual interest, such as the "oil- and coal-producing countries," "island nations threatened by rising sea waters," and "rainforest preservation advocates." Once he divided the seven thousand delegates into a manageable number of representatives, he clarified political processes for informing, consulting, and negotiating and produced one of the most effective global mega-conferences ever.

4. Protect Yourself from Being Exploited

No matter how hard you work to build a positive identity, there is always the danger that people will use identity politics against you. So it is critical to take preemptive action to shield your identity from harm. Three strategies prove particularly useful here.

Name the Dynamic—and Propose an Alternative

If you sense that identity politics is destroying a relationship you value, name the dynamic—and suggest a way to achieve inclusive relations. Consider the marital conflict between Kathy and Joe, the couple whose respective mothers provoked strong emotions through one-sided backing of their children. Kathy might say to her mother, "Mom, you know I love you, and I appreciate your support. But every time I fight with Joe, you put him down, and it only fuels my anger toward him. Next time I come to you upset, can you help me see things from his perspective, too?" It takes courage to make such a statement, but it can mean the difference between respect and rancor or, in a worst-case scenario, even marriage and divorce.

Advocating for inclusive politics is equally conducive to reconciliation in the international sphere. Several years ago I facilitated a private meeting in Jordan between Israeli, Palestinian, and broader Arab leadership to discuss avenues to promote resolution to the Israeli-Palestinian conflict. As these leaders discussed strategies to import a more powerful security apparatus to stabilize the region, one frustrated panelist, a former Arab head of state, burst out, "Will Israel be stronger with a wall surrounding it—or with twenty-two Arab embassies in its capital?" His point was controversial but powerful: Inclusive politics can build bridges of connection.

Enhance Your Structural Power

Politics is about power, and power often resides not in *who* you are but in *where you are positioned* in a social network or ladder of influence. People often shield themselves from political harm by aligning with powerful individuals in their social networks and ladders of influence. The boss's inner circle usually has greater job security than the employees at the bottom of the ladder.

If you are David facing Goliath, seek to strengthen your structural power. One method is to build a political coalition. Look for people with a similar agenda and combine forces. During the Cold War, for example, a number of states banded together to form the Organization of Non-Aligned States (OAS), which was not formally aligned with either the United States or the Soviet Union. OAS served as a counterweight to the imperialistic and colonialist tendencies dividing much of the world at the time.

A second method is to establish a role for yourself that positions you in a place of political influence with respect to your counterpart. A case in point comes from Bineta Diop, the African Union's special envoy for women, peace, and security, and a colleague on a project I launched to build a global curriculum on conflict prevention. She described to me how, as war flared in the Democratic Republic of the Congo (DRC) between the government and rebels, women were its primary victims, and many of them wanted to contribute to the peace negotiations. So Diop and her organization, Femmes Africa Solidarité, mobilized senior female African leaders to meet with President Kabila, then in his midthirties. They drew political strength from their stature, age, and gender. "As your mothers and sisters, we are motivated by peace," Diop boldly stated to President Kabila, commanding his attention, "and we want to advise you." Their meeting lasted several hours, and the president lent his support to their plan to meet with the rebels. This and related efforts paved the way for the increased participation of women in political negotiations in the DRC, including in the Sun City talks that resulted in an agreement on many key issues.

A third method to strengthen your structural power is to pursue social agendas that protect your identity from harm. For example, you can work to institutionalize new laws, organizational policies, or household rules. This process takes time, but the payoff can be tremendous. In the

United States, for example, the Civil Rights Act of 1964 outlawed discrimination based on race, religion, sex, and national origin. Though discrimination still exists, such social policies provide a critical shield of protection.

Some advice for Goliath is also in order. The fact that you have power *over* the other party does not mean you have maximized your strategic position. You often can expand your influence by sharing power *with* the other side. Rather than compelling the other side to do what you want (coercion), you can come together to get things done (cooperation).

Establishing cooperative relations tends to be a good long-term political strategy. Coercion threatens the other side's autonomy, leading to potential resistance and resentment; it may work in the short term, but tends to be ineffective in the long run. Cooperation, in contrast, expands each side's sense of autonomy. Coming together to deal with differences only deepens the overall emotional investment in resolving the conflict and honoring its outcome. Managers, for example, can better motivate employees through cooperation than through coercion, as employees feel greater affiliation to the company and expanded ownership over the product of their work.

The same principle can enhance success in the political context. Consider the leadership approach of Julius Nyerere, the first president of Tanzania. More than 125 ethnic tribes live in the nation, creating an environment ripe for divisive identity politics. But Nyerere prioritized national identity over tribal identity. He shared governmental power with major tribes so no single tribe could hold full authority. He outlawed public census of people's tribal affiliations; ordered compulsory military service for all classes and tribes; and made it clear that he was president not because of his particular ethnic background, but because of his leadership abilities. These efforts were successful: Despite persistent waves of violent conflict across other parts of Africa, Tanzania remained peaceful.

Forge Good Political Relations

The final—and most powerful—way to shield your identity from harm is to proactively build friendly relations with your counterpart. This is the

Relentless We, back again. Two countries with a history of tension should expend considerable resources building good relations, and the wisest elected officials should meet with their political rivals *before* taking office, building constructive relations that allow for cooperative work on divisive issues in the future. A former student of mine took this advice to heart: She went on to hold a top congressional post, and before settling into the job she met with her political counterpart in a farmhouse on the outskirts of the city. She later told me that that get-together was critical to her later success in bridging the political divide.

A good relationship is sincere, amicable, and resilient to tension; it allows for differences to be safely discussed. But such relations require maintenance. The marital couple who fails to work through their day-to-day grievances should be prepared for a blow-up. And the negotiator trying to broker peace must maintain communication with concerned parties—or be ready to deal with crisis.

The Relentless We really must be relentless.

In Sum

Identity politics is a matter of power, and power is *relational*: You acquire it through your relations with others. Negative identity politics traps you in adversarial relations that can spiral your conflict toward the Tribes Effect. Positive identity politics, on the other hand, can foster cooperative relations. The underlying strategy of positive identity politics is straightforward: *Define who you are, not who you are not. Then persistently position yourself to maximize partnership and minimize resentment.*

Section 3

Bridging the Divide

Integrative Dynamics—a Four-Step Method

There is nothing quite like listening to the late, great jazz musician Dizzy Gillespie. As he brings the trumpet to his mouth, puckering his lips and expanding his cheeks like two balloons, the sound that flows through his instrument feels rhythmic and melodious, then as choppy as a car hitting bumps in the road, then flowing again like water in a stream. As a drum sizzles softly in the background and a piano accents three off notes, Dizzy hits a potent staccato—*bop-ditti-bop-bop-BOOM*—disrupting the rhythm once again and then striking a downward scale with penetrating speed and bravado. This wild array of sounds and beats, discordant and discombobulated, frenzied and fanciful, weaves together in a strikingly integrated whole, a harmonious trail of musical whims.

Jazz finds harmony in dissonance. The dissonance remains, but is held together by a deeper, integrative force.

This insight is crucial to resolving an emotionally charged conflict. To heal broken relations, you need to find transcendent unity. While your core identity and the other's may *feel* completely incompatible, do not let the Five Lures undermine your sense of what is possible. You have the capacity to create harmony within yourself and in your relations with others. Once you believe in the possibility of transcendent unity, you open yourself up to finding it. Dizzy Gillespie undoubtedly had off nights, searching in vain for that elusive well of creative energy. At times he undoubtedly was dissatisfied with his own performance; transcendent unity can be elusive. But his "on nights" were flawless. He integrated Afro-Cuban rhythms with Afro-American jazz, bopping up and down scale after scale in lightning-fast tempo and creating a musical whole much larger than the sum of its discordant parts.

Conventional Methods of Conflict Resolution Are Insufficient

Two conventional methods of conflict resolution—positional bargaining and problem solving—are insufficient to achieve transcendent unity in an emotionally charged conflict.

Positional Bargaining?

In positional bargaining, you and the other side take firm, opposing stances, cling tightly to them, and stubbornly refuse to concede. This method works best in straightforward transactions. When purchasing a new car, for example, the buyer requests a lowball price, the dealer responds with a higher one, and both sides volley back and forth until finally agreeing on a number somewhere in the middle. Everyone walks away relatively happy.

Positional bargaining falls short, however, when issues of identity are at stake. Identity implicates indivisible issues of meaning, memory, and narrative. To reduce identity to a tradable commodity that can be compromised is to undermine its very essence. For almost anyone, such existential compromise would seem repugnant. Imagine two leaders negotiating a sacred piece of land:

Politician A: If you sacrifice 20 percent of your religious values, we'll give you 20 percent more land.

Politician B: I will never agree to that! I suggest we do an even 10 percent sacrifice on religious values. You add a 20 percent increase in respect for my people, and we will guarantee a 5 percent decrease in humiliation of your people for two years.

Politician A: Only if you include a clause in the contract noting that you'll wipe out all negative memories of my people. Is it a deal?

The entire premise of the above negotiation—that core identity can be quantitatively adjusted and traded—represents a fundamental methodological flaw. Yet even at Davos, the leaders held to entrenched positions and presumed that their task was to persuade others to join their tribe, until positional bargaining produced an explosion.

Problem Solving?

A second common method of conflict resolution, *collaborative problem solving*, encourages you and the other side to look beneath your respective positions for underlying interests and then to devise an agreement that best satisfies those deeper motivations. But this approach also has serious deficits in the face of an emotionally charged conflict.

Consider one of the most well-known anecdotes in the field of negotiation. Two young sisters fight over an orange. "I want the orange!" yells one. "No, it's mine!" responds the other. They tug back and forth. Along comes their mother, frustrated and tired. Should she cut the orange in half? Tell the sisters that no one gets it? Eat it herself? Well versed in problem solving, she finally asks each child, "Why do you want the orange?" The younger sister sniffles and says she needs its vitamin C to help cure her cold. The older sister says she is making a pie and needs the rind. Aha! The solution becomes clear. By looking behind the girls' stated positions to determine their underlying interests, she can give each daughter what she wants without compromise.

Problem solved! Or is it? I used to think so, until I became a parent. I have three young boys who have a knack for sibling rivalry, and problem solving tends to be no more than a temporary solution. In the real world, the mother in the above anecdote could expect, only minutes after resolving the orange dispute, that the girls would begin to argue over who should get the bigger cookie or the last piece of pie or some other issue. In other words, *the mother may have solved the problem, but not the fundamental dynamic.* The emotional intensity of each sister's commitment to getting her way suggests deeper concerns—ones that involve identity. Who is stronger? Smarter? More loved? Until such issues are confronted and dealt with, any solution to the presenting problem will only temporarily forestall a new conflict.

To overcome an emotionally charged conflict, an alternative method of conflict resolution needs to be found—and Dizzy Gillespie's discordant harmony offers a way.

The Power of Integrative Dynamics

To reconcile strained relations, summon the power of *integrative dynamics*—emotional forces that pull you toward greater connection, with the most stable connection being transcendent unity. In this state of mind, you move beyond the pull of opposing perspectives, beyond the duality of us versus them. Integrative dynamics link you and the other side together as *one*, separate but united. Just as the Five Lures divide you from the other side (regardless of your similarities), integrative dynamics connect you (regardless of your differences).

Integrative dynamics hold the power to convert your relations from adversarial to collegial, shifting the habitual center of your emotional energies from enmity to amity. Achieving this requires an emotionally intense process to transform your relations until positive sentiment occurs outside your conscious will, leaving you feeling as if a dark cloud had suddenly lifted. I view this process as a *relational conversion*, for through it you effectively alter the emotional space that exists between you and the other side. As in a religious conversion, the key is to believe change is possible and to surrender yourself to it. You will still feel afflictive emotions, but if you trust in the potential of integrative dynamics, your healing instincts will follow.

Integrative dynamics pulls you toward a communal mindset, which is characterized as:

1. *Cooperative.* Rather than viewing the other side solely as a threat, you are able to identify ties of connection and highlight them to foster cooperative relations. You do not disregard difference, but you do not turn it into a basis for division.

2. *Compassionate.* A communal mindset invokes compassion toward your own plight, as well as toward the suffering of your counterpart. In a conflict, some people may suffer more than others, but everyone feels a degree of pain. Compassion is a humanistic ideal, because it demonstrates that your motives extend beyond self-interest. As your connections improve, compassion naturally flows between you and the other party.

3. *Open.* In a communal mindset, you are open to connecting with others. The walls of your identity become porous, allowing you to learn about the other side's concerns and to share your own. Rather than getting mired in a battle over core identities, you permit yourself to imagine new, creative approaches to relate to each other.

Divisive Mindset (the Tribes Effect)	Communal Mindset
1. Adversarial	1. Cooperative
2. Self-righteous	2. Compassionate
3. Closed	3. Open

Integrative dynamics comprises a four-step approach to reconcile damaged relations and resolve identity-based differences. The chart on the next page depicts these steps and how they interconnect. In brief, the process begins with your engaging in a unique method to understand how you and the other side each view your relations in the conflict. Once your narratives feel heard and acknowledged, you jointly work through emotional pain. As your relations thaw, opportunities open up to build authentic connections, which provide a basis for recasting your relationship within a mutually affirming narrative. Subsequent chapters guide you through each step.

Principles of Integrative Dynamics

Before discussing the specifics of integrative dynamics, it is helpful to get a big-picture understanding of the method and its goals. There are several key principles to keep in mind.

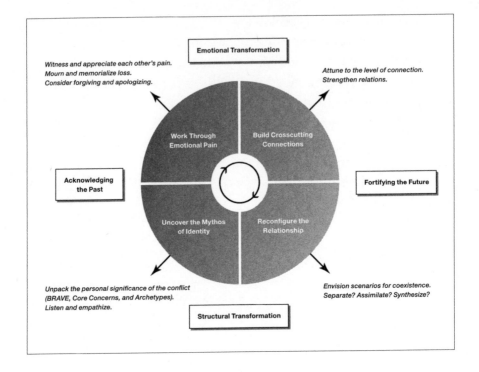

1. The Objective: Strive for Harmony, Not Victory

In an emotionally charged conflict, you may aspire to win over the other side, but this is unlikely to create conditions for a stable peace. Your victory is the other's loss, and their subsequent resentment typically inspires some form of vengeance.

The goal of integrative dynamics is to produce harmonious relations with the other side *and* within yourself. Substantive differences over land or other tangible issues can be solved, but differences in identity must be harmonized. You cannot bend the other's will to your beliefs, but you can change the nature of your relationship, viewing your differences within a framework of transcendent unity.

2. The Path to Harmony Is Nonlinear

While I depict integrative dynamics as a neat cyclical process consisting of four linear steps, this description is more a convenient guideline than a strictly accurate description. To foster integrative dynamics, you will have to move back and forth through these steps in an emotionally volatile flight: You may despise your spouse one day, feel a hint of forgiveness the next, return to a state of livid righteousness the third day, and remorsefully reconnect a week later.

Nor are these four steps intended to be exhaustive, for there are innumerable paths to reconciliation. But rather than offering you a thousand-page tome that would leave you with too much information to be of practical use, I have identified critical elements that are, on the whole, both memorable and applicable, whether you are trying to negotiate a marital dispute or an international clash.

3. The Path to Harmony Comprises Both the Past and the Future

An emotionally charged conflict tosses us into a sea of bitter history and future fears, where we must confront a fundamental choice: Should we focus on healing the past or cooperating on joint activities that promote future relations?

One school of thought, characteristically that with a psychoanalytic bent, argues that failure to deal with the past condemns us to repeat it. If an ethnic minority sees itself as the historical target of social abuse and discrimination by "the powers that be," it is unlikely to embrace full and enthusiastic citizenship without financial and symbolic restitution for perceived injustice. Even with such restitution, the past may still haunt the group's sense of communal belonging.

Another set of scholars argues that raising ghosts of the past merely recycles old conflicts. The thinking here is: "What's done is done. It's better to solve current problems jointly and build strong new relationships than to rehash old ones." Collaborative problem solving takes a stance in this direction, focusing disputants on devising forward-looking solutions to pressing problems.

So which academic camp is right? Both: Past and future are both important. Past experience absolutely affects your present emotional relations, just as present emotional relations affect your future ones. The question is how to honor the past and build a better future. Integrative dynamics approaches this problem by looking backward *and* forward. The first two steps of the method are past-focused, deconstructing identity narratives and coming to terms with relational wounds. The latter two steps are forward-looking, reconstructing relations to strive toward transcendent unity.

4. The Path to Harmony Requires Emotional and Structural Transformation

Resolving an emotionally charged conflict requires you not just to release afflictive emotions, but also to change the structure of your relations. A woman in an abusive relationship may take part in therapy with her husband and successfully release much of her anger and pain, but if there is no change to their patterns of interaction, the abuse will continue. Similarly, the leaders of two disputing factions may negotiate their political differences, but if their home communities cling to adversarial perceptions of each other, the conflict will only continue. Thus, afflictive emotions and divisive structures are barriers to conflict resolution, and each is addressed within the method of integrative dynamics.

The Making of a Mountain

Integrative dynamics can be understood through a comparison to geology. Beneath our feet lie massive plates of earth that create continents and islands. These plates are like parts to a moving jigsaw puzzle, constantly drifting ever so slightly in response to subterranean forces. When the edges of two plates collide, they produce powerful geologic activity, whether in the form of a damaging earthquake or the creation of a mountain.

Now imagine that these plates represent our core identity drifting through social interactions. Most of the time we enjoy relative peace of mind. But when two people's identities clash, the result can be a reverberating emotional tremor. The question is: Will the clash result in an earthquake or a mountain?

An earthquake is destructive, harming us and others by shaking the very foundation of our identities. The mountain is constructive, combining our identities into a whole greater than the sum of the parts. Integrative dynamics creates the conditions for a clash of identities to result in a mountain.

10

Uncover Your Mythos of Identity

Humans are innate storytellers. From the moment you are born, your family wraps you in stories about your identity—naming you, teaching you about your culture, and inculcating in you a historical web of allies and adversaries. These stories lend coherence to your life and shape to your identity.

Of all the stories that fuel conflict, none affects you more than your *mythos of identity*—the core narrative that shapes how you see your identity in relation to that of the other side. In a conflict, you are likely to regard yourself as the victim and the other as the villain. You fill in the details of this mythos with personal grievances and accusations. Of course, the other side also sees the conflict through a mythos—and in theirs *they* are the victim. Unless you transform the fundamental way you relate to each other—your mythos—your conflict will remain.

But to characterize your mythos solely as a liability is to tell only half the story. Just as atomic energy can be used productively to generate electricity, your mythos can be used to bring about reconciliation. The more deeply you appreciate each other's mythos, the more space you create to build positive relations. The other's "irrational" behavior becomes understandable.

This chapter presents a unique method to uncover each party's mythos. As it turns out, merely acknowledging grievances is not sufficient to resolve an emotionally charged conflict. You need tools to unpack the symbolic significance of the conflict and reshape your relations, yielding a more successful dialogue and enabling you to defuse even the most explosive conflict.

The Unconscious Power of Mythos

The mythos you project onto a conflict has a powerful, unconscious impact on how your conflict unfolds, as I witnessed while facilitating a negotiation exercise for global leadership at an international conference in Europe. I randomly stratified the fifty attendees into economic classes, ranging from elites to lower-income groups. The elites were given substantial resources; the lower classes were given nearly none. Attendees had three rounds to trade resources with whomever they wanted to maximize their independent financial success. As the elites compounded their wealth, the lower classes' frustration grew.

Prior to round three, I announced a surprise twist. The elites had by now acquired so much wealth that they would be given the opportunity to formulate *new* rules for the final round of bargaining: They could redefine the value of resources and restrict who could negotiate with whom. I invited them to meet in a nearby room furnished with comfortable couches, champagne, and Swiss chocolate.

They were overjoyed—but only momentarily. As they left the main conference room, the lower-income groups hissed and booed. An angry businessman stood on a chair and shouted, "We can't trust them!" Another yelled: "Let's start a revolution!" A third urged, "Let's steal their stuff!" And in fact, the moment the elites left the room, a participant stole one of their folders.

Strikingly, the elites spent twenty minutes in their room discussing how to reconfigure the bargaining rules to benefit the lower classes—*not* themselves. But by now the underclass had worked itself into such a vertigo-like frenzy that as the elites reentered the main room, jeers drowned out their voices. The lower classes accused them of abusing power while the elites responded contemptuously and defended their good intentions. Everyone had begun shouting, and I realized that the final round of negotiation would never happen. It took a good ten minutes for the group to calm down so that we could debrief.

What caused these global leaders to end up in virtual class warfare? Each side's mythos of identity was a significant factor. The lower classes admitted to seeing themselves as victims of a dictatorship, a mythos to which they attached even before the elites announced the new bargaining rules. In other words, they *presumed* the elites would exploit them—when in fact the elites had no such intention. For their part, the elites attached to the mythos of saviors serving the helpless. In their private discussion over champagne and chocolates, they brainstormed how to "rescue" the lower classes and applied top-down decision making. No rules prohibited them from consulting with the lower classes, though they never thought to do so. Thus, each side drew on a mythos that misread the other's intentions— and produced an emotional thunderstorm.

How a Mythos Works

To unearth a mythos, you must first understand its basic properties.

A Mythos Frames Your Emotional Reality

In a conflict, your mythos shapes your deepest emotions into a coherent narrative that feels unassailably true. Should others attempt to delegitimize it, they had better brace themselves for your wrath. Consider the conflict between the elites and lower classes in the negotiation exercise. The elites tried forcefully to convince the lower classes of their interest in the common good, but the lower classes held to their own mythos and refused to countenance any contradictions.

Your mythos can change as circumstances change. As the lower classes in the negotiation game revolted against the elites, their mythos transformed from "victims" to "revolutionaries." This new mythos framed their emotional reality just as viscerally as had the old one.

A Mythos Is Rooted as Much in Biology as in Biography

While Sigmund Freud viewed conflict as mainly the result of social experiences from our early lives, as is the case with the repetition compulsion, other schools of thought have contended that conflict has a biologically based component. In other words, innate characteristics of the human species may contribute to conflict.

Psychiatrist Carl Jung suggested that humans all share a collective unconscious, which houses "a fund of unconscious images" that exists independent of personal experience. These images, known as archetypes, encapsulate prototypical characteristics of humanity. Just as birds know how to fly south for the winter, humans have intrinsic templates to navigate the social world. We all respond emotionally to such archetypes as birth and death; mother, father, hero, and devil; and stories of creation and apocalypse. Though my specific conscious image of the archetype "mother" may differ from yours, we share a primordial understanding of its emotional meaning.

Jung is in good company in his conviction that humans share innate structures for making sense of the social world. Neuroscience has been discovering an ever-expanding set of hard-wired, species-wide brain mechanisms that affect our social behavior. Advances in epigenetics suggest the existence of nongenomic sources of biological inheritance. Renowned linguist Noam Chomsky has demonstrated that we have both deep structures for understanding the meaning of language and surface structures for communicating its content. And ethological studies have revealed patterns of social behavior that are intrinsic to all animals—humans included.

A mythos weaves archetypal images (biology) with your current context (biography) to deepen your emotional reality. Imagine a couple invites their respective families to a hotel ballroom and asks them to watch as they walk slowly from the back of the room to the front. That would be a fairly undramatic event. But if this was the couple's wedding day, the same situation would resonate with deep emotional meaning for the gathered crowd. The couple would evoke archetypes that cohere into a powerful narrative about human bonding: The families would assume the role of witnesses, and the betrothed become mythic lovers being joined through a sacred ceremony.

A Mythos Deepens the Personal Significance of Your Conflict

In every age, people have identified with primal myths that revolve around plots of love, jealousy, resentment, and humiliation. A mythos infuses these plots into the context of your current conflict. As you project your personal biography onto an archetype, you root yourself simultaneously in your own experience and in an enduring stream of shared human experience. While your conflict may feel unique—and it is unique at that moment in time—its underlying themes are timeless.

In fact, a conflict may *draw* you into mythic time. As you unconsciously take on the role of a mythic hero or martyr, you transport your psychological reality to the era of the original myth itself. You come to see no emotional distinction between the mythic archetype and the reality that now confronts you, and you enter what religious historian Mircea Eliade calls an *eternal return*. I view Eliade's concept broadly: Anytime you project a mythical storyline onto your conflict—whether from an ancient text or recent history—you engage in an eternal return. While an outsider may view your conflict as a "technical border dispute" or "organizational rift," you experience it as a mythic struggle between good and evil.

Strategy: Creative Introspection

Creative introspection is a straightforward method I have developed to help you uncover each side's mythos. This process borrows techniques from great artists, who express their archetypal fantasies and fears through tangible stories and other works of art. Similarly, in a conflict you can seek to translate unconscious archetypes into concrete images that will help you better understand each side's relational identity. In Jung's words, your goal is to activate your "mythopoeic imagination"—your ability to create narratives and images that surface unconscious experiences.

The chart on page 144 depicts the key steps of creative introspection: Establish a space for genuine dialogue on controversial topics; identify what's at stake in the conflict; uncover the mythos driving each side's fears and anxieties; and revise the mythos to improve relations.

1. Establish a "Brave Space" for Genuine Dialogue

Common wisdom suggests that you create a "safe space" to discuss controversial issues, but this strategy can backfire. A safe space can become *too* safe if ground rules sanitize your feelings to the extent that they allow

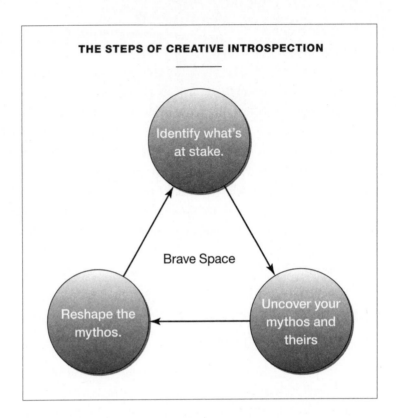

you to avoid tough topics. For example, consider the common ground rule that it is acceptable to halt a conflict by "agreeing to disagree." This rule may help you *feel* safe, but it gives everyone the license to opt out of intense dialogue. It also can favor the more powerful party, who can simply say, "I don't care about your perspective. I simply agree to disagree"—and the conflict persists.

To genuinely address the deeper issues in an emotionally charged conflict, dialogue should feel emotionally unsettling. I therefore recommend that you and the other side establish a "brave space," a learning environment that emboldens you to embrace controversy, take personal risks, and reconsider perspectives. In this atmosphere, emotional vulnerability is a sign not of weakness but of strength.

The rules in a brave space are not much different than those in a safe space—agree to a code of confidentiality, share genuine feelings, listen openly, be respectful—but the framing matters. People are more likely to discuss emotionally sensitive issues within a framework that prioritizes personal courage rather than one that emphasizes the illusion of safety.

2. Identify What's at Stake

Search for what is personally motivating you and the other side to clash. At first glance, your conflict may appear to be a straightforward battle over a resource, policy, or other substantive issue. The challenge is to unearth the deeper stakes in the conflict. You may argue incessantly with an arrogant colleague—until you learn that he was bullied as a child and longs for social respect. Understanding his deeper need for status can boost your patience with him and help you bridge the emotional divide.

Recognize the Depths of Human Motivation

There are three basic dimensions to the human experience, and each has its own machinery for motivating you. The uppermost level emphasizes rationality while the middle focuses on emotionality and the deepest accentuates spirituality. The deeper layers hold the greatest personal significance, and you will fight hardest to protect them. Should you fail to address them in a conflict, resolution becomes more difficult to attain, and an agreement can easily unravel.

Rationality is the tier of logic, intellectual understanding, and systemic analysis. It motivates you to action through *reasons*. In a conflict, you and the other side each have reasons for doing what you are doing; in the field of negotiation these are called *interests*. While people's positions may be at loggerheads in a given conflict, their underlying interests tend to be much more compatible.

Emotionality brings personal intensity to the world around you. Your emotional experience in a conflict is often the result of unmet "core concerns," fundamental relational needs. Roger Fisher and I have found that five core concerns tend to stimulate many emotions that arise in a conflict: appreciation, affiliation, autonomy, status, and role. If a core concern is met, we feel positive emotions and are more inclined to cooperate; if it is not met, we tend to feel distressed. When I work with corporate and government leaders, I often have them analyze their conflicts to discover unmet core concerns driving each side's emotions. As a result, the leaders find hidden sources of discord, and the other side's irrational behavior becomes more understandable and manageable.

Spirituality may be the most complex of these layers and the most pertinent to resolving an emotionally charged conflict. The spiritual dimension is not necessarily concerned with the divine per se, but represents a *deeper sense of purpose*. Whereas a clash of rational perspectives leads to animated debate, a spiritual clash can lead to zealous opposition.

Spirituality motivates you through a *calling*—a gut-level directive about how best to fulfill your life's purpose. It summons you, sometimes in a delicate whisper and sometimes with a shout, compelling you to walk *this* path, not *that* one. To respond to a calling is thus to pursue an action that expands your sense of emotional wholeness. You identify with something larger than yourself—family, nation, ethnicity, religion, ideology—that beckons you to action, "telling you" what you must do to feel emotionally whole, no matter the cost.

Your rational mind may answer this call, and your emotional mind may urge you forward. But the calling radiates from the inner sanctums of your identity, from what the religious might term the "soul." You can close your ears to this calling or drown it out with the noise of everyday life, but by ignoring it, you fail to take advantage of this significant guide to reconciliation.

Seek to Understand the Conflict's Deeper Significance

As you contemplate the rational significance of the conflict, you will discover core concerns at stake, which in turn will provide groundwork for discovering the conflict's spiritual significance. To unearth these three layers of the conflict, explore the following questions on your own, and then with the other side:

1. What interests are at stake? Look beneath positions to the underlying interests behind them. For example, John and Sarah, senior partners in a small company that is experiencing financial difficulty, disagree about firing two employees. "For the company to survive," John says, "we have to lay them both off." Sarah disagrees. "No," she insists. "Firing them will erode the heart and soul of our company." John grows angry, asking her why she has to be so oppositional. But while John and Sarah have taken contrary positions, their interests are in fact compatible. They both want to save the company costs, maintain its essence, and preserve their partnership. They weigh options for mutual gain and decide upon a feasible one: to retain both staffers while moving their office to a less pricey building.

2. Which core concerns feel personally at stake? Examine which concerns may be fueling the strongest emotions in your conflict. Do you feel unappreciated for your perspective? Treated as an adversary? Excluded from decision making? Demeaned in status? Cast in an unfulfilling role? Then step into the other's shoes and envision which of their core concerns might feel unmet.

Before John and Sarah were able to problem solve, they had to escape the lure of vertigo. Sarah did so by becoming aware of unaddressed core concerns in herself, but also in John. She realized that she was feeling unappreciated for her perspective; her autonomy felt impinged upon as John "told" her what to do; she felt treated as an adversary; her status felt belittled; and her role in the company felt insubstantial. She realized that John probably felt exactly the same way. This self-reflection on core concerns helped to calm her strong emotions, creating a space for problem solving.

3. Which pillars of identity feel personally at stake? Discovering the spiritual layer of your mythos can be an intense process, requiring you to look inward and be honest about what you perceive. But through spiritual insight, you can discover aspects of yourself that substantially affect your behavior—aspects you may have known little about or denied altogether.

To become aware of your spiritual experience in the conflict, reflect on your pillars of identity. Which of your fundamental beliefs, rituals, allegiances, values, or meaningful experiences feel threatened? Which pillars are calling you to action?

You also can ask yourself *comparative questions* to better understand what really matters to you in the conflict. If you have established a good rapport with the other side, you then might ask them the same questions:

- What do you most wish others would understand about your experience?
- How does this dispute personally differ from previous ones?
- If you were to look back on this dispute five years from now, what would you see that you cannot now see? What would you view as most important?
- How would a good friend of yours describe your experience in this conflict?
- How would your mother describe your experience in this conflict— and what would she be most concerned about for you? What do you think she does not understand about your perspective?

You may feel confident that the other party is driven solely by rational, emotional, or spiritual concerns, but do not be fooled: All three are typically significant. The chart on page 149 suggests some additional questions to help you decipher the deeper meaning of a conflict.

Even a rationalist can experience the spiritualist's world. Not long ago, I bumped into my colleague Mooly Dinnar at a café. His father had died a week earlier, after falling and suffering a brain hemorrhage. Though Mooly is not particularly religious, he revealed how his father's final moments of life took on mystical importance. His father's health had deteriorated rapidly, so Mooly caught the next flight overseas to see him. Upon landing, he discovered that his father had fallen into a coma; the doctors had been saying for the past ten hours that he could die at any moment. Mooly rushed into the hospital room and took his father's hand. *Dad, I'm here. I love you. We're all here around the bed now with you, and love you.* His father let out his last breath. Mooly felt awed: It was Memorial Day and the eve of the Sabbath; these events together symbolized for him the transcendent meaning of his father's life and death.

Core Identity	**Relational Identity**
Which of your . . .	**In what ways do you feel . . .**
1. **beliefs** feel attacked?	1. **unappreciated** for your perspectives or effort?
2. **rituals** feel endangered?	2. constrained in **autonomy** to act or feel as you would like?
3. **allegiances** feel strained?	3. **disaffiliated**: alienated or treated as an adversary?
4. **values** feel threatened?	
5. **emotionally meaningful experiences** or memories feel delegitimized?	4. disrespected in **status**?
	5. cast in an offensive **role**?

Questions to Decipher the Deeper Significance of a Conflict

Listen to Learn—Even in the Tough Moments

Conflict can feel unsettling, but do not let that frighten you away from listening to the other side's narrative. Embrace your discomfort: It is an important signal of emotional learning. All too often, a person asks a good, open-ended question but then interjects with a defensive rejoinder only moments later. Your goal is to listen to *understand*, not to rebut.

While active listening is a popular method, it is insufficient in an emotionally charged conflict. If you mechanically repeat back the other's words, you demonstrate only that you can hear what they are saying, without showing an understanding of its deeper meaning. In an emotionally charged conflict, it is this deeper meaning that aches to feel heard. Simply parroting back the other party's feelings of rejection can leave their mythos unacknowledged. So rather than parroting, listen proactively for how the other's identity is wrapped up in the conflict.

The most important part of listening takes place within you. Righteous indignation, shame, and judgmental thoughts may so preoccupy your attention that you literally are deaf to the other party's message. It is therefore critical to make a practice of assessing your emotional state every few minutes, taking note of hurt feelings, physical tension in your body, and angry thoughts. By paying attention to these experiences, you can sideline them and deal with them *after* you fully attend to the other's experience. The result is that you become a more powerful listener and avoid knee-jerk reactions.

After listening carefully to learn the other's narrative, share yours—but remember your goal: to have the other party hear and acknowledge it. The best way to do so is to express yourself with nonthreatening language. For example, rather than complaining, "You are a complete fool for accusing me of abusing power," you might say, "A big part of me feels angry at your accusation. Here was my intent. . . ." You avoid distancing the other person and also indicate that while "a big part" of you is angry, your emotions are complex; you leave open space for reconciliation.

3. Uncover Your Mythos—and Theirs

To reach a durable resolution to a conflict, you must transform how you fundamentally view your relationship with the other side—your mythos of identity. Two leaders may sign a peace accord, but if they essentially view each other as adversaries, their agreement won't stick. Your mythos of identity unconsciously casts you and the other side as archetypal opponents relating to each other in predictable ways: You might see yourself as David confronting Goliath or as a victim held hostage by a captor, but in either case you are confronting the disempowerment you feel in the face of a powerful adversary. To regain control over your conflict, you need to uncover these archetypes and the mythos giving them form.

There are several practical benefits to discussing archetypes. First, they allow you to step outside yourself to see your relationship at a distance. It becomes easier to imagine changes to the relationship, because you are talking not directly about yourself but about metaphorical images.

Second, archetypes let you discuss emotional issues through the proxy of symbolic images rather than talking directly about your own emotions. People in conflict are often reluctant to share their feelings; they dislike being vulnerable and fear saying things that may provoke a hostile reaction. Discussing archetypes can quell this fear.

Third, archetypes are easy to remember. During a conflict, it can be difficult to stay fully aware of every detail of each side's emotions, complaints, wishes, and fears. An archetypal image, on the other hand, is memorable, visual, and packed with emotional information. You may not recall the other side's complex emotions, but you can easily remember that they saw *you* as Goliath. The archetype can help you to swiftly contextualize subsequent exchanges and promote empathic understanding.

Finally, uncovering an archetype can open your mind to see beyond your own pain. While conflict narrows your attention to your own suffering, a focus on archetypes expands your capacity to contextualize your conflict. You see yourself as not just a lone victim of conflict, but a character in a primal drama. The question confronting you is transformed from "Why me?" to "Why us?" Why do we humans suffer at the hands of the powerful? Why do we humans grieve the loss of love? The archetype takes the isolating sting out of conflict.

I find this approach especially comforting. If my wife and I get into a fight, I remind myself that it is in keeping with the way of the world: Couples argue; they always have and always will. Mia and I are not alone in our emotional distress, but are reenacting an age-old archetypal drama. To contextualize the conflict within the broad scope of human experience is to keep the situation in perspective.

Now that you understand the importance of archetypes, you can use them as a tool to uncover each side's mythos.

Create a metaphor to depict your conflictual relations. What image do you feel represents your emotional experience in the conflict? Perhaps you feel like a powerful lion or a powerless child. What image best represents the other party? Try to invoke characters from mythology, a childhood fairy tale, or a spiritual story—the more creative, the better. You might envision the other party as a sneaky monkey, violent windstorm, or tough boxer.

If you have established a brave space, consider working with the other party to conceive these images. I have facilitated this process with disputants in ethnopolitical conflict and have been surprised at their ability to construct mutually agreed-upon images. But the most valuable part is that in creating their images, they must listen to each other's perspectives, acknowledge differing views, and account for them in their shared decision.

Several years ago, I led a workshop in the Middle East to tackle divisions that had flared up between Shias and Sunnis in the region. Tensions ran so high that explicit discussion of the topic in question would almost inevitably have resulted in an unproductive argument. I accordingly divided participants into several groups, each charged with finding a metaphor to depict Shia-Sunni relations. Thirty minutes later, each presented its results. One group depicted conflict between the two sides as a cancer destroying its own body, while another saw it as a chronic brother-brother rivalry. This latter image resonated with the entire group and shifted the conversation to how to heal a fraternal rift. After one participant suggested that only leaders from "within the family" could facilitate reconciliation, the group envisioned structures in which Shia and Sunni leadership could meet, exchange views, and conceive of reconciliation processes. Although the issues surrounding reconciliation were complex, exacerbated by geopolitical rivalries, the exercise helped the participants clarify the nature of the challenge so they could more effectively address it.

There are a variety of creative methods to help you find a fitting metaphor. For starters, choose any image and shape it to your situation. You might select an option from the illustrative archetypes chart on page 157, such as a lion, and consider how to fashion it to express the specifics of your emotional experience in the conflict. Are you a young lion threatening the old guard? Or a wounded lion, suffering but maintaining a tough facade?

Another method is to invent a metaphor with a trusted ally. This method worked well with Jung's patients. Jung spent years studying world mythology, so when patients shared with him their problems, he had a rich store of myths to draw upon to depict their archetypal experience. Your own confidant need not be a Jungian scholar on mythology; a creative friend will do.

You also can depict your image through art. Flip through a few magazines to find an image that resonates with your experience in the conflict, or take a risk and draw an image of yourself. The result can be enlightening.

In a negotiation course with midcareer executives, I asked participants to sketch how they viewed themselves in a current conflict. The images they came up with were striking and included everything from a determined soldier to a frightened child.

How do you know if you have found the "right" metaphor? The key is emotional resonance. You want to choose one that resonates with your emotional experience in the conflict. Perfection is not the goal; no image will fully encapsulate your feelings. So brainstorm until you create a metaphor that resonates enough to feel useful.

Clarify the relationship between the images. Now that you have a metaphor, think about the nature of the relationship between the images. Perhaps it feels like a turf war between angry lions? Or a competition for the love and attention of the pride's leader?

Professor Vamık Volkan and his colleagues from the University of Virginia and the Carter Center experimented with the power of metaphor in an international context, facilitating unofficial dialogue between leaders from Russia and Estonia soon after the collapse of the Soviet Union. During one of their sessions, they asked the Estonian and Russian participants to devise a metaphor to describe the relationship between their countries.

The delegates came up with two images—an elephant to represent Russia and a rabbit to represent Estonia—and pondered the dynamics between the rabbit and elephant. The animals could be friends, they reasoned, but the rabbit must always remain vigilant, because the elephant could unintentionally step on it. "With the elephant-rabbit metaphor," Professor Volkan and colleague Joyce Neu observed, "some Russians came to see Estonians not just as ungrateful for the Soviet Union's past help but also as understandably cautious." The Estonians worried about losing their newly gained autonomy, and each country struggled to define its mythos amid shifting political sands. Exploring metaphors enabled these leaders to safely discuss their relationship. Rather than directly sharing their feelings, they indirectly communicated them.

To sharpen your metaphor, consider how it could better convey the conflict's full significance from each party's perspective. Ensure that the images represent not just the rational interests at stake but also emotional and spiritual ones. As you move back and forth between analyzing the significance of the conflict and refining the metaphor, you will clarify the essence of your mythos of identity.

Of course, you will not always agree with the other party over which archetypal images best depict your relations. You may see yourself as a docile cat, while they are more prone to view you as a hostile lion. If you have diverging images, discuss why each of you depicted the relationship as you did. In fact, a useful exercise is to have each side envision archetypes depicting its best guess at how the other side would envision the relationship, then to discuss these images.

4. Revise Your Mythos

The final step of creative introspection is to revise your mythos. At this stage, you keep the same images you and the other side have created for yourselves—your core identities remain secure—but reshape the relationship between those images, much as the Russian and Estonian delegates reinterpreted relations between the elephant and rabbit.

Envision better relations between the images. Consider this conflict between my wife and me. "We are not connecting," Mia tells me, and I agree. We share our personal experiences and realize we both feel frustrated and alienated. I am busy teaching and writing my book; she is working nonstop to take care of our kids and the home. On the occasions when we do have two minutes to talk, we do not click. Despite sharing our narratives, however, our disconnection persists.

Later that day, we have a different type of conversation, painting images of how we each feel in the context of our conflict. We decide that I am like a cloud, floating in the world of theory as I write my book, while Mia is an anchor, grounded as she attends to an endless stream of family tasks. Already we each feel more appreciated. The mood lightens.

We playfully envision how the cloud and anchor can better communicate. At times, the anchor may need to take a helicopter to the clouds—but not for so long that it runs out of gas. At other times, the cloud may need to float down to the ground. We also discuss the possibility of the two of us joining as a kite that is anchored as it floats in the sky. Notice that our scenarios were not logically sound—would an anchor take a helicopter ride?—but that does not matter. Creative introspection is about catching the emotional *essence* of your relational experience, no matter how dissonant the combination of metaphors.

Translate insight into action. Consider how you can practically apply your new perspectives to your relationship. In my conflict with Mia, we each appreciated the other's hard work in the service of our family and broader social values. We also realized that we were communicating in two different languages: I was speaking theory, and Mia, pragmatics. We decided that we would each "visit" the other's world for at least ten minutes each day: The anchor would visit the clouds to talk about theory, and the cloud would visit the anchor to discuss everyday life. These steps brought us closer together.

This same process of creative introspection proved helpful in my consultation with Maria and Gail, a mother and teenage daughter who struggled to connect. They would fight for days on end, would threaten to "never talk again," and then finally would make up—only to have another bout a week later. When we discussed archetypal images that they felt captured the essence of their relational dynamic, Gail saw herself as a small fish, always being threatened by an aggressive shark. Her mother agreed—except she saw herself as the small fish.

When I asked them to describe the nature of the relationship between the shark and small fish, they had a lively conversation about each other's frustrations, but both expressed a strong desire to improve relations. Gail suggested that they figure out how to become two friendly sharks that aggressively protect each other's feelings. Her mother agreed, and we went on to explore how to translate this into action.

Sharing their feelings had failed time and again with this mother and daughter; they had quickly gotten caught in the repetition compulsion and spiraled into vertigo. Their relationship had by now become so battered that the indirect route of creative introspection proved a particularly safe and effective path to reconciliation. The mother could now listen behind Gail's angry words for the deeper dynamic at play, while Maria realized her anger was mere armor to protect her identity from harm.

How to Uncover a Mythos

Call to mind your conflict. Complete the questions below to create a metaphor that depicts your relationship with the other side.

1. I feel like a _____(image) because _____

    _____

    _____.

2. I see the other side as a _____ (image) because _____

    _____

    _____.

3. Describe how the images interact: _____

    _____

    _____.

4. What metaphor might the other side use to depict how they see their relationship with you?

    _____

    _____.

Family Relations

- Disobedient child
- Divorcée
- Disloyal sibling
- Demanding parent
- Subservient child
- Betrayed spouse
- Excommunicated family member
- Adopted child
- Widow
- Distant cousin
- Rival relative

Stock Characters

- Savior
- Trickster
- Witch
- Healer
- Hero
- Infidel
- Villain
- Patient
- Thief
- Adviser
- Vampire
- Mischievous child

Illustrative Archetypes

Greek Mythology

- Olympians—Sat on Mount Olympus and held power over the mortals below.
- Zeus—Used his supreme power to ensure stability and security among the gods and mortals.
- Sisyphus—Condemned to repeatedly haul a boulder up the side of a mountain, only to watch it roll back down as he approached the top.
- Hera—Deeply resented her loved one's betrayal, as she was forced to tolerate Zeus's incessant infidelity.
- Tantalus—Could never obtain that which was to keep him alive, as he was bound to a tree with its fruits forever out of reach.
- Theseus—Negotiated in good faith, but was duped into an eternity in hell.

Animal Kingdom

- Alpha Lion—Leads a pack to prey on lone zebra.
- Great White Shark—Among the sea's most fearless predators, will feast on anything that lingers.
- Mouse—Resourceful in the face of attack, compensating for size with nimbleness.
- Elephant—Dominating in stature, but quite gentle in behavior.
- Wolf—Chases large prey until they fatigue and then pounces.
- Cheetah—Quick, graceful, and ferocious. Attacks swiftly, but gives up just as rapidly.

But What if They Are More Powerful?

A mythos is not just a narrative, but also a tool for wielding power. The basic principle is simple: Whoever controls your mythos controls you, so it is little wonder that the other side in a conflict may try to shape your mythos to serve *their* objectives. This is identity politics at its most perilous. Consider how an emotionally abusive husband crafts a narrative of dominance over his wife, making her feel that she cannot leave the relationship without getting hurt; she sees no space to voice her dissent. Or consider how racial narratives in the United States, such as the Jim Crow segregation laws, have given whites disproportionate access to goods, services, and networks of social influence.

Reclaim Power over Your Mythos

In most conflicts, each side will feel that the other side is mischaracterizing their identity or demeaning them in some way. To reclaim power over your mythos, follow these steps:

First, become aware of the mythos the other side imposes on you. The wife in the emotionally abusive relationship may come to realize that her husband is trying to define her as dependent and submissive. He is Zeus on Mount Olympus; she feels like a feeble, helpless mortal. To come to this realization, she asked herself what identity her husband was defining for her and whether that was an acceptable role in their relationship.

Second, identify the sources of the other side's power. Does the other side have the following types of power?

1. *Legitimate power*: They hold a position of authority over you.

2. *Expert power*: They have specialized knowledge or credentials.

3. *Referent power*: They have influential interpersonal connections.

4. *Reward power*: They have the ability to reward you.

5. *Coercive power*: They have the ability to threaten, punish, or impose sanctions on you.

6. *Informational power*: They have access to information you or others want.

In our example, the wife realizes that her husband's mythos anoints him as the sole *legitimate power* in their marriage—the only one who can decide whether it is acceptable to go out for dinner, enjoy a vacation, or determine weekend activities. He draws upon *expert power* in claiming he "knows better" than she does about what is good for their marriage. He uses *reward power* by giving her a weekly "allowance" as long as she takes care of family duties. And he commands *coercive power*, threatening to cut her off financially should she leave the relationship.

Third, identify sources of power you can draw upon. The wife attends a weekly support group that broadens her social network and enhances her *referent power*. She realizes that she, too, can act as a holder of *legitimate power* in her relationship, an important decision maker in choosing the fate of their marriage. She consults with a lawyer to learn more about her financial and legal rights, enhancing her *informational power* and decreasing her husband's *coercive power*. She boosts her own *coercive power* by arranging to stay at her sister's home should her husband refuse to change his ways.

Finally, reclaim control over your mythos. The wife approaches her husband, voices her frustrations, and demands that he modify his behavior—or she will leave the relationship. The warning is credible; she has re-empowered herself. The husband threatens to cut off financial resources, but she is well prepared. He demeans her as "incapable of surviving outside the relationship," but she is confident in her support network. The fear of losing his wife motivates him to accede to her demands, and he reluctantly joins with her to reconfigure their relationship, a process that requires time as well as deep and intensive personal deliberation and dialogue.

But What If the Other Side Resists Dialogue?

You cannot force the other side to reveal their mythos, nor can you force them to listen to yours. In fact, if you are trying to reconcile with a party who feels they are more powerful than you, you should *expect* resistance. They may fear that if they agree to speak with you, they open themselves to the possibility that you may undermine their narrative—their source of power.

The best approach is to tactfully persuade the other side to engage in dialogue; threats may bring them to the table, but in a state of resentment. Here are a few suggestions to break through the other's resistance to dialogue:

- Before you talk to the other party, clarify your purpose in wanting to have a dialogue. Is it an internal desire to heal your pain? A curiosity to understand their perspective? A moral obligation? You may be able to satisfy your need without opening a dialogue, such as by independently healing painful emotions.
- Launch a conversation with them about how to conduct a dialogue about tough relationship issues; thus you discuss not your conflict itself but rather the process of talking about it.
- Invite them to an off-the-record dialogue. Conversation out of the spotlight is safer.
- Should they still refuse to talk, you might share your perspectives with them in the form of a personal letter—and request they reciprocate.
- Seek a shared ally who can encourage joint dialogue. Or enlist a mutual friend, colleague, or other trusted third party to organize and facilitate it.
- View this entire process as an opportunity for personal learning that requires patience and compassion.
- If the situation is an institutional concern, strive to change the institutional structures, such as discriminatory laws or policies, to create more space for your voice to be heard and dialogue to take place.
- As a last resort, you may have to exit the relationship—but before doing so, know where you are going.

Putting It All Together: An Office Example

Uncovering your mythos of identity in a conflict takes work—and a willingness to approach the conflict with a creative spirit. It may seem childish to characterize yourself as a bent spoon or a timid rabbit, but the effect of shaking up your perspective on a difficult situation can be profound. That is exactly what Adam, a respected executive, realized after he and I worked together.

Adam had just left the helm of a nonprofit to try his hand in the corporate world. The attitude of his new supervisor, Jerry, was in no way easing the transition. "He's out to get me," Adam said. "Two weeks ago Jerry asked me to put together a proposal for an important client. I spent a week working on it, day and night, over the weekend, neglecting my family. I sent it to him, and the next day he criticized a few minor details and said he didn't think I had what it took to make it in this business. I was *fuming*."

We identified Adam's main interests in the conflict, which were keeping his job and positioning himself for a promotion. We explored his core concerns, including his desire for Jerry's appreciation of his work. And we discussed his spiritual calling in the conflict: to be someone who serves his community.

Then we turned to the question of archetype. "How might you depict your relationship with Jerry through metaphor?" I asked. Adam thought a moment, then said, "He's the charter member of an exclusive club, and everyone in that club is rich and successful and motivated by money. He sees me as the impostor, an interloper doing anything to become a member of the club. To him I'm just the nonprofit guy, a guy who's not a *real* corporate player. I don't think he believes I have the grit for this line of work."

"Do you?" I asked.

"Of course," said Adam, his tone defensive, hesitant.

"*Do* you?" I persisted.

"To be honest," Adam said, "I've been having doubts about whether I'm meant for the corporate world. I'm not sure I fit in. But that doesn't give Jerry the right to slam my performance."

"Of course it doesn't," I agreed. "But there are a few issues on the table. One is the question of whether you *want* to work here. Another is what Jerry's perspective is all about. A third is what you can do to improve your situation."

Our conversation dug deeper into Adam's mythos of identity. What was his core relational narrative in this conflict? Did he feel like a sellout for having left the nonprofit sector? Did he doubt his ability to survive in the jungles of business?

We then shifted to his boss's perspective, looking for hints of *his* mythos. Adam happened to know that Jerry's parents were both community activists. I suspected that Adam's own community-driven spirit might be threatening to Jerry, calling into question his corporate career path. When interacting with Adam, Jerry might feel like an impostor or, even worse, a traitor to his family's values, triggering the Tribes Effect.

The use of metaphor helped Adam think about how to pursue his career aspirations in a way that supported his identity. After our conversation, he invited Jerry to lunch and broached the issue of his conflicted feelings about corporate life. To his surprise, Jerry opened up about his own struggles, explaining that he saw his job as a way to feed the family and dedicate the rest of his life to community service. Had they never taken the time to have this conversation, they might never have formed a connection—and Adam's job might have been in peril.

In Sum

The first step in reconciling tense relations is to better appreciate each other's perspectives on the conflict. But rationally discussing each other's interests is insufficient to understand the deeper emotional issues at stake. Even discussing emotions directly is not enough, as people tend to use the same words to describe drastically different experiences. We can "fear" a rainy day, or a bomb dropping on our heads.

So this chapter presented creative introspection as a method to help you shed light on the emotional narrative fueling your conflict. There is nothing more real to either party, nor more emotionally powerful, than a mythos of identity. It is an archetypal story planted in a contemporary context, a narrative both universal and personal, that sheds light on matters of deep significance. By uncovering each party's mythos, you take a huge stride toward bridging the divide.

11

Work Through Emotional Pain

Before you embark on a journey of revenge, dig two graves.

—CONFUCIUS

At the height of the U.S. Civil War, a battle-weary Confederate soldier reflected in quiet despair, "How can one forgive such enemies as we are contending against? Despoiling us of our property, driving us from our homes and friends and slaying our best citizens on the field are hard crimes to forgive. At any rate let me have a chance to retaliate and then I can forgive with a better grace."

The soldier struggled with two possible narratives for how to respond to the misery in which the South found itself: One beckoned him to forgive, pure and simple, by the grace of God. A competing narrative, much more emotionally compelling, urged him to take justice into his own hands. Seek an eye for an eye—*then* grant clemency.

The soldier's dilemma is our own. Forgiveness appeases our conscience, but retaliation feeds our thirst for revenge. As much as we may want to reconcile with a family member or colleague, hurt feelings urge us to strike back, to even the score. Like the Confederate soldier, we may feel compelled to avenge, sometimes so strongly that we feel we have no choice in the matter.

But we do have a choice. This chapter presents a method to *work through* emotional pain and unburden yourself of the necessity to avenge. It's not easy to shake away deep resentment, but while doing so may go against your every retaliatory instinct, the effect is liberating—and far more productive than the alternative.

On Working Through

The best way to heal emotional pain is to work through it. The pain is frozen within you, and addressing it transduces negative emotions into a positive relational force, just as a lamp transduces electrical energy into light. This process requires you to look within to locate and understand your emotional pain, and then to gain control over it. The process can be frightening, for you may confront inner demons beckoning you to cling to grievance and retaliate with all your might. But while you can ignore a cut on your hand and it will still heal, ignoring those inner demons makes things worse. Pain compounds pain, and past a threshold point your world explodes.

Are You Ready? Check Your BAG

Your emotional fate rests with you. You cannot let go of a grudge if you are not emotionally ready to let go of it. So inquire within: What's your best alternative to a grudge? (I call this your BAG.) Compare your life as it is now, holding the grudge, with a realistic vision of life without it. How would things be different, and possibly better?

Your grudge has a purpose. When the other party offends your identity, they undermine your moral order—your sense of right and wrong—and you naturally feel demoralized and driven to retaliate. To *not* retaliate can feel disloyal to your own suffering. But to sustain a grudge requires intense personal energies that, ironically, can eat away at your own well-being and integrity.

So check your BAG: What would it feel like to unburden yourself of your toxic emotions? How would you relate to the other side? The choice is yours: Decide whether you are ready to let go of the grudge. You have the power to work through your pain or ignore it. If you feel ready to work through it, you will need to journey through three stages: (1) bear witness to emotional pain, (2) mourn loss, and (3) contemplate forgiveness. In short: witness, mourn, forgive.

Stage 1: Bear Witness to Pain

To *bear witness* means to acknowledge a person's emotional pain, no matter how hard that reality is to accept. It is useful to start by bearing witness to your own pain, then engaging with the other side in the same process, which involves seeing the pain, entering into it, and deciphering its meaning.

See the Pain

Look for two aspects of emotional pain: *raw pain* and *suffering*. Raw pain is the visceral feeling you get when your romantic partner says, "I don't love you anymore." Your chest tightens, your throat constricts, and your head pounds. Suffering is how you make sense of that pain, quietly worrying, *What's wrong with me?*

To detect raw pain, monitor your emotions and bodily sensations. Envision yourself back in the heat of your conflict, and slowly scan your body from head to toe, looking for points of tension. Do your shoulders feel tight? Do you have a knot in your gut? What you find may startle you. Anger can so consume your attention in a conflict that you fail to notice the physical manifestations of other powerful emotions such as shame, humiliation, or self-pity. It is tempting to deny these painful feelings, but until you acknowledge them, you remain at their mercy.

Once you identify your emotional pain, look for signals of suffering— how you make sense of your pain. Be attentive to the things you tell yourself when you feel hurt: *I can't believe he did this to me! He'll pay!* Note fears of inadequacy hiding beneath your angry thoughts: *Why do these things always happen to me? Maybe I'm destined for a life of misery.*

But while pain is unavoidable, you *can* reduce your suffering. Your inner critic tends to be your biggest critic. The secret is to become aware of it—to slow down its "whirling machinery" of self-denunciation—and talk back. Do not let your inner critic have the last word. The next time you get into a heated argument, observe the stream of thoughts running through your head and slow them down so you can listen to them carefully: *He's such an idiot! Why does he always give me a hard time? Maybe I'll never fit in here.*

Then question your self-criticism. Call to mind an *inner advocate*—your loving mother or a cherished mentor—and respond to the criticism with that person's supportive commentary: *You tried your hardest and have a lot to offer the world. Just because he doesn't see your strengths doesn't mean you don't have them.*

Enter into the Pain

Remember a simple motto: *To heal, you must feel.* You cannot bear witness to pain if you tiptoe around it. That is why problem solving alone is insufficient: It solves problems, not pain. You can resolve emotional pain only if you confront it directly and make sense of what you feel.

Find the courage to experience your pain. Anger is easy to feel, because it enables you to blame someone else for your misery. But emotions that call attention to your shortcomings, whether shame, guilt, or humiliation, are more difficult to acknowledge. You may be tempted to bury these emotions, because experiencing them is necessarily painful. But again: To heal, you must feel—the insecurity of your jealousy, the mortification of your shame, the heaviness of your sorrow.

While you must enter into your pain, do not allow yourself to drown in it. One strategy to navigate this line is to imagine yourself simultaneously playing two roles: diver and lifeguard. As the diver, you plunge head-first into your pain, observing and experiencing all that you see in the same way that a scuba diver absorbs the sights of the fish and coral reef. As the lifeguard, you remain above the surface to protect the diver. The moment the diver appears at risk of drowning in emotions, the lifeguard pulls the diver back to the surface. In other words, know when to take a break from your emotions—go out for a walk, read the news, catch your breath. The sea will be waiting when you are ready to head back in.

Consider enlisting the help of a professional therapist in understanding your emotional pain. This is especially important if you feel overwhelmed, overcome by personal crisis, or afraid for your physical or mental safety. A good therapist can supply the necessary safety and skill to work through intransigent emotions.

Decipher the Meaning of the Pain

Begin by clarifying the origin of your pain. Who said or did what to injure your emotional well-being? Was there a single traumatic incident, or is your pain the result of long-standing abuse? Then decode the function of that pain. When I get a headache, for example, it tells me I need to reduce stress. Similarly, emotional pain sends a message about what is missing or broken in your life. Look for its message. If you experience a strong urge to avoid a superior who disparaged one of your ideas, your pain may be telling you that you require more praise than you realized.

After bearing witness to your own emotional pain, turn your attention to the other's pain. Imagine yourself in their shoes. What might they be feeling? Why? If you are trapped in the repetition compulsion or vertigo, it can be difficult to empathize with them, but keep trying.

You cannot, however, force the other side to heal. The will to heal is a personal choice. A common misstep is to push the other side to find common ground and "cool" the conflict, but should they feel aggrieved, they may feel that you are depriving them of their righteous anger and trying to neutralize the leverage that comes with being angry and ready to use force.

In that case, the best you can do is to establish an environment conducive to emotional healing—a brave space to bear witness to each other's pain. This space may be facilitated by a mutually respected third party, such as a trusted family member or professional mediator. If you both feel comfortable exploring each other's pain without a third party, it is important to establish ground rules to promote productive conversation. For example, a married couple I know posted the following ground rules on their refrigerator:

- Share emotional pain one at a time;
- Listen nonjudgmentally to each other and repeat the other's key points;
- Take emotional risks;
- Remember to care for each other; and
- Remember the "escape clause"—that either of us can call for a break if overwhelmed.

Stage 2: Mourn the Loss

The second stage of working through emotional pain is to mourn the loss you have incurred. Any conflict involves loss: A divorcing couple must mourn their thwarted vision of a life together; a pair of reconciling siblings must mourn the years they spent apart; battling armies must mourn their casualties of war. Mourning is, in essence, the emotional metabolizing of loss. If you fail to mourn, you remain trapped in a time capsule of painful emotions. For a better future, you need to take emotional stock of your loss and come to terms with it.

Recognize the Loss

Notice what you have lost and what can never again be. Your conflict may have cost you a friend's trust or your idyllic marriage. Such loss can feel disorienting, sometimes devastating, in the same way that the death of a loved one leaves you reeling: *Is she really gone? How can this be?*

To mourn is to come to accept that what was in the present is now in the past. But while you may *intellectually* understand that your friend betrayed you or your spouse left you, coming to *emotional terms* with this actuality is extremely difficult. As you confront existential reality, your relational identity must transform.

I watched this process unfold when close family friends suffered the loss of their teenage daughter, Nora. For years they underwent therapy to grieve her loss. But they left Nora's room as it had been when she died: her dresses strewn on the floor, her diary by her bed. Then, one rainy Tuesday, they woke up and knew the time had come to recognize their loss and put Nora's belongings into storage. While their love and pain endured, they had made an emotionally painful but necessary stride in acknowledging the reality of their daughter's death.

Come to Terms with the Loss

The pain of loss will endure until you come to terms with it—until you emotionally resolve to the fact of your loss. This requires you to move beyond recognition to emotional acceptance. A key challenge here is that the intense pain of loss can compromise your ability to confront it. In fact, when your brain records a traumatic experience, it tends to inactivate your language encoding, preserving the experience as an emotional imprint, a wholly nonverbal impression. But without words, you literally cannot come to terms with your pain and claim control over it.

So find the words. Ask yourself: *Why is this loss so painful to me? How can I best make meaning of it?* You might discuss these questions with a trusted friend or journal your thoughts to put language to your feelings.

Coming to terms need not be done solely through words, however. *Ritual* is a powerful tool to release your pain and put closure to your emotional experience. Through ritual you perform a solemn ceremony to support your internal transformation from a state of loss to acceptance. In the Jewish religion, for example, to mourn a person's death, the immediate family of the deceased sits shivah for seven days, remaining in their home and receiving a stream of friends and family who bring food and drink.

The most potent rituals connect to the basic elements of our planet: fire, water, earth, and air. In the Christian rite of baptism, for example, an infant is immersed in water to symbolize admission into the church. The dead are often buried in the earth. Religions such as Hinduism use cremation, destroying the dead body in fire. And many spiritual traditions spread the ashes of the dead into the air.

To come to terms with loss, you can memorialize it. A nation may honor its fallen soldiers with a monument. Grieving parents may preserve their dead child's memory through a nonprofit foundation. You also can begin to accept loss through art, whether composing a song of sorrow, drawing a picture of rage, or writing a short story of nostalgia. Some of the world's most impassioned stories and songs were born of loss. To commemorate is to turn your pain from an all-consuming experience into a contained entity, a tangible structure that puts one chapter of life to rest while conceding that the pain it caused will never be forgotten.

Just as you need to mourn loss, so does the other side. Give them the space to express their grief. Behind their sharp attacks may reside a longing to regain that which, through the conflict, they have forever lost.

Stage 3: Contemplate Forgiveness

Forgiveness is the third stage of working through emotional pain—and typically the most demanding. The Confederate soldier cited at the beginning of this chapter felt victimized and duty bound to avenge the emotional cost incurred by him and his comrades. How, he wondered, could he ever pardon the perpetrators of these transgressions without first exacting his vision of justice?

That soldier was unaware of a crucial truth: To forgive is to free yourself of victimhood. Remaining consumed by anger holds you captive to those who perpetrated it. Forgiveness unchains you and frees up space in your mind to attend to worthier concerns. If you spend 40 percent of your time replaying old wounds, nursing your rage, and plotting revenge, you have only 60 percent left to spend on more beneficial activities. And while a desire for vengeance keeps you firmly stuck in the past, forgiveness frees you to live in the present.

To forgive, you need not concern yourself with the dictionary definition of the term, but rather with developing a practical plan of action to advance reconciliation. For example, you might prepare an expression of forgiveness: *Despite what has happened—which I will never forget—I am prepared to let bygones be bygones, to abandon the idea of revenge, to talk with you, and to work together toward a better future.*

The Unique Qualities of Forgiveness

To forgive is not to absolve. A father may forgive his daughter for staying out past curfew, but he will still ground her for the weekend. The Confederate soldier may forgive his enemies for their actions but can still hold them accountable in a court of justice.

To forgive is likewise not to forget. A bank may forgive your debt, but it will still keep a record of the loan. Two nations may fight on opposite sides in a brutal war, but after they reconcile, each group's history books will still record what happened.

Forgiveness is a process. There is no quick path to forgiveness. It requires time, effort, patience, and the recognition that your motivation to forgive will ebb and flow. A friend may betray your trust, and you may resist forgiving him for years—until suddenly, one unexpected day, your grudge softens.

No one can force you to forgive—not even yourself. Author C. S. Lewis tried to forgive someone for thirty years, and when he finally felt ready to do so, he realized that "so many things are done easily the moment you can do them at all. But till then, simply impossible, like learning to swim. There are months during which no efforts will keep you up; then comes the day and hour and minute after which, and ever after, it becomes impossible to sink."

It is tempting *not* to forgive, for you hold the key that can allow the perpetrator back into your moral community. That person once held power over you—violating your dignity—but now the power dynamic is reversed. South African writer Pumla Gobodo-Madikizela observed that "just at the moment when the perpetrator begins to show remorse, to seek some way to ask forgiveness, the victim becomes the gatekeeper to what the outcast desires—readmission into the human community."

To begin the process of forgiveness, open yourself to the possibility of forgiving. Imagine how your relationship might feel if you do so. Consider the pros and cons of forgiving—and not forgiving—and record them using the chart below. Next, check with your gut: What would it *feel* like to release yourself from your grudge? Compare that feeling with the anger currently weighing you down. Contemplate what feels right. Talk with a confidant, and examine your dilemma from every angle. Over time, clarity will emerge.

Should I Forgive?	
If yes:	**If no:**
What are the pros?	What are the pros?
What are the cons?	What are the cons?

Finally, decide whether to (1) forgive, (2) withhold forgiveness, or (3) revisit the question at a later date. Think through your decision carefully, and listen to your heart. Should you decide to forgive, you will feel freer and more empowered—but that will not be the end of the story. You will still need to release your anger, and the best way may be to invoke compassion, to feel concern for the other's suffering. So when you feel the pull of anger, ask yourself: *Do I want to cause suffering to myself and others, or to embrace compassion?*

But What About the Unforgivable?

Philosopher Hannah Arendt proposed that certain behaviors are so beyond the pale that they can only be the product of what Kant calls "radical evil," a malevolence so terrible that it has abandoned all claims to ethics. As a Jew who fled her homeland of Germany in the face of rising nationalism and anti-Semitism, Arendt witnessed the Holocaust from a distance and could not shake off the notion that this deed was so extreme, so absurdly offensive to humanity, that it was an act of radical evil that was, in her words, both "unpunishable" and "unforgivable."

Like Arendt, I believe that certain conflicts may produce such intolerable pain that the transgression *feels* unforgivable. But I also believe that assuming with unquestionable finality that we can never forgive another is ultimately a self-fulfilling prophecy. Healing can take generations, until emotional wounds are transformed into scars of remembrance. But forgiveness always lies within the realm of possibility.

Apology: The Other Side of Forgiveness

A sincere apology is perhaps the most powerful tool for restoring positive relations. An apology is an expression of regret, a message that you wish you could take back the actions that hurt the other party—so much so that you are willing to sacrifice your pride in the interest of reconciliation.

Whereas forgiveness is an internal decision, an apology is an *interpersonal* acknowledgment of regret. You can forgive in any conflict, with or without the perpetrator present, but you cannot apologize to an empty room. To apologize is to communicate directly to another person that you are sorry—and mean it.

To Offer a Genuine Apology, Follow a Few Guidelines

A sincere apology comes from the heart, but several guiding principles can prove useful. Before you apologize, examine these guidelines and think how you might authentically communicate them. The more you can integrate them into your apology, the more effective your communication will be:

1.   Express honest remorse.

2.   Acknowledge the impact of your behavior.

3.   Communicate that you accept responsibility.

4.   Make a commitment not to repeat the offense.

5.   Offer reparation.

Decide whether to apologize privately or publicly. A private apology makes it easier to build affiliation and puts neither of you at great risk of losing face. In complex cases of *restorative justice*, the perpetrator of a crime may meet privately with the victim to explore perspectives on the offense and even to apologize for the wrongdoing. At other times, apology may best be made publicly, especially when the injustice is political and collective. South Africa's Truth and Reconciliation Commission provided a platform for victims of political violence to tell their stories of grievance and for perpetrators to admit to and apologize for their wrongdoing. In some cases, victims even forgave the perpetrators.

Offer an Apology, Not an Apologia

If you are going to apologize, be straightforward. Do not muddle it with remorse and defensiveness. In Plato's book *The Apology*, Socrates stands trial—having been accused of corrupting the minds of youth, disbelieving in gods recognized by the state, and inventing new gods. At his hearing, he delivers an *apologia*, a Greek word referring to a speech in defense to an accusation—in other words, the opposite of an apology. For example, the spouse who arrives home late for the birthday dinner would be ill-advised to say, "I'm sorry I hurt your feelings by showing up late, but I had a project I needed to get done." This contradictory communication may appear on its surface to be an apology, but its subtext is clear: I take no responsibility for hurting you.

In Sum

An emotionally charged conflict causes pain for everyone involved—which is precisely why it demands understanding and compassion. By bearing witness to each party's emotional pain, mourning the loss incurred, and moving toward forgiveness, you can begin to heal. As poet Roethke observed, "In a dark time, the eye begins to see."

12

Build Crosscutting Connections

In 1991, a man named Cyril Ramaphosa received an invitation from a friend to join him for a weekend of fly-fishing. Cyril loves the sport and readily accepted the invitation. Three hours into the trip, his host informed him that Roelf Meyer and his family would be joining them for lunch on Saturday.

These events would be of little interest to most people—if not for the fact that Cyril Ramaphosa was secretary general of the African National Congress and Roelf Meyer was the minister of defense for the then-ruling National Party of South Africa. Two weeks hence, the two men were scheduled to begin negotiating some of the most contentious issues regarding the transition to a multiracial, democratic state.

On that Saturday afternoon in the South African outback, however, politics was not the only thing on their minds. Roelf's son asked Cyril, "Will you teach me how to fly-fish?" Cyril agreed, and off they all went. Roelf also decided to try his hand at the sport, but when he cast his line in the wrong direction, the hook caught his ring finger and pierced his flesh. He turned to Cyril and asked plaintively, "What do you do now?"

After Cyril's wife, a nurse, tried unsuccessfully to disengage the hook, Cyril knew what had to be done. "Get me a pair of pliers," he told her. He poured Roelf a glass of whiskey and said, "Okay—drink this, look away, and trust me." He then yanked the hook out.

Two weeks later, on opposite sides of the negotiation table, the leaders found themselves at an impasse. Over the years, the National Party had imprisoned a great number of people who resisted apartheid, including African National Congress leader Nelson Mandela and many of his colleagues. By 1991 many, but not all, of them had been released. The National Party was willing to free the remaining political prisoners if the

ANC ceased its use of armed resistance; the ANC, in turn, refused to stop using armed resistance until the prisoners were released. The negotiation came down to a question of who would accede first.

Roelf leaned over the table and told Cyril, "I hear you saying: *Trust me.*"

He ordered release of the prisoners, and one week later the African National Congress announced an end to its armed struggle.

The backbone of reconciliation, as this anecdote so powerfully illustrates, is human connection. When people fight, they typically view their connection as adversarial, as *us* versus *them*. But even in the midst of an emotionally charged conflict, there are ways to establish positive connections that deepen relationships and transcend self-interest. The key is to build what I call *crosscutting connections*.

The Power of Crosscutting Connections

Relationships can be fortified through diverse links between you and another. The more numerous and meaningful these links, the stronger your relationship. Cyril and Roelf connected through their fishing adventure, their conversations in the outback, and their common role as negotiators. These varied connections inspired trust and enabled creative problem solving. Within their cocoon of connection, they were able to argue *more* vociferously; they each felt secure enough in the relationship to express their concerns uninhibitedly and to share information. You likewise will be better positioned to influence an ally than an adversary. Friends listen more willingly to friends than to enemies.

To help you foster cooperative relations, this chapter presents a strategy for proactively building crosscutting connections. The method shows you how to (1) evaluate your current level of connection, (2) envision what better relations might look like, (3) decide whether to change your relationship, and, if so, (4) draw on three tools to strengthen it.

Step 1: Evaluate Your Current Level of Connection (Using the REACH Framework)

Human connection has different levels of depth; the deeper your bond, the more likely you will stick together even during the turmoil of conflict. To help you gauge the status of a relationship, I have developed the **REACH Framework**, which provides a simple guide to assess your emotional closeness. While your sense of closeness ebbs and flows—you feel intimate with your spouse this morning but distant in the afternoon—the following pages will help you attune to these dynamics.

The REACH Framework

This model distinguishes between five levels of connection, which form the acronym REACH—a reminder to *reach* for connection. In ascending order of emotional depth, the levels are:

(1) recognition of existence;

(2) empathic understanding;

(3) attachment;

(4) care; and

(5) hallowed kinship.

Level 1: Recognition of existence. Does the other party treat you as invisible, or acknowledge your existence? In the movie *The Jerk*, Steve Martin plays Navin Johnson, a down-and-out gas station attendant trying to find his place in the world. One day a new phone book arrives at the gas station, and Navin jumps for joy when he finds his name inside. "I'm somebody now!" he shouts. "Millions of people look at this book every day! This is the kind of spontaneous publicity—your name in print—that makes people!" His delight underscores the power of the most fundamental form of human connection: recognition of existence.

We all want to feel that we are "somebody"—a person who is visible and heard, a meaningful part of the world. Picture yourself attending a meeting with colleagues during which they disregard everything you say. Or imagine yourself at the dinner table with your family, and as hard as you try to get a word in, no one even looks your way. The sense of anguish you feel in such situations is palpable. Ethnopolitical groups can experience extreme frustration when denied political recognition or excluded from diplomatic discussions. To feel unrecognized is to feel like a nobody—and nobody wants that.

Level 2: Empathic understanding. Does the other judge your emotional experience as irrelevant, or authentically appreciate it? To empathize is to inhabit the emotional landscape of another person. You sense his or her felt experience and understand the emotional significance he or she attaches to it.

There are two kinds of empathy. *Cognitive empathy* refers to an intellectualized understanding of someone's emotional experience, but one that does not inspire an emotional response. Picture a psychopath about to victimize a teenage girl: He charms her into his car with his keen cognitive understanding of her vulnerabilities, reading her emotions but experiencing no emotional resonance of his own. If you feel *emotional empathy*, in contrast, you co-experience the other party's feelings. The brain is equipped with circuitry to make this possible, and this circuitry is especially active in meaningful relationships. German neuroscientist Tania Singer has shown that even if you simply watch your romantic partner receive a zap on the hand, *your* neural networks activate, and you experience the emotional tone of their pain.

Level 3: Attachment. Does the other perceive you as expendable, or emotionally irreplaceable? Through attachment, you experience an enduring bond. Perhaps the greatest pain in a marriage is to discover that your spouse is having an affair, signaling that you are replaceable. Attachment implies cohesion; emotional glue connects you to the other party. This is why attachment is so useful for reconciliation: It leads to cohesive relations.

Look for two telltale signs of attachment. First is a *yearning to stay emotionally connected.* My four-year-old son, Liam, constantly clings to his mother's leg while she types on the computer or cooks dinner, not daring to stray more than a few yards from her. Some divorced couples continue to fight long after their divorce, in part to feed their unwavering feelings of attachment. This yearning to sustain an attachment helps explain seemingly irrational behavior. A classic example is the disgruntled wife who packs her suitcase, announces that she has had enough of the relationship, and storms out the door—only to be followed by her husband, who yells, "I can't live like this either! Wait a minute, and I'll go with you."

The second sign of attachment is *separation anxiety*. When your need for emotional connection goes unmet, internal alarms of anxiety begin to sound. For little Liam these translate into a tantrum: "Mama, HOLD ME!" When he reconnects with his mother, opiatelike painkillers activate in his brain, reinforcing his attachment and bringing a smile to his face. The same alarms of anxiety wail for the divorced couple who cannot stand being together but cannot bear being apart.

Level 4: Care. Do you sense that the other is indifferent to your fate, or cherishes you? At one end of the spectrum, the other party values everything about you; their love is unconditional. The extent to which another willingly makes sacrifices for your welfare is a good indicator of their degree of care for you. I know a mother in Florida who was so deeply worried about her teenage son, a cocaine addict, that she had the police arrest him; she sacrificed her relationship out of concern for his life.

"The opposite of love is not hate, it's indifference," wrote Nobel Laureate Elie Wiesel. As a Holocaust survivor, he realized that for Jews in concentration camps in World War II, perhaps the only thing more painful than the insufferable cruelty of the Nazis was the international community's initial indifference to their plight.

Level 5: Hallowed kinship. Does the other view you as ideologically incompatible, or as a kindred spirit? Hallowed kinship is a transcendent bond based upon spiritual or ideological ties. Malcolm X initially scoffed at the notion of racial integration but then traveled to Mecca and observed "tens of thousands of pilgrims, from all over the world. They were of all colors, from blue-eyed blondes to black-skinned Africans. But we were all participating in the same ritual, displaying a spirit of unity and brotherhood that my experiences in America had led me to believe never could exist between the white and the non-white."

Nationalism is another example of hallowed kinship. The soldier on the battlefield risks life and limb to save a fallen comrade, motivated not just by care for the individual but also by patriotism. Indeed, any transcendent experience, religious or otherwise, can serve as the basis for hallowed kinship. When my first child, Noah, was one year old, I brought him to the beach at dawn, and together we watched the sun cast its rippled reflection across the ocean. I felt a sense of hallowed kinship with him and with the natural beauty surrounding us.

Take Stock of Your Connection

Now that you have a better sense of the five levels of connection, you can use them to evaluate the quality of your own relationships. Start by thinking of someone with whom you are in conflict, such as a family member, colleague, or neighbor. Take an honest look inward to assess your current level of connection. How recognized do you feel? How emotionally understood do you feel? Do you feel attached? Do you care for them? Feel hallowed kinship with them?

Consult the chart below, which can help you analyze relational tension. In a family business, for example, you may feel that your sibling does emotionally understand you, but not to the extent you would like. This suggests an empathy gap (level 2). Within each level of the framework, place a C at the place along the line where you perceive your *current* connection to be. Then ask yourself: What is my *desired* connection within this level? Place a D at that spot. The gap between your current and desired degrees of connection represents the amount of tension you feel. Note any gaps between your perceived and desired level of connection.

Now step into the other's shoes and imagine how connected they feel to you. Do they feel you recognize them? Emotionally understand them? Revisit the chart below, considering their perceived level of connection—and whether they aspire for more or less.

Level of connection	Spectrum of possible feelings
1. Recognition	Invisible————————————Fully acknowledged
2. Empathy	Emotionally judged————————Appreciated
3. Attachment	Replaceable—————————— Irreplaceable
4. Care	Insignificant—————————————Cherished
5. Hallowed kinship	Spiritually separate————————Spiritually unified

Step 2: Envision Better Relations

Once you evaluate your current level of connection, envision the type of relationship you desire. The more detailed your image, the more successfully it can transform a conflict. Ultimately, you want to cultivate a shared vision of cooperation so palpable that it feels not just realistic, but inevitable.

A shining example comes from Dr. Martin Luther King Jr., who had a bold dream of a possible future for race relations. Standing at the Lincoln Memorial at the height of racial divisions in the United States, he did not merely criticize current government policies, but instead articulated his vision of a racially integrated nation, imagining that "one day on the red hills of Georgia, the sons of former slaves and the sons of former slave owners will be able to sit down together at the table of brotherhood." Dr. King understood that to break free of the shackles of social division, Americans needed an inclusive social model in which to believe.

As you create your own vision of better relations, keep in mind the following guidelines:

1. Make it vivid. A vivid vision is concrete and holds emotional resonance. Imagine a short video clip depicting your vision of better relations. Are you in good humor as you talk with your ex-spouse? Are you working together companionably with your workplace rival on a project? Are you sitting side by side with your neighbor to discuss your boundary dispute?

2. Suspend judgment. Do not critique your vision. In the heat of conflict, any thought of reconciliation can feel unrealistic. But without some vision of reconciliation, you condemn yourself to continued conflict. Just as you do not judge your dreams while asleep, do not judge your visions while awake. Your goal is to imagine a vibrant picture of what the future *could* look like. Allow yourself to picture fresh possibilities.

This process can help resolve conflicts at any level. I facilitated a workshop for Israeli and Palestinian leadership from the public and private sectors, in which I challenged the group to create concrete visions for what peace could look like twenty years in the future. At first skepticism ran high, and several participants complained that the exercise would be a waste of time, as peace felt unattainable. But I encouraged them to think creatively, however unrealistic their ideas might seem, and they obliged.

Within ten minutes the room electrified, and when the group presented their ideas an hour later, the results were striking. Participants enthusiastically described possibilities for joint economic ventures, interlinking social organizations, and new political collaborations. Because they had been tasked with envisioning specific measures of connection rather than abstract arguments over political rights, the group worked with great enthusiasm. The possibility of peace was within their grasp, which led this influential group to support a broader, ultimately successful initiative to break the impasse in formal negotiations. Despite the fact that the political negotiations faltered, the group continued to meet and work together toward their visions of peace.

Step 3: Decide Whether You Are Willing and Ready to Change

You cannot just jump from vision to action without attending to a critical middle step: determining whether you and the other side are both *willing* and *ready* to deepen relations. Too often parties agree to new forms of political or personal connection, only to renege on their commitments because they are not truly eager and able to implement them. So ask yourself the following two questions:

Do You Have the Will to Deepen Your Connection?

Will is the deliberate intention to do something. There are two types of will—emotional and political—and you want to check each to gauge your willingness to connect with the other party.

Emotional will refers to the intention to open up emotionally in a conflict for the sake of increased connection. If the pains of conflict run deep, you may discover that the wells of emotional will are currently running dry. That is understandable; emotional will changes over time, and today's resistance may transform into tomorrow's readiness.

Then turn your attention to your *political will*, which refers to your commitment to take *action* to improve your connection. You may emotionally desire reconciliation with an estranged sibling, but find yourself unable to muster the determination to pick up the phone to begin the process.

Similarly, the manager of a research department may want to resolve tension with the marketing department, but resist expending political capital to make that happen.

After determining the degree of your will to change, make a decision: Are you *actually willing to change?* A definitive "yes" opens you up to the possibility of increased emotional connection. A definitive "no" indicates you might avoid pursuing further connection at this time. Incertitude will only set you up for future relationship problems. Imagine a priest asking the bride, "Do you take this man to be your lawfully wedded husband?" and she answers, "I do—but only under a few specific conditions that I'd like to further discuss." That marriage won't work. Nor will your attempt to deepen connection, unless you enter into it with clarity of will.

Are You Ready to Deepen Your Connection?

The answer is likely to be yes if you feel open to empathizing with the other side's emotions and sharing your own. But if you have the will to deepen your connection but not the emotional readiness, problems can brew.

A good example is a romantic relationship in which the man is eager to get married but the woman is not. Her reluctance may have nothing to do with her love or commitment—it may just be that she needs more time. Though emotional readiness is an abstract concept, it is a state most of us become familiar with over the course of our lives. We intuit the "right time" to get married, buy a house, have children, change jobs, or make other major life decisions. We don't consult a clock to tell us the right time to make such decisions; they come from within.

If you want to improve a damaged relationship, boost your readiness to connect. Start by looking for ways in which you are resistant to change. Do you fear closer connection, feel resentful, or harbor unresolved pain? Then work through that resistance. While mediating conflict in Northern Ireland, for example, politician George Mitchell helped disputants not only prepare *for* change but prepare *to* change, realizing that emotional readiness required that the parties involved open themselves to novel ways of relating. Mitchell worked with international leaders to prepare institutions and citizens for the new reality of peace. These preliminary efforts proved essential to the negotiations that ultimately led to a peace agreement.

Step 4: Strengthen Your Connections

The philosopher Arthur Schopenhauer once mused about the way in which porcupines keep warm on a cold night: They huddle close enough to share body heat but keep enough distance to avoid being pricked by one another's quills. The same notion applies to finding the "right" level of human connection. I call it the *Schopenhauer Principle*: If you want to improve your relationship, get close enough to benefit from a positive connection, but not so close that you invade each other's space. Adopt the habit of assessing your level of connection and reflecting on whether you are getting too distant—or too close for comfort.

When you want to deepen your relationship, draw on three forms of connection: physical, personal, and structural. These are applicable across a wide range of contexts, whether you seek to reconnect a divided family, organization, or nation, and are essential to build robust crosscutting associations. Though you cannot manufacture authentic connection, these three dimensions create the conditions for positive exchange.

Form of Connection	Associates Us Through . . .
1. Physical	Geographic proximity
2. Personal	Emotional closeness
3. Structural	Shared group membership

The Power of Physical Connection

A physical connection is the proximity of your body to the other's body. Such proximity is a good indicator of the way you and others conceive of your relations. As you discuss your conflict, do you sit side by side as a single unit, or square off on opposite sides of a long table? Even small differences in spatial orientation can have a big impact. The next time you eat dinner with a friend, sit closer than usual and watch the effect—he may appear uncomfortable and unconsciously back away. In a serious negotiation, the ramifications of such miscalibrated proximity can be disastrous.

Become aware of physical barriers to connection. Physical proximity can have a powerful, unconscious impact on your sense of connection. In an organization, the mere fact that employees are situated on different floors of the same building is enough to give rise to tribal division. Even employees on the same floor may feel more allied with cube mates than colleagues around the corner. On a larger scale, physical divisions can reinforce societal ones: Think of the Berlin Wall, a concrete political barrier between East and West Germans, or the racial segregation in the United States mandating that black people sit at the back of the bus and patronize separate establishments.

As social psychologist Henri Tajfel has demonstrated, the mere sorting of people into groups can create a preference by members for their own group. This finding is replicated in the Tribes Exercise: Before the tribes start their negotiation, they are seated in six different clusters of chairs, creating the perception of distinct groups. Tribe members immediately feel more aligned with their own tribe and distant from the others, both physically and emotionally. Surprisingly, no group has ever taken it upon itself to suggest rearranging the seating into one big circle that would include all the participants. I am confident that if anyone did so, the walls of division would shake.

Design the setting to promote connection. When you meet, arrange the seats to encourage cooperation. Is one of you on a raised dais looking down at the others, or are you side by side? Sitting around a circular table or on the same side of a table tends to generate greater connection than being on opposite sides or at different levels. You might similarly designate specific spaces at work or home for different types of conversation. I know a consultant who offered useful advice to a brother and sister who co-managed a large company but fought constantly over everything from management decisions to personal grudges. As their communication deteriorated, their business suffered. The consultant told them to settle business disputes at the office and family disputes at home, and to schedule a time for each. This simple instruction worked, because it helped the siblings compartmentalize their differences and deal with each in its own sphere.

The Power of Personal Connections

For Srđa Popović, whose youth resistance movement helped organize the revolution that overthrew Yugoslavian president Slobodan Milošević, personal connections were critical. The day before any protest, his organization would have a select group of university students meet with the police chief and explain, "Here's what we are going to do. We know you will have to arrest us, and we will have security there to make sure everything is in order." In this way the revolutionaries methodically built affiliation with the police and military and engaged them in their cause.

When we connect, we identify with each other's emotional experience, which makes us feel closer. Whether we are trying to finalize an important business deal or reconcile an enduring conflict, long-term success can come about only through personal connection, and five strategies are particularly useful for promoting it:

1. Relate to significant aspects of their life. Ask questions to discover what is emotionally important to the other party. Your goal is to move beyond their formal self to learn what they might reveal to a good friend. Your questions should come from a place of genuine curiosity, stretching the conversation beyond their curriculum vitae to more personal topics:

"Do you have siblings? Kids? Tell me about them."

"What do you do for fun?"

"Where did you grow up? Do you still have ties there?"

It is important, however, to move gradually into the realm of the personal. Start with a safe conversation about the weather, traffic, today's news—impersonal subjects—to raise the comfort level, then gradually inquire about the other party's personal life. As they share, listen for cues about what is meaningful to them. What are they trying to express? What do they want to talk about? If they keep driving the conversation back to a particular topic, recognize that as a clue as to what they emotionally prioritize.

As you discover what topics are most significant to them, find a link between their experience and your own. If, for example, the other party reveals that his or her mother died a few months ago, you might respond, "I'm so sorry. I remember when we were all together over the holidays and what a wonderful woman she was. Do you feel like talking about her?"

2. Reveal meaningful aspects of your personal life. The flip side of inquiry is revelation. By opening up about your own life, you demonstrate your humanity, providing information with which others can identify and encouraging them to share.

When revealing facts about yourself, try to connect to aspects of the other's life. "I understand how taxing it can be to raise kids. I have three little boys, and while I love them to death, they are utterly exhausting!" Describe events colorfully so that the other person gains a good sense of what they mean to you emotionally. "Just yesterday, I came home and discovered that four-year-old Liam had painted our entire kitchen floor with blue paint. It took us two hours to clean things up." Muster the courage to share both your strengths *and* your weaknesses. You can let the other know areas of your life of which you are proud—"My son just got admitted to college!"—but balance these with acknowledgments of your vulnerability. "I worry about how well he will adjust to life away from home."

3. Attune to personal chemistry. In a conflict situation, notice when you feel a natural, easy connection with the other party. This personal chemistry will improve your conversation and decision making. On the other hand, if your personal connection feels out of sync, consider soliciting someone who *does* have good chemistry with the other party to serve as an intermediary. For example, some years ago I was asked to mediate an ongoing conflict between a head of state and a leading businessman. The government official so despised this business leader that he refused to have direct communication with him. These two men had to address important policy differences, but their conversations had stalled. Reconciliation eventually took place through deputy advisers who did have good chemistry.

4. Notice bids for connection. Become aware of the other side's "bids for connection"—subtle attempts to affiliate with you—and respond to them. For example, a husband asks his wife if she wants to watch television and she says no; she needs to make dinner. When the husband explodes in response, the wife cannot understand his "irrational anger," nor, for that matter, can he—until they recognize that his invitation was a subtle bid for connection that went unmet, leaving him feeling rejected and shamed. Happily married couples typically extend more bids for connection and respond more often to them. Even in an international dispute, the most effective diplomats are extremely attuned to subtle hints of conciliation and the moderation of negative rhetoric.

5. Create rituals of connection. You enact countless rituals every day without realizing it, whether hugging your kids before they head to school or sitting down for the nightly family dinner. Rituals enable you to deepen your relations over time through predictable, meaningful interaction. So consider introducing them into a conflictual relationship. They need not be time-consuming, just repeated and meaningful. In a romantic relationship, for example, you might ritualize the postconflict healing process, giving each other a massage. During a large-scale conflict, you might ritualize aspects of the negotiation process, such as by starting each meeting with a minute of silence to respect all the victims, or eating meals together, or committing to communicate once a week even in difficult political times.

The Power of Structural Connections

Structural connections—the third mode of connection—are based on shared membership in an organization. Are you and the other party colleagues in the same club, institution, or nation? While personal connections focus on emotional closeness, structural connections focus on inclusion. You can draw on three main strategies to promote these links:

Look for points of commonality with the other party. You may have been born in the same town and attended the same school, or you may enjoy the same hobby. Points of structural commonality need not be monumental to promote a positive connection. Years ago, at a water park in the Middle East, I was waiting in a long line to go down a big slide when the man behind me asked, "Where are you from?" "The United States," I answered. "Me too!" he replied with great enthusiasm. There are millions of U.S. citizens, and in the United States that connection would have little significance. But in that foreign context, the simple commonality of nationality kindled a thirty-minute conversation.

Create a community of tribes. Disputants in a conflict often overlook the possibility of creating a new, inclusive group to deal with partisan differences. In only one iteration of the Tribes Exercise did all the participants come together and devise a strategy to revolt against the instructions of the alien. *But* no group has ever thought to turn the alien from adversary to partner, such as by launching an Intergalactic Council on Tribal Cooperation—with the alien as its distinguished founding member.

In real life, divided groups of any size can unite under the aegis of shared loyalty. Our loyalties may pull us toward the familiarity of our family, friends, or cultural tribe. But it is possible to create a *community of tribes*, an overarching framework within which many groups can join in common allegiance. The most effective strategy is to identify symbols to unite these groups into a community. Countries, for example, comprise a spectrum of tribes, each with its own culture and heritage—yet national identity often reigns. Why? Because, as esteemed social psychologist Gordon Allport notes, "nations have flags, parks, schools, capitol buildings, currency, newspapers, holidays, armies, historical documents"—symbols that mentally anchor the unique character of a nation in people's heads and hearts.

There are many examples of divided groups who have reconciled and created an overarching community of tribes. In the wake of World War II, several European countries decided to pursue greater continental unity. After numerous international integration efforts, the Maastricht Treaty formally established the European Union, a governing body linking states across Europe in a range of cooperative economic, legal, educational, military, and health-related activities. To solidify its reality, the European Union introduced a flag and common currency, established a capital in Belgium, and created a diplomatic corps. While the European Union has not eroded differences in culture or language among its member states, it has inspired regional economic growth and cohesion based on each region's specialties and traditions.

Another example of the power of a large-scale structural body comes from the Middle East. I was an instructor and adviser to the Israeli-Palestinian Negotiating Partners network, founded in response to the failure of the Camp David II negotiations. As part of this network, Israeli and Palestinian participants spent a week in Cambridge, Massachusetts, where they learned methods of negotiation and had the opportunity to build relations within and between groups. Few of the participants had met prior to the workshop, but in the course of it they worked together on the same side of negotiation cases, talked informally at social events, and played the role of "students" in lectures. These kinds of activities helped them to see each other not as adversaries but as colleagues working collaboratively on shared problems. The results of this program were concrete and striking. For example, the deadly thirty-eight-day standoff at the Church of the Nativity in Bethlehem was resolved through negotiations behind closed doors between Israeli and Palestinian members of this network.

Highlight transcendent connections. The most powerful structural connections rise above everyday concerns and usher us into hallowed kinship. A transcendent connection binds us through mutual reverence for a higher meaning or ideal, whether spiritual, historical, cultural, natural, or communal. The congregation in a religious ceremony experiences a transcendent connection to a sacred power, just as a couple watching a beautiful sunset experiences a transcendent connection with the world around them. Two parties may even hold very different spiritual convictions but bond around the shared feeling of religious awe. By finding ways to join ourselves in transcendent connection, we can more easily work through long-standing conflicts and pave the way for peaceful coexistence.

As civil unrest reached a crescendo in South Africa's apartheid era, Archbishop Desmond Tutu centered his efforts on fostering transcendent connection, drawing upon the traditional African concept of *ubuntu*, which teaches that "my humanity is inextricably bound up in yours." As his country sought to escape the shadow of racial division, *ubuntu* arose as a powerful social force, helping people to transform from adversaries to brothers and sisters rooted in a shared spiritual tradition, moving through a traumatic history and navigating toward an interconnected future.

In Sum

When I think of how to strengthen positive connections, I picture the ice skates my son Noah wears during his hockey games: The laces are so tightly intertwined that it takes us a good five minutes after a game to undo them. Similarly, crosscutting connections help you and the other side remain connected. As you create more crosscutting links—and more diverse ones—you increase the strength and resilience of your relationships, which in turn helps to constructively resolve your most emotionally charged conflicts.

Reconfigure the Relationship

Imagine you get a phone call from the mayor of New York City. Only nine short years have passed since Islamic extremists crashed two planes into the World Trade Center skyscrapers. "I need your help," the mayor tells you. "We have to figure out how to resolve the Park51 controversy. I'm calling a meeting of key people involved—will you facilitate?"

A developer has purchased an old Burlington Coat Factory in Lower Manhattan in hopes of converting it into a fifteen-story mosque and Islamic cultural center called Park51. But protests have erupted over the location, which is roughly two blocks from the site of the fallen Twin Towers. Many opponents feel that erecting an Islamic center so close to Ground Zero will tarnish the site's sanctity and emotionally distress people who lost a loved one in the attack. But proponents of the project, equally passionate, argue that the mosque will send a global message that the actions of the nineteen terrorists are not representative of Islam and that the United States fundamentally supports religious tolerance.

The task is clear: to help the opposing parties find a viable resolution to the Park51 controversy. But why should either side compromise?

In this book, we have explored ways to resist the Five Lures of the Tribal Mind and promote integrative dynamics, including surfacing each side's mythos of identity, working through painful emotions, and building crosscutting connections. Though these strategies will all serve to improve your relations, in any conflict you will still have to figure out how to solve the actual problems at stake without compromising your core identity. In this chapter I introduce the **SAS system**, a simple framework to help you resolve such issues.

You Cannot Solve the Problem from Within It

As core identities come under threat, conflict can easily turn into a *zero-sum battle*: Either the other side bends to your identity, or you bend to theirs. Because you are unlikely to betray *your* identity, you see only one viable option: Get the opposition to cave. But they are no more likely to bend to your identity than you are to theirs, which leaves you both in a troubling stalemate. Money and other tangible assets may be negotiable, but core identity is not. As the Tribes Exercise suggests, most people would rather blow up the world than sacrifice their selves.

So how *do* you negotiate the nonnegotiable? Is it even possible?

It is, and the key insight to remember in doing so is: You cannot solve a problem from within it. You need to shift your objective from "winning" an identity battle to reconfiguring your relationship so that your core identity and the other side's can coexist. But coexistence alone is not your goal—a family, for example, can coexist for years in misery. To truly resolve identity-based divisions, you need to reframe your conflict as a quest for *harmonious coexistence*, thus opening up the possibility for resolution without compromise.

Reconfiguring Your Relationship

There are three steps to the SAS system: (1) Clarify how identity is at stake; (2) envision scenarios for harmonious coexistence; and (3) evaluate which scenario best fosters harmony. Once you complete these steps, you will be in a strong position to problem solve even the most substantive issues.

Clarify How Identity Is at Stake

Recall how the Five Lures can hook you and spiral your conflict out of control. You may initially be merely irked with a colleague for excluding you from a meeting, but within minutes vertigo and the repetition compulsion work you into a rage. So search for the conflict's deeper significance—the mythos of identity. It is often the case that the conflict at hand, while important in itself, is a proxy for an identity-based concern. The controversy over

Park51 concerned the building's practical function, but it served as a proxy for deeper questions of national identity: Who is American? Who belongs in the United States, and who is an outsider? What is the role of Islam in American society?

Because such issues are difficult to discuss directly, the building became an *emotional proxy*—an object through which people could express their wishes and fears about the shape of their identities. A proxy is a safer subject to consider than a direct conversation about identity. In this case, the mosque is a tangible quantity; you can argue about whether it should be placed two blocks or ten from Ground Zero. But the moment you explicitly share your personal perspectives on identity itself, you open yourself to a direct attack on your ego.

Strive to understand the deeper motives driving each side to conflict. A helpful starting point is to explore how a highly charged issue might be an emotional proxy for a question regarding identity. Is your interdepartmental battle really about resource distribution—or is it ultimately a conflict over which division the board sees as more central to operations? Is your argument with your sibling really about your inheritance—or about whom Mom loved most?

The need to understand deeper motives was very much on my mind a few years ago, when I consulted for a young couple, Linda and Josh, whose marriage was teetering on the brink of dissolution. They had met in college, dated for three years, and then married. Their relationship was fine until their twin girls turned four and became old enough to know about Santa Claus. The problem was that Linda is Protestant, and Josh is Jewish. As the holidays neared, they faced the perennial issue of how to celebrate in a way that worked for both partners. The more Linda pleaded to have a Christmas tree, the more Josh refused. They talked about it endlessly, read negotiation books to help them find a win-win solution, and sought advice from friends. But before long their resentments had grown so deep that finding a compromise seemed impossible, especially now that their daughters were also involved in the matter.

I sensed that the battle over the Christmas tree was a proxy for deeper differences in identity that the couple needed to work through, and I asked them, "What parts of your identity feel threatened in this conflict?" I listened for which of the Five Pillars of Identity seemed most under siege for each of them: beliefs, rituals, allegiances, values, or emotionally meaningful experiences.

Linda explained that she was only ten years old when her mother died, leaving her father as the sole caretaker. Linda felt a strong allegiance to him, recalling the ritual of waking up each Christmas to piles of gifts. The tree had become a proxy for Linda's close relationship with her father, who emotionally nourished her; its absence would feel like a betrayal. For Josh, winter inspired an allegiance to his parents and grandparents to uphold Jewish rituals and values. He imagined their disappointment if they learned of a Christmas tree in his home, with his little girls awaiting Santa's gifts. To him, the tree symbolized a betrayal of his own blood, a shameful desecration of his family roots.

While this discussion helped both Linda and Josh see why the other had been so resistant, and renewed their connection as a couple, the practical question of how to deal with the Christmas tree still had to be resolved.

Envision Scenarios for Harmonious Coexistence

The SAS system provides three approaches to coexistence: separation, assimilation, and synthesis. No one method is right for all circumstances, but the following three questions will help you devise a wide range of possible scenarios to address your conflict.

1. What would it look like to separate your identity from theirs? If you are in a troubled marriage, you may decide to live apart for a while or file for divorce. If you have an invasive neighbor, a fence can help. A first step in ending a war is to withdraw troops. Even in my own family, what do I do when my older two boys fight? Separate them.

But physical separation is not the only possible route. You also can pursue psychological forms of separation, such as fencing off discussion of specific issues from your relationship. When I was a teenager, my mother habitually peppered me with personal questions about girls I was dating. I would tell her, "That's off limits," which kept those issues out of our relationship. Nations sometimes use the same tactic, setting aside contentious matters to preserve good relations and avoid military escalation.

2. What would it look like to assimilate to their identity, or vice versa? To assimilate is to incorporate a part of their identity into yours. While separation keeps your identity intact, assimilation expands it. For example, a friend of mine who emigrated to the United States from Russia quickly assimilated to pragmatic, fast-paced American culture, but also maintained his national identity by speaking Russian at home and regularly enjoying shashlik and borscht.

You can assimilate to another's core identity through conformity or conversion. In conformity, you play by the other's rules without internalizing them. During President Barack Obama's state visit to Japan, he bowed deeply upon meeting Emperor Akihito. In other words, the president conformed to Japanese ritual but did not take on that behavior as an integral part of his identity; he did not bow to other state leaders he met. In conversion, in contrast, you *internalize* aspects of the other's core identity, as when a missionary persuades an individual to adopt a new religion as his or her own. Because conversion is a choice you make, your core identity remains uncompromised. You have changed your identity, but not by force.

3. What would it look like to synthesize identities? The third route to reconfiguring your relationship is synthesis: You redefine your relationship with the other side so your core identity and theirs coexist. You are separate and connected, autonomous and affiliated. Consider the great number of ethnic groups that live within the United States, each with a distinct cultural history but all identifying as American.

I encountered a creative example of synthesis during a visit to South Korea. After I conducted a workshop in Seoul, my host took me to the Jung district in the heart of the city. She pointed out the old city hall, an austere concrete structure erected during the Japanese occupation of Korea. After South Korea gained independence from Japanese rule, the seat of Seoul's municipal government remained in the building. In 2005, however, Mayor Lee Myung-bak called for construction of a new city hall. But what would be done with the old one?

The citizens of Seoul were split. Some advocated for its demolition: Why keep this vestige of Korea's painful past when a new building could eloquently express its modernization? Others opposed its destruction, arguing that all aspects of Korean history deserved acknowledgment. For each side, the city hall served as a proxy for South Korean identity.

As my friend led me past the building, I realized that the municipal government had resolved this identity-charged dilemma through synthesis. They converted the old structure into the Seoul Metropolitan Library, which rested in the shadow of a new city hall—a modern glass edifice whose curvature resembled an enormous wave cresting over its predecessor. Together, the two buildings presented a story about South Korea's multifaceted identity, juxtaposing its dark past and radiant present.

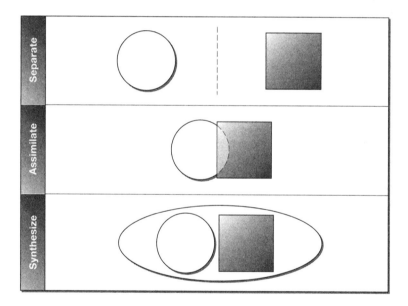

Revisiting the Christmas tree. Linda and Josh had reached an impasse over how to resolve the dilemma of the Christmas tree. To help them explore possible scenarios for harmonious coexistence, I introduced them to the SAS system. Although each of them held fixed spiritual beliefs, they were open to exploring ways to bridge their divide. I explained that their goal was to brainstorm a wide variety of options, from realistic to far-fetched, in hopes that creative thinking would help them find one that felt right. I also asked them not to evaluate the merits of each scenario; that would come later.

The couple began by envisioning scenarios of separation. They could both pretend the conflict did not exist, fencing off this irreconcilable difference from their relationship for most of the year and dealing with it only when Christmas neared. Alternatively, one or the other could agree explicitly to the other's desire but harbor resentment. Or they could take the more unusual step of actually dividing their home. "In this part of the house," they could agree, "we will celebrate Christmas. In the rest, we'll celebrate Hanukkah." Or they could seek a lawyer and initiate a divorce.

Next, they considered scenarios of assimilation. Josh could convert to Linda's religious beliefs and become a Protestant. Or he could accept the Christmas tree in the house, either living with a sense of betrayal to his ancestry or figuring out how to accommodate the tree within his beliefs. Conversely, Linda could agree to conform to the rituals of Judaism, remaining faithful to her Protestant denomination but observing Jewish rituals. Or she could convert to Judaism.

Finally, the couple envisioned a scenario in which to synthesize their differences. They could buy a tree for their house, jointly decorate it with their kids, and each ascribe personal meaning to it: Linda could view it as a Christmas tree, Josh as a festive Hanukkah decoration.

Evaluate Which Scenario Best Harmonizes Differences

I gave Linda and Josh a few minutes to reflect on the scenarios and then to assess the options. The question I asked them to focus on was: "Which scenario—or combination—seems most compelling and feasible for both of you?"

Weigh the pros and cons. As Linda and Josh came to realize, there is no perfect approach to coexistence. Separation can reduce the emotional intensity of a conflict: Separate the troops, and crisis is averted. But while separation can be useful for *making* peace, it can become an impediment to *keeping* it. In Northern Ireland during the period of bloody hostility known as the Troubles, "peace walls" of iron, brick, and steel were built to protect areas that had served as flash points for violence. During a recent visit to Northern Ireland, I was surprised to see peace walls still standing, more than a decade after the Good Friday Agreement; in fact, the number of walls had actually risen after the peace accord. The walls kept communities safe, but at a psychological cost to an integrated society.

Similarly, while assimilation allows you to join with the other, it can give rise to long-term resentment. If you conform to the other's identity but grow to resent it, the backlash can be intense. Imagine that Josh decides to accept the presence of the Christmas tree, but then experiences a change of heart once he sees it in their home. Resentment begins subtly but then engulfs him, spinning him into vertigo as he asks himself, *Why did I have to betray my roots?*

The advantages of synthesis are many. If you and the other side can find a way for your identities to coexist, your relationship can withstand strong headwinds. You become increasingly interconnected and feel an obligation to stick together through good times and bad. Because you are "in it together," the incentive to sabotage your relationship has been neutralized.

Yet even synthesis is not a panacea. It can be extremely difficult to identify a mutually agreeable area of connection within which adversaries can coexist. How, for example, can a government synthesize differences with a terrorist organization? There is also the risk that the more powerful party may attempt to impose itself on the weaker power; the two will have joined at the cost of the weaker party's interests. Finally, maintaining a synthesized identity requires conscious long-term effort. Marriage is a great example of synthesis, but the mere act of saying "I do" is not enough to sustain a relationship.

Don't battle over the relationship; jointly build it. It is hard to reconcile a conflict if, say, you want to synthesize and the other side demands that you assimilate. Any mismatch between preferences will result only in more conflict. Opponents of Park51 demanded that the mosque be erected farther from Ground Zero; they wanted separation. Proponents of the project leaned toward synthesis, advocating for the original location but including in the mosque a community center with prayer space and a memorial for victims of the attacks.

Rather than battling over scenarios, try to devise ways to restructure the relationship to address each party's fears and wishes. Linda and Josh followed this advice and ultimately found a solution that combined the three approaches to coexistence. They agreed not to have a Christmas tree in their own home, but to celebrate Christmas each year at Linda's father's house in Georgia. This was consistent with each spouse's mythos of identity: Linda, Josh, and their kids would get to experience Christmas with Linda's father, honoring Linda's attachment to ritual while respecting Josh's beliefs. Meanwhile, Linda reaffirmed her premarital commitment to raise their children in the Jewish faith, which allayed Josh's fears of betraying his heritage. The couple came to understand and accept each other's identities, weaving differences into the relationship and growing in the process. To be sure, their agreement was a work in progress—but progress had been made.

Beware of power struggles. People like power, and they fear losing it. Thus, the powerful often want others to assimilate to their ways, whereas the powerless prefer synthesis. The resulting clash can become explosive. A case in point is the Treaty of Versailles, the agreement that ended World War I. The victorious nations sought to "utterly humiliate and destroy their enemies—mostly Germany," excluded the Germans from peace negotiations, and imposed sanctions that drained the German economy. Germany felt humiliated, which set the stage "for a leader such as Adolf Hitler and his ultranationalist agenda to rise to power, something that was unimaginable just twenty years earlier."

Recognize when you are engaging in a struggle for structural power—the authority to legitimately tell others what to do. Many negotiations do not involve structural power: When you haggle over the price of a new car, you are not negotiating the dealer's level of authority; you cannot force him to give you the price you want. But if a minority group seeks greater decision-making authority, they are negotiating for more structural power. Similarly, when two owners of a company fight for more than 50 percent equity in their company, their conflict involves structural power; only one of them will have the ability to dictate company policy.

The most heated conflicts usually involve a power struggle, because the powerful fear losing power and the powerless crave more. So proactively seek to rebalance power relations. Here are a few suggestions:

- *Avoid humiliating the other side, especially when you are more powerful.* After World War II, the victorious nations sought not to disgrace the defeated nations, but to help them rebuild and reintegrate into the global community through the Marshall Plan.
- *Seek institutional change.* The Civil Rights Act mandated equal treatment of black and white people in the United States.
- *Enlist a mediator.* A mediator can level the playing field and ensure each party has equal airtime to voice their views, problem solve differences, and reconfigure the relationship for mutual satisfaction.
- *Remember the necessity of sacrifice.* Remind yourself that harmonious coexistence requires each party to relinquish some degree of autonomy for the sake of harmonious coexistence.

Back to Park51

Just before you and the mayor hang up, he reminds you, "New York and our nation are counting on you." You begin preparations for the meeting you will facilitate—designing the agenda, contacting invitees, reminding each that the meeting will be private and off the record. However, you are concerned, having realized that there appear to be only two possible solutions: Either the proponents or the opponents of the project will prevail. Very few mutually agreeable scenarios have been presented, and those that have—such as using the site as both mosque and memorial—have been roundly rejected.

A few days later, twelve of the parties involved in the debate gather for a two-day workshop at a hotel in upstate New York, out of the media spotlight. After explaining the purpose of the workshop, you describe the Five Lures and facilitate a two-hour discussion of how they might be escalating the conflict. Participants discuss how the nation and media have fallen into a state of vertigo around Park51; how the repetition compulsion may be at play in reaction to the trauma of September 11; and how there is a taboo around explicitly discussing the range of attitudes toward Islam in American society. Individual members of the group also realize that the issue feels like an assault not just on their own sacred values, but also on the sacred values and beliefs of the other parties involved. A couple of brave souls even acknowledge that Park51 may have been usurped for purposes of identity politics, recognizing that a few outspoken politicians have exploited the issue as midterm elections near.

Next, you lead the group through a rough version of integrative dynamics, starting by having each participant share his or her mythos of identity for five minutes, then opening the floor for others to pose questions about that perspective. You ask each participant to answer the question "What is the personal significance of Park51 to you?" You remind the other participants to listen carefully and respectfully; the goal is to learn, not debate.

As each person speaks, a common theme emerges: The parties all feel emotionally pained and fearful. The September 11 attacks have profoundly affected the way people view their identity and security. In light of the shared sentiments in the room, you ask everyone to join in a moment of silence for the victims of the attack. As silence falls, you feel the group's dynamic shift. They are sharing in mourning, an important step in working through emotional pain. They are fortifying their human connection.

The members of the group discuss what has driven them to speak out on the controversy, each participant diving deeper into his or her own motives. By midday, the group seems ready to problem solve practical differences. You introduce the SAS system and establish two ground rules: (1) brainstorm as many scenarios as possible, and (2) do not evaluate ideas yet. You start by asking the group: "What are some ways to deal with Park51?"

The group envisions possible solutions, and two separation-based scenarios emerge: move the center to a location farther from Ground Zero or keep it within the old facility. Assimilation scenarios include making Park51 a cultural center; turning it into solely a memorial for victims of the terrorist attack; and incorporating the mosque into the Park51 community center. Synthesis scenarios include making Park51 a center for all religions; keeping it as an Islamic cultural center but adding a memorial for victims of the terrorist attack; and doing what former president Bill Clinton proposed: "Dedicating this center to all the Muslims who were killed on 9/11."

You ask the participants to jointly evaluate which scenarios might prove most satisfactory to everyone involved. A positive-spirited debate ensues as the list is narrowed to the three most promising scenarios. You share these with the mayor, who responds enthusiastically: Each scenario is preferable to the binary scenarios dominating the public debate. The mayor privately discusses the ideas with the key stakeholders, who agree to move forward with one of the three recommended scenarios—and who ultimately choose one that synthesizes concerns implicit in each stakeholder's mythos of identity.

In Sum

Can you negotiate the nonnegotiable? My answer is yes. The SAS system allows you to disentangle your core identity from your relational identity in order to reconfigure your relationship. Your core identity is largely fixed, so attempting to negotiate it is unlikely to be productive. Instead, concentrate on adjusting your relational identity, transforming the way in which you and the other party coexist.

The SAS system offers three tools for reconfiguring your relationship while keeping your core identity intact: separation, assimilation, and synthesis. Each of these alternatives has pros and cons that must be carefully evaluated. Your goal is to identify, and then develop, the scenario that best serves each party's mythos of identity.

So remember: You cannot solve a problem from within it. By applying the SAS system, you can step outside the conflict in order to resolve it.

Section 4

Reconciling Irreconcilable Differences

Managing Dialectics

An age-old Native American legend tells of a grandfather who shares a secret with his grandson: "I have two wolves fighting within me. One is a wolf of love and kindness. The other is a wolf of hate and greed."

The boy's eyes open wide. "Which will win?" he asks.

The grandfather pauses for a moment and responds, "Whichever I feed."

Reconciliation involves a dialogue between people—but the hardest part takes place within yourself. In any conflict, you have to decide which wolf to feed. Can you release your grievances, forgive, and move forward? Do you trust the other side enough to welcome them back into your good graces? Are you fundamentally willing to change? The answer to these questions resides not in any textbook, but in your heart of hearts.

What makes these questions especially difficult is that they involve contradictory impulses. While you want to resolve your conflict, you also want to protect yourself. To invite the other side back into your life is risky, for they *have* opposed you. They *have* hurt you. How can you be sure they will not do so again? The vulnerability required to transcend your differences, therefore, causes unavoidable ambivalence about reconciliation. Even the most compassionate among us will experience a desire for vengeance; the gentlest soul will acknowledge a hint of resentment; the most accepting will feel a twinge of judgment.

I call these competing impulses *relational dialectics*. They are the wolves within you—and they pull your emotions in two different directions: toward the relationship and away from it. In a conflict, contradictory impulses can be neither avoided nor resolved, as they are part of your human architecture. But once you become aware of them, you can decide which to feed.

A Brief History of Dialectics

The concept of dialectics dates back thousands of years. The Greek philosopher Heraclitus of Ephesus proposed a *unity of opposites*: the notion that everything in the world is determined by its opposite. In U.S. politics, for example, the Republican Party's agenda can affect that of the Democratic Party, and vice versa. This is the essence of dialectics: the nature of how two opposing perspectives relate to each other.

Philosopher Immanuel Kant took the concept a step further. He proposed that ideas develop in three stages: a *thesis* bumps up against an *antithesis*, producing a *synthesis*. This simple, elegant formula sheds light on the evolution of ideas, history, economics—just about any field of thought. A medieval fisherman supposes that the flat world ends at the horizon (a thesis). But then one day he sails a ship so far that he eventually arrives on the opposite coast of his homeland, causing him to reexamine his assumption (antithesis). Ultimately, he concludes that the world is round (synthesis).

Despite Kant's brilliance, his theory had holes—or, to put it in dialectical terms, his thesis was not without antithesis—and German philosopher Georg Wilhelm Friedrich Hegel attempted to fill them. Hegel believed that the concept of an antithesis was too fuzzy, so he proposed that an idea progresses through three states: abstract, negative, and concrete. An initial thesis is abstract and untested and lacks the "negative" precision of trial and error. Every idea, no matter how thoughtful, contains an intrinsic incompleteness. The idea that the world ends at the horizon contains an internal error, a "negative," that is overcome only through a new idea that brings the dialectic to completion. Once the abstract meets with the negative, a more concrete synthesis emerges.

Dialectics present you with necessary ambivalence, an inescapable conflict within yourself. But they need not prohibit you from reaching resolution—if you know how to manage their contradictory forces.

Navigating a Bundle of Contradictions

Several dialectics dominate the emotional world of conflict: *acceptance versus change; redemption versus revenge;* and *autonomy versus affiliation.* You seek redemption but harbor vengeance. You try to accept the other party but hope they will change. You build affiliation but feel constrained within it. To deal with these dialectics effectively, adopt a three-pronged strategy.

First, become mindful of the dialectics struggling within you. If left unattended, the pull of dialectics can sabotage even your most satisfying agreement. So remain aware of how they are affecting you. Do you feel resistant to reconciling? Hesitant to change?

Second, feed the force that gets you where you want to go. If you want to improve your relationship with your ex-spouse, perhaps because you share parenting duties, first recognize the internal battle simultaneously pulling you toward both redemption and revenge. Then, to rebuild your relationship, focus on redemption, even as you accept that years of accumulated anger may saturate your heart with calls for vengeance. Acknowledge the hostile feelings—but do not feed them.

Third, recognize that dialectics affect the other party, too. By becoming aware of their dialectical challenges, you can help allay their fears about reconciling with *you.* For example, you can let your ex-spouse know that you understand how hard it must be to build a partnership with *you* after all the pain you have inflicted in the past.

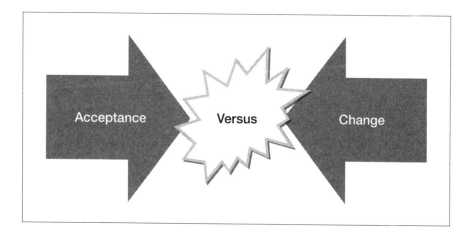

Dialectic #1: Acceptance Versus Change

Most conflicts hinge on two essential truths: (1) everyone involved wants to be accepted, and (2) nobody wants to change. Consider the situation facing Susan and Ron, a couple married for thirty years, as they sit on the couch watching television. Susan says, "My New Year's resolution is to lose twenty pounds—and I have to start by curbing my snacking. Will you help me?"

"Sure," Ron says with a supportive smile.

"Oh," Susan snaps back, "so you think I snack too much?"

Ron, startled, finds himself caught in a dialectic that exists within Susan's mind. Underlying her request for support were two potent questions: *Should I accept myself as I am, or change? Does Ron accept me as I am, or does* he *think I should change?* By supporting Susan's New Year's resolution, Ron unwittingly undermined his support for her.

Of course, dialectics have no "right" answer. Had Ron replied, "You don't need to lose weight. You're perfect the way you are," Susan might well have said, "Why can't you support me?"

We Crave Acceptance

When you feel accepted for who you are, blemishes and all, you feel both comforted and liberated. You no longer need to worry about what you say or how you behave. You have confidence that, no matter what, the other person will support you.

When you feel judged, you experience the opposite. Judgment is the enemy of acceptance. Everyone possesses an emotional radar system that is alert to any hint of nonacceptance. Whenever someone accuses you of an "unfair" feeling, "wrong" thought, or "defective" character trait, you feel unaccepted. And it hurts.

But the most painful form of judgment comes from within. You fail to accept parts or all of yourself, harshly judging your own behavior, feelings, or thoughts and concluding that you are inadequate. Psychologist William James dismissed one of his own books as "a loathsome, distended, tumefied, bloated, dropsical mass, testifying to nothing but two facts: 1st, that there is no such thing as a science of psychology, and 2nd, that William James is an incapable." James was one of the most venerated minds of his era, yet even he was susceptible to harsh criticisms of his work and, by extension, of himself.

It is extraordinarily difficult to break free of self-criticism. You eventually become trapped in a self-perpetuating pattern of flawed thinking—what psychologists call *cognitive distortions*: The more you criticize yourself, the more you find yourself worthy of criticism.

We Resist Change

Conflict saturates you with tension, making you want to alter the other party's behavior—but not your own. You believe you are right, so why should *you* change? But because the other party has precisely the same rationale, the more you each demand that the other change, the less each of you feels accepted. In Hegel's words, you each feel the other side casts a "negative" to your perspective, some error or gap, leading you both to stubbornly maintain your positions.

Time and again in the Tribes Exercise, I have witnessed how the pressure for change collides with the yearning for acceptance. In the first round of the exercise, tribal leaders often try to persuade other tribes to join theirs, emphasizing the appeal of their own tribe while discounting the merits of others. What these leaders fail to account for, however, is just how resistant identity is to change. The more external pressure a tribe feels to change, the more they demand that other tribes accept them as they are. A battle of autonomy emerges, with each tribe insisting that the others accept theirs as the leader. The result is a nearly inevitable clash.

The Five Lures further diminish your motivation to change. Vertigo, for example, thrusts you into a warped world of confrontation. The repetition compulsion pulls you deeper into divisive patterns. Taboos prevent you from even talking about change with the other side. And both an assault on the sacred and identity politics strengthen the lines of division.

Acceptance or Change?

By recognizing the acceptance/change dialectic, you can improve the way you and the other party deal with tension. I advised a couple, Marshall and Betty, who struggled with chronic intense fights. Marshall explained how Betty would unexpectedly lose her temper and how he would attempt to placate her by saying things like "Calm down, we can work this out." But Betty would only grow angrier in response, causing Marshall to withdraw.

Neither party felt accepted for his or her style of emotional expression. Betty was comfortable expressing anger, whereas it made Marshall anxious. He had grown up in a conflict-avoidant home; his family rarely expressed strong emotions. Betty's parents, in contrast, regularly blew up at each other but always reconciled. The more Betty expressed anger, the less Marshall accepted her, and the more Marshall tried to change Betty's anger, the more unaccepted she felt, which only further fueled her anger. This couple was caught in a disastrous spiral, at the heart of which lay the dialectic of acceptance versus change.

After I presented this observation to Marshall, he began to view the relationship in a new light. When the couple next fought, Marshall responded in a different way. He recognized and accepted his feeling of discomfort with Betty's anger, but did not act on it or attempt to placate her. To his surprise, Betty's anger softened. By accepting their dialectical struggles, Marshall helped to reconfigure their relationship.

To reconcile an emotionally charged conflict, both acceptance and change are necessary; the key is knowing what to accept and what to change. It is an uphill battle to change someone's core identity—people resist changes to essential beliefs and values. But accepting a tense, unproductive relationship serves no one.

Therefore, aim to accept the other's core identity as is, nonjudgmentally acknowledging their values and beliefs. Meanwhile, seek to reconfigure your relationship, embedding each party's core identity in a broader relational narrative. Marshall restructured his marital relationship by recognizing, but not responding to, Betty's anger—and that strategy worked.

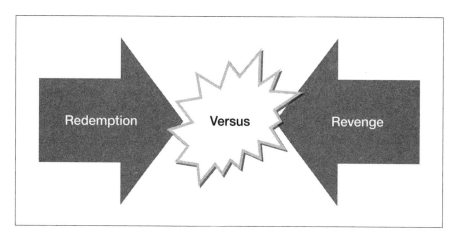

Dialectic #2: Redemption Versus Revenge

If you prick us do we not bleed? If you tickle us do we not laugh?
If you poison us do we not die? and if you wrong us shall we not
revenge?

—WILLIAM SHAKESPEARE, *THE MERCHANT OF VENICE*

Imagine sharing a deep, dark secret with a close friend, only to discover that she has posted it on her website. You are aghast. The moment she betrays you, the dialectic between revenge and redemption commands your attention. On the one hand, a gut-level force compels you to retaliate to restore your sense of moral order, perhaps by posting some of her secrets on your website. On the other hand, because she is a friend, an inner voice urges you to confront her and talk things out. To which voice should you listen?

The challenge is to disentangle impulse from action. Even a trivial offense to your identity can trigger a strong impulse to avenge. If you fail to notice the impulse, you remain at its mercy. But while you cannot avoid the impulse, you can thoughtfully consider how to respond.

To become aware of the impulse to avenge, take note of any fantasies you have of retaliation. If your boss constantly demeans you, do you daydream about exposing his flaws to the world? Fantasies have no limits; they can be antisocial or shocking. A small part of you may enjoy these daydreams, for they mollify a wounded ego and invoke a sense of justice: Your boss made you suffer, and now you want to administer him a dose of his own medicine. But whether you decide to actually retaliate is a wholly different matter.

The Upside of Revenge

Revenge can empower you by giving you access to justice, power, and catharsis.

Justice. Revenge motivates you to rectify injustice, to "even the score." Relatives who exclude you from a holiday party should not expect to receive an invitation to your next family reunion. The flames of revenge are stoked through a desire not for contrition from the offending party, but for punishment. You want your relatives to viscerally experience emotional pain comparable to that which you suffered at their hands; and you gain the satisfaction of knowing that they now truly understand—and are paying for—your suffering. Justice feels restored.

The threat of revenge can also deter future injustice. If the school bully knows your daughter will slug him if he insults her, he might think twice about doing so again. In fact, your daughter may threaten to respond to him with excessive force. While her threat may seem irrational, it creates a wide wall of deterrence that can promote cooperation.

Power. Revenge galvanizes you to improve your standing in relation to the other side. Your daughter challenging the bully may be a way for her to assert her dominance and reorder the social hierarchy. This hunger for increased status can supersede the desire for justice.

Catharsis. Revenge provides you with a means of catharsis—purging you of painful emotions. As a result, you feel free from the chains of victimization, released from humiliation and shame. In fact, researchers at the University of Zurich have discovered that as you enact revenge, blood flows increasingly to your brain's reward centers, including the caudate nucleus and thalamus—the same parts of the brain that are activated if you take a hit of nicotine or cocaine.

The Downside of Revenge

While revenge offers gratification on several fronts, scientific research and anecdotal evidence cast doubt on its ultimate efficacy.

Lopsided justice. Revenge can indeed promote a sense of justice—but only for you. The other party will perceive your justice as their injustice, triggering a cycle of mutual retaliation. Even if you are convinced that you are inflicting suffering on the other side in proportion to that which they inflicted upon you, they are likely to see your punishment as excessive. As my grandmother used to say, "If it's your finger, it hurts more." In other words, you judge your own pain as more severe than do those who see it from the outside. This makes the belief that revenge will prevent further offenses an unlikely proposition.

Short-lived empowerment. While revenge can briefly empower you, the perpetrator-turned-victim is likely to begin quickly to scheme their own ways to retaliate. For example, as a husband seeks revenge on his ex-wife—for instance, refusing to let her back in the house to collect her favorite painting—he is energized with empowerment. A day later, however, he finds himself facing the deflating reality of new legal charges.

Fleeting catharsis. The sweet taste of revenge does not linger for long. Scheming to avenge the misdeed of a nasty spouse or colleague may feel revitalizing, but research suggests that after we retaliate, we actually feel *worse* than we had anticipated: We question our own morality and increasingly ruminate about the offender. Furthermore, the cathartic experience of revenge is but a momentary distraction from the emotional pain of loss. A soldier who has seen a comrade die in battle may feel a wave of cathartic justice as he shoots the perpetrator in retaliation, but he still must live with blood on his hands, the heightened threat of the enemy retaliating, and the unchanged reality that his comrade is forever gone.

Venting: A Middle Ground?

Instead of seeking revenge, you may decide to vent your anger. You grab a pillow, imagine it as the person who hurt you, and pound it; you then talk to a close friend and spill the gory details of how you feel you've been wronged. Surely these popular forms of catharsis work, right? Wrong. A massive body of scientific evidence has demonstrated that venting anger actually backfires: The more you vent, the stronger your desire for revenge.

Venting assumes that your anger is like steam in a kettle: If you open up the lid to release the steam, the pressure will be reduced. But anger does not function like that. The more you think about all the ways you feel wronged, the more you work yourself into an emotional frenzy. Rather than releasing anger, venting reinforces it.

Professor Brad Bushman designed an unusual study that underscores this point. The subjects were instructed to write an essay on abortion, either pro-life or pro-choice. A student in another room then evaluated the essays and returned them with a handwritten comment: *This is one of the worst essays I have ever read!* Unbeknownst to the participants, there was no student in the other room—an experimenter had actually written the comment as a way to anger the participants. Experimenters then divided the subjects into three groups—one hit a punching bag while thinking of the (fictitious) despised student evaluator, a second hit the punching bag while thinking about becoming physically fit, and a third sat quietly for two minutes.

All three groups then put on headphones and played a computer game against the (fictitious) student who had graded their essay. The loser in each round of the game would be blasted with a loud noise, while the winner got to choose the duration and intensity of the noise. The game was rigged so that the subjects won half the time. So which group set the volume the loudest? The bag punchers were equally aggressive whether they had just been thinking about their despised counterpart or their own physical fitness—and these results point to the dangers of venting anger.

Of course, there are other forms of catharsis that are much more effective. A massive amount of evidence in clinical psychology points to the value of talking about your feelings as a way of making meaning of them. While venting focuses on getting rid of anger, better-designed methods of catharsis use the power of dialogue to understand your anger and work through it, such as those described in the previous chapters on integrative dynamics. The key, however, is in your mindset.

Focus on Redemption, Not Revenge

Whereas vengefulness undermines relationships, redemption makes space for a communal spirit. To redeem a relationship requires you to believe in the possibility of reconnection, making amends, and restoring positive bonds. But redemption is more of a mindset than a skill. It is characterized by *courage* to recognize your insecurities, *compassion* for others' suffering, and *moral determination* to build better relations. The potential for redemption resides within everyone. Here are concrete ways to help yourself access it.

1. Summon the courage to look inward. At an international conference some years ago, I spoke with a top political negotiator in the Israeli-Palestinian conflict. As we explored some of the sensitive issues surrounding the conflict, his cheeks reddened, his arms flailed, and the cadence of his speech accelerated. As I watched this display I finally asked him, "Do you think emotions are impacting you in the conflict?" He bristled and replied, "Absolutely not!" It was a clear case of refusal to look inward. On some level his analysis was right—structural factors were major causes of the conflict in question—but within this outwardly rational problem he and the other stakeholders were at an emotional standstill. It takes courage to objectively examine our fears and insecurities in order to open the door to redemption.

2. Feel compassion for others' suffering. You may not agree with the other party's beliefs or actions, and you may even be disgusted by their words or deeds. But remember, they are human, and in an emotionally charged conflict, you can be certain that they too are suffering. Being sensitive to their anguish is the single best way to restore positive relations.

In a state of compassion, you empathize with another's suffering and feel the desire to relieve it. The Buddha saw compassion as "that which makes the heart of the good move at the pain of others." The Latin roots of "compassion" mean "to suffer with." Compassion emotionally moves us to action.

While the capacity for compassion lies within each of us, the challenge is to evoke it. But how can you feel concern for someone who has intentionally hurt you? For starters, remember that feeling compassion for someone does not preclude your seeking justice for any wrongdoing he or she might have done.

Second, inquire into the other's suffering. You might ask, "How has this conflict personally affected you?" Listen not to defend, but to understand.

Third, imagine stepping into the other person's *situation*—not just their shoes—and identify with their suffering. Recently I flew from Boston to Chicago, and several rows behind me a four-year-old girl wailed continuously. Fellow passengers and I shared sympathetic glances, yet there was little we could do but bear it. Then it suddenly occurred to me that I was viewing this girl as a tribal outsider, an object to which I felt opposed. I decided to imagine that she was a part of my own family, and soon my annoyance turned to compassion. I walked down the aisle and tried to distract her with a few clownish faces. Her crying stopped for a few minutes, and her mother looked up in appreciation.

A fourth way to evoke compassion is to build even a trivial emotional connection. Pairs of students in a laboratory experiment who sat across from each other and merely tapped their fingers in synchrony to musical tones were 31 percent more likely to volunteer to help their partner in a tedious forty-five-minute follow-up task than those subjects in pairs who did not tap fingers in synchrony to the music. The synchronized tappers spent on average seven minutes helping, while the asynchronous tappers spent only one.

But how do you find compassion for a *reprehensible* adversary? I posed this question to Ambassador Lakhdar Brahimi, a distinguished diplomat who has negotiated political stability with dictators and militants in Afghanistan, Iraq, Syria, Liberia, South Africa, and Yemen. We were members of a council exploring methods for promoting global conflict resolution. With characteristic thoughtfulness, Ambassador Brahimi reflected on the question and said, "I find something admirable in them." He proactively seeks to recognize the humanity in everyone he meets and works to appreciate something about them, whether their dedication to parenting or their loyalty to a cause.

Another effective method to awaken compassion is to draw on contemplative practices. One well-researched technique is known as the loving-kindness meditation (LKM), which encourages the bolstering of positive emotions through systematic cultivation of kindness toward yourself and others. This technique may sound insubstantial, but hard science supports its positive effect. Eminent neuroscientist Richard Davidson and colleagues found that the practice of LKM strengthens brain circuitry linked to empathic sensitivity, and Professor Barbara Fredrickson found that LKM is associated with "increases in a variety of personal resources, including mindful attention, self-acceptance, positive relationships with others and good physical health."

To practice LKM, begin by cultivating a feeling of loving kindness directed at yourself. Embrace it and allow it to flow throughout your body. Now imagine radiating this same positive feeling toward your loved ones. After a few minutes let this compassion emanate to colleagues, acquaintances, and strangers. Then call to mind people who distress you, and extend your compassion to them.

In sum, an emotionally charged conflict will tempt you to seek revenge. Don't fight these feelings, but don't succumb to them. Let this be your mantra: Focus on redemption, not revenge.

3. Invoke moral determination to improve relations. To counteract the temptation to avenge, approach redemption with moral determination: Grit your teeth, hold fast to your goal, and don't let go. You can do so by first defining your guiding values and then sticking to them. This second part is the key. In the Tribes Exercise, for example, tribes regularly claim to espouse such profound values as equality, harmony, and compassion, but these values vanish when they begin negotiating.

Take a few minutes to list the three to five values you most cherish, such as dignity, compassion, equality, justice, security, and respect. Post them on your refrigerator as a daily reminder. As you manage your next conflict, reflect on whether you live consistently with those values. If not, revise your behavior or redefine your values.

In some conflicts it can help to jointly define a shared set of values. For example, spouses embroiled in a pattern of conflict might sit down in a time of peace and identify three core values that define their relationship—dignity, fairness, respect, kindness, compassion, and so on—and agree to hold themselves accountable for honoring them. In effect, the spouses create a *social covenant*, a mutual commitment to the moral foundation of their relationship. In subsequent conflicts, the mere fact of having that social covenant can heighten their respect for each other.

However, not all relations are so easily reconciled. The greatest barrier to seeking redemption lies in the belief that the other side simply cannot be redeemed. You condemn their behavior as immoral and regard them with such vehement disapproval that an emotional connection feels not only unbearable but impossible. To seek redemption in such cases, therefore, requires *moral fortitude*, the internal strength to tolerate a connection with someone whose moral code you condemn.

This was the challenge facing my colleague Robert Jay Lifton, a distinguished scholar who interviewed dozens of Nazi doctors accused of committing horrific medical experiments on men, women, and children. This work tested Lifton's moral fortitude, particularly because he is Jewish. He told me that as he embarked on this study, he consulted his mentor, the esteemed psychologist Erik Erikson, who remarked, "You know, you may even make contact with their humanity." To truly grasp the psychology of Nazi doctors, Lifton would have to enter their psyches to understand how they had justified these atrocities to themselves and rationalized medical torture as a virtuous act.

Lifton is a dedicated humanist, but even he discovered thresholds to redemption. These interviews gave him "regular nightmares," and he went on to explain that his "greatest challenge arose during a trip to Bavaria to interview one of history's most repugnant Nazi doctors. I arrived at his door and met this charming elderly man who had never been tried for his crimes. From the moment he opened the door, I felt this strange affinity for him. Of course, I felt deeply ashamed of this feeling, knowing what I knew about his past. But the man generously hosted me and answered all of my questions with complete candor."

The dialectic between redemption and revenge soon came to a head. Typically, Lifton refrained from sharing meals with interviewees, which was his way of separating the necessary objective rapport he needed to establish for his research from his moral condemnation of the subject's actions. But on this particular day, Lifton was in the middle of the Bavarian woods, miles from any restaurant and fearful of losing valuable time for his interview, so he accepted. As he notes, "The next hour was one of the most difficult of my entire research experience. Divested of our rather clearly defined interview roles, we were suddenly thrust into a social situation and reduced to making small talk." He felt self-condemnation for being on "such seemingly affable terms with this man and his monstrous ideas," but concluded that his research goals justified his actions. He later acknowledged, "I have no regrets."

However resilient an individual's moral fortitude might be, not all relationships are readily redeemable. Political leaders on opposing sides of a conflict may recognize the social, economic, and long-term political value in restoring good relations, but also recognize that extending their hand in peace will effectively be political suicide. What should they do?

In such cases, it is best not to abandon one's determination but to channel it in a different direction. In politically fraught conflicts, a third party may have to be enlisted to "force" an agreement. The two political leaders may appoint their deputies to meet privately with an official from a neutral country who can help them iron out an agreement. The third country's leader can then invite the conflicting countries' leaders to a summit, where they finalize the agreement and have decisions that are politically sensitive "imposed" upon them.

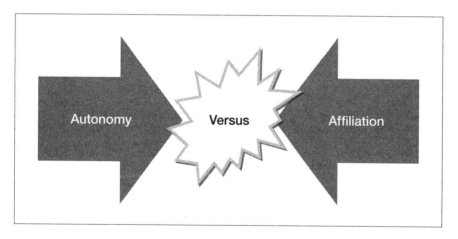

Dialectic #3: Autonomy Versus Affiliation

A mystique surrounds the number one. When two people marry, they join as one. When a child is conceived, two lives create one. When organizations merge, two entities become one. But this process of affiliation brings with it an inherent tension. Spouses feel beholden to each other; the child longs for independence; and the merged organization strains to integrate its original entities.

This dual desire to be one *with* another (affiliation) and one *from* another (autonomy) represents the third dialectic. I believe this is the essential dialectic of coexistence—and it confronts us with two dynamics that can escalate conflict: one that threatens your autonomy and another that endangers your affiliation.

The Turf Battle

Every organization grapples with turf battles—fights to protect or expand domains of autonomy. The fact that employees work within the same organization, which affiliates them, also limits the space for independence. Autonomy becomes a finite resource for which people compete; if someone encroaches on their turf, they pounce.

Consider a common scenario: The CEOs of two companies agree to merge their companies. On paper the merger guarantees skyrocketing profits, but as these two executives implement the agreement, the situation turns disastrous. The newfound affiliation has given rise to a turf battle: Because the employees have not been properly inducted into the newly merged organization, they have maintained loyalty to their original ones. They have effectively become two tribes, panicking over the potential loss of their members' jobs, authority, and culture. As a result, they begin to battle for power, wreaking havoc on both productivity and morale.

Leadership in an effective corporate merger must recognize the inevitability of turf battles and take proactive action to prevent them. As company leadership formulates a merger strategy, it should appoint cross-departmental, multilevel consultation groups to devise ways to increase the chances of the merger's success. They can develop policies to ensure that members of each "tribe" hold key roles within the new entity. Institutionalizing the consultation groups will help create a new corporate identity in which everyone feels connected. Turf battles will still erupt—the autonomy/affiliation dialectic is inevitable—but can be blunted through preemptive efforts to enhance everyone's sense of affiliation to the new organization and autonomy within it.

The Space Invasion

Whereas a turf war is a battle over autonomy, a space invasion is a battle over affiliation. In this scenario, tension emerges because you feel so emotionally smothered by a relationship that you cannot separate your identity from that of the other. Excessive affiliation impinges upon your autonomy.

Space invasions are unavoidable within families. When my friend Peter's mother-in-law visited for a few days, the two of them got along fine. But when she later moved in for six months, tensions ran high, and he found no time to be alone with his wife and kids. Soon enough his mother-in-law was weighing in on every family matter. From her perspective she was providing helpful ideas; from his, she was impinging on his ability to make decisions. Peter knew that if he raised his frustration with his mother-in-law, he risked offending her. If he didn't, his autonomy would continue to feel compromised. He felt trapped in a lose-lose situation.

But he was not. Peter and I spoke about the matter, and he decided that, rather than endangering his relationship with his mother-in-law, he would discuss the matter with his wife. She empathized with him and spoke privately with her mother about how best to structure everyone's roles. The mother-in-law understood and distanced herself from some of the family decisions. Having Peter's wife raise the issue constructively defused the space invasion.

Unless you're able to manage the tension between autonomy and affiliation, it can become all-consuming. This became clear to me several years ago when I co-led an executive education program at Harvard for senior business and government executives. My co-facilitator and I ran the Tribes Exercise, and while we typically have participants negotiate without a microphone, we had one available that day. The unexpected ramification was that the microphone enabled delegates to speak one at a time, reducing chaos and encouraging everyone to listen to one another. From the outset of the intertribal negotiation, a delegate named John took positive advantage of this situation and led the discussions. He stood at the middle of the room, handed each tribe the microphone to share its attributes, flip-charted the results, and facilitated a consensual decision-making process.

In the middle of the final negotiation round, John turned to me and said, "We've all come to agreement."

"Really?" I asked, skeptical. All six delegates nodded, pointing to John's tribe as the chosen one. I asked everyone to return to their seats so we could review the exercise, whispering to my co-facilitator, "This is going to be a boring debrief!"

It turned out I was wrong.

I opened the discussion by asking the group, "How are you feeling?"

A businessman at the back of the room raised his hand and, pointing to John, asked, "Why did *you* get the microphone?"

"Yeah," remarked another participant before John could respond. "Who authorized *that*? In the first round we all had a chance to use the microphone. In the second round you monopolized it!"

"You didn't pay attention to what I said!" complained a woman at a neighboring table, arms crossed. "You were like a dictator!"

"But I saved your life!" John protested.

A businessman from the back row, who had been shaking his head, suddenly stood and shouted, "I would rather *die* than be in a tribe with people like you!"

As a hush fell over the room, I asked the businessman to explain what he meant by that statement. He said he had been deeply offended by the degree to which John usurped everyone's autonomy during the negotiation. Although John's intentions had been positive—he was, after all, trying to save the world—he had failed to respect everyone's independence. Consequently, the businessman and a majority of participants felt disempowered, humiliated, and ready to fight back.

But what *should* John have done? He was, after all, in a double bind. By taking on the leadership role, he saved the world—but at the cost of inciting great animosity toward him. Had he not assumed leadership, the world most likely would have exploded. Neither option seemed good. Though John's leadership helped the tribes reach agreement, I have no doubt that had this been a real-life situation, the rage these tribes now felt would have ignited a civil conflict.

In Sum

To resolve an emotionally charged conflict, you must cultivate a communal mindset. But like a ship keeping its direction on the high seas, that mindset requires you to constantly monitor the push and pull of dialectics. You must balance acceptance with change; focus on redemption, not revenge; and most of all, strive for affiliation and autonomy, for us and them, for now and always.

That is the path to reconciliation.

Fostering the Spirit of Reconciliation

Every mythos must have its end, and we have come to ours. We have journeyed into the world of conflict resolution and discovered tools along the way to neutralize the divisive forces of conflict and stimulate integrative dynamics. But a book is just a book: Theory is useful only if it is actually used. So put these ideas into practice, trying them out to see what works in your particular conflict. Keep in mind, though, that reconciliation is not social engineering: Your heart needs to be fully involved in the process. The *spirit* of reconciliation is ultimately what makes it work. And so I leave you with a few essential principles:

1. Reconciliation Is a Choice

No one can force reconciliation upon you. It begins as a feeling that change is possible. That feeling may be hard to cultivate, because the Tribes Effect conspires against you—but it is not an invincible force. You can break its spell if you so choose.

To foster change, become what Norman Vincent Peale calls a "possibilitarian." Enlist your imagination in a quest for the *positive possible*. While knowledge confines you to what *is*, imagination opens you to what *can be*. Einstein was right in asserting that imagination is more important than knowledge.

2. Small Changes Can Make a Big Difference

The ripple effects of reconciliation are far-reaching. Each fight you resolve in a productive manner trickles up into the world. Reconciling with a family member creates the possibility for better relations at work, which can in turn spread to your community at large, and then on to the world. As Indian philosopher Krishnamurti noted, "A stone can change the course of a river."

3. Don't Wait

If a conflict distresses you, give it the attention it deserves. The fundamental struggle of reconciliation is not with other people, but within yourself. Internal resistance is the greatest obstacle to peace, and no one can overcome that for you.

In *The Wizard of Oz*, young Dorothy struggles to return home to Kansas from the magical land of Oz. At her great moment of despair, Glinda the Good Witch appears and tells her that she always had the power to go home. "Then why didn't you tell her before?" asks the Scarecrow. The Good Witch responds, "Because she wouldn't have believed me. She had to learn it for herself."

There is no quick fix to bring about reconciliation. It is a process you must work through with thoughtful deliberation, and you need to start somewhere. Rather than blaming others and watching your relationships suffer, ask yourself, *What might I do now—today—to bring this conflict one step closer to resolution?* Dorothy's journey ended where it began: in the comfort of her own home. Should you take the journey to reconciliation, you too will end where you began: within yourself. But in the process you will have achieved self-transcendence.

Years after the exercise at Davos, I bumped into the deputy prime minister who had participated in the Tribes Exercise. He told me that his group's failure to save the world had truly shocked him. As a result, he initiated the practice of preparing for his every upcoming negotiation by reflecting not just on rational strategy, but also on deeper issues of identity at stake for the other side—and for himself.

This is the key to overcoming the Tribes Effect. The world did not have to explode at Davos, and it need not explode in your own life. The potential for reconciliation rests firmly in your mind and in your heart. It is up to you to decide whether to use it.

Acknowledgments

"No man is an island" wrote poet John Donne, whose words resonate with my experience in writing this book, which has required me to research the field of conflict resolution from a variety of perspectives and through interaction with a great number of people. I feel honored to have traveled the journey with this inspiring community of family, friends, and colleagues:

Community of scholars. I am grateful for all I have learned through my collaboration with the late professors Roger Fisher of Harvard Law School and Jerome D. Frank of Johns Hopkins University, who shared in my grandfather's belief that the impossible is just a little bit harder. I am grateful to Bob Mnookin, chair of the Program on Negotiation at Harvard Law School (PON), and Jim Sebenius, director of the Harvard Negotiation Project, who have provided invaluable intellectual support and unflagging encouragement. I deeply appreciate the tremendous support and insights of Susan Hackley, managing director of PON, and James Kerwin, assistant director.

The broader PON community of scholars has opened my mind to a wide range of important aspects of negotiation, and I could write a chapter on how each person has influenced this book's thinking in important ways, but for sake of brevity, let me simply express my heartfelt gratitude to Eileen Babbitt, Max Bazerman, Gabriella Blum, Robert Bordone, Hannah Riley Bowles, Diana Chigas, Jared Curhan, Florrie Darwin, David Fairman, Mary Fitzduff, Marshall Ganz, Shula Gilad, Debbie Goldstein, Sheila Heen, David Hoffman, Kessely Hong, Peter Kamminga, Herbert Kelman, Kimberlyn Leary, Alain Lempereur, Jennifer Lerner, Jamil Mahuad, Deepak Malhotra, Brian Mandell, Melissa Manwaring, Hal

Movius, Bruce Patton, Howard Raiffa, Nadim Rouhana, Jeswald Salacuse, Frank Sander, David Seibel, Ofer Sharone, Bosko Stankovski, Doug Stone, Guhan Subramanian, Lawrence Susskind, Gillien Todd, William Ury, Joshua Weiss, Michael Wheeler, and Robert Wilkinson. Thanks to the PON staff and consultants: Warren Dent, Abigayle Earnes, Alex Green, Beth Hankes, Kristy Hanstad, Polly Hamlen, Keith Lutz, Gail Odeneal, Katie Shonk, Shiona Sommerville, Nancy Waters, and Tricia Woods.

The ideas in this book also have benefited through collaboration with some of the greatest minds in the field of psychology. I am deeply appreciative of the intellectual and moral support of eminent neuroscientist Scott Rauch, president and psychiatrist in chief of Harvard-affiliated McLean Hospital. And no words can describe my admiration for Dr. Philip Levendusky, the iconic director of the psychology department at Harvard Medical School/McLean Hospital, who has been a beacon of support and guidance. My research also has benefited from the exceptional input and support of Thröstur Björgvinsson, Bruce Cohen, Cathie Cook, Sue DeMarco, Jason Elias, Lori Etringer, Judith Herman, Lisa Horvitz, Robert Jay Lifton, Michael Miller, Steve Nisenbaum, Cecelia O'Neal, Rachel Penrod-Martin, Mona Potter, Bruce Price, Richard Schwartz, and Bruce Shackleton.

The wider Harvard system has been a source of intellectual inspiration, including the Harvard Global Health Institute and its affiliated faculty and staff, with special thanks to Ashish Jha, David Cutler, and Sue Goldie. I was honored to receive a Burke Global Health Fellowship, which provided me with the opportunity to refine this book's theory and translate it into curricular activities. Additionally, as I have explored deeper dimensions of conflict resolution, I have benefited from participation in the Harvard Divinity School's Religion and the Practice of Peace initiative, spearheaded by Dean David Hempton and doctoral student Elizabeth Lee-Hood.

Some of my greatest learning has come through research collaboration with my Harvard students, whose fresh perspectives and sharp minds keep me on my toes and have helped me see my own blind spots. Special thanks to current and former research assistants and associates at the Harvard International Negotiation Program: Amira Abulafi, Sarah Abushaar, Vladimir Bok, Marissa Brock, Alexander Dagi, Harleen Gambhir, Jenny Gathright, Bushra Guenoun, Melda Gurakar, Amy Gutman, Eric Hendey, Joseph Kahn,

Adam Kinon, Mariah Levin, Brooke McLain, Abigail Moy, Joy Nasr, Kendra Norton, Jasmine Omeke, Ashley O'Neal, Miranda Ravicz, Sarah Rosenkrantz, Jonny Tan, David Tang-Quan, Ty Walker, Kelsey Werner, Bessie Zhang, and Ali Zu'bi. Thanks also to my teaching fellows at Harvard: Michaela Kerrissey, Kashif Khan, Sorapop Kiatpongsan, and Mihan Lee, as well as to Rebekah Getman, head teaching fellow and assistant director of special operations at the Harvard International Negotiation Program.

International community. The World Economic Forum, an independent international organization, has proven to be an important real-world laboratory from which I have conducted practice-based research. I am indebted to its inspiring founder, Professor Klaus Schwab, who sees our world as not just disparate parts, but rather as a global system. It was with his encouragement that I conducted the tribes exercise at Davos.

This book has benefited through my collaboration with many distinguished scholars and international political and business leaders with whom I have worked in conjunction with the World Economic Forum, including Bertie Ahern, David Aikman, Bruce Allyn, Kwesi Aning, Louise Arbour, Ronit Avni, Selene Biffi, Betty Bigombe, Tony Blair, Kvell Bondevik, William Boulding, Jaime de Bourbon Parme, Lakhdar Brahimi, Caroline Casey, Miniya Chatterji, Andrew Cohen, Jennifer Corriero, Chester Crocker, Raghida Dergham, Kirill Dimitriev, Bineta Diop, John Dutton, Mary Galeti, Katherine Garrett-Kox, Pierre Gentin, Mack Gill, James Gilligan, Hrund Gunnstein, Julian Ha, David Harland, Shamil Idriss, Martin Indyk, Parag Khanna, Steve Killelea, Tim Leberecht, Andrew Lee, Geir Lundestad, Daniel Malan, Jessica Matthews, Michèle Mischele, Mirek Miroslav, Amre Moussa, Christian Mumenthaler, Oksana Myshlovska, Priya Parker, Aaron Peirora, Jonathan Powell, Gilbert Proust, Mary Robinson, Alvaro Rodriguez, Marie-France Roger, Karim Sadjapour, Herbert Salber, Maria Schmitt, Dennis Snower, Jiro Tamura, Mabel van Oranje, Paul Van Zyl, Jim Wallis, Stewart Wallis, Scott Weber, Victor Willi, Yan Xuetong, and Kyle Zimmer, along with a long, long list of inspiring Young Global Leaders of the World Economic Forum.

My international work has been enhanced through collaboration with

Yasar Jarrar and Khaled El Gohary, my longtime collaborators in the Middle East, as well as through partnerships with visionary peace builders Shafik Gabr, Bowei Lee, and their inspiring families. I am indebted to Romero Britto, who has joined my Harvard class on multiple occasions and worked with my students to create visual masterpieces depicting the key principles in *Negotiating the Nonnegotiable*. Finally, I would like to express my gratitude to the inspiration of many other friends and colleagues, including Tom Abraham, Melissa Agocs, Oliver Amrein, Ulrich Aschoff, Dan and Simona Baciu, Michelle Barmazel, Andre Bisasor, Melissa Broderick, Javier Calderon, Monika Christen, Irene Chu, Peter Coleman, Nadia Crisan, Jennifer Delmuth, Alexandra Dimitriadis, Lior Frankiensztajn, Mariko Gakiya, Yolanda Garzon, Dean Tom Gibbons of the Northwestern School of Professional Studies, David Grunfeld, Maya Hallett, Julien Hawary, Ashraf Hegazy, Paul Henry, Louis Herlands, Patrick Hidalgo, Angela Homsi, Chris Honeyman, Gowri Ishwaran, Walid Issa, Vera and Ivan Janik, Kyle Jones, John Kennedy, Ihab Khatib, Shiv and Urvashi Khemka, Chairman Younghoon David Kim, Claire King, Audrey Lee, Evelin Lindner, Vanessa Liu, Mary McDavid, Oliver McTernen, Beat Meyer, Matthew Miller, Jennifer Morrow, Michael and Esther Mulroy, Sandro Muri, Joan Myhre, Joseph Nye, Juraj Ondrejkovic, Judah Pollack, Sonja Rauschütz, Javier Rojo, Catalina Rojas, Suzanna Samstag, Zoe Segal-Reichlin, Ofer Sharone, Karim Souaid, Kevin Steinberg, Erica Suter-Ganz, Jiro Tamura, Stephanie Teterycz, H. E. Abdulla Al Thani, Liz Tippett, Rui Pedro Tropa, Gustavo Luis Velasquez, Rory Van Loo, Frank White, Deborah Whitney, Rebecca Wolfe, Yan Yanofsky, Craig Zelizer, and Katie Marie Zouhary.

Community of reviewers. An all-star cast of international scholars and practitioners critically reviewed *Negotiating the Nonnegotiable* and provided detailed, incisive feedback: Mina Al Oraibi, an internationally renowned journalist; Professor Cary Cherniss, co-director of the Consortium for Research on Emotional Intelligence in Organizations; Catharyn Gildesgame, vice president for strategic planning and implementation at McLean Hospital; Jamil Mahuad, former president of Ecuador; Professor Robert McKersie, Sloan School of Management, MIT; Professor Leonard Riskin,

University of Florida and Northwestern University; Professor Mary Rowe, founding ombudsperson at MIT; Jeff Seul, chairman of the Peace Appeal Foundation; and numerous Harvard student researchers.

The publishing community. The tribe at Viking has been spectacular. Rick Kot, editor extraordinaire, ensured that every word and argument on these pages was written as sharply and persuasively as possible. He mentored me through the publishing process, took my phone calls day or night, and truly aspired to make this book as solid as it could be. Rick, my deepest thanks.

The Viking team has helped to turn the overwhelming process of publishing into a positive adventure. My thanks to Brian Tart, Andrea Schulz, Carolyn Coleburn, Meredith Burks, Kate Stark, Lydia Hirt, Mary Stone, Chris Smith, and Diego Núñez.

There is a hidden gem in the publishing world: Katie Arnold-Ratliff, articles editor at *O, The Oprah Magazine*. I enlisted her editorial assistance early on, and she took what amounted to an editorial hacksaw and trimmed pages, paragraphs, and words to make for easier reading; I trusted her instincts, and the book is much the better because of it.

Guiding me through the complex labyrinth of the publishing world are my remarkable agents: Andrew Wylie, Sarah Chalfant, and Jackie Ko.

Writing a book is one thing; spreading the ideas is another. My thanks to Harry Rhoads, Jr., Christine Farrell, and the Washington Speakers Bureau, as well as to Mark Fortier, Courtney Nobile, and the rest of their publicity team, for helping me to get my ideas out to a broader audience.

Sacred community. The inner circle of my family tribe is my source of sustenance. No one has influenced my way of understanding the world more than my parents. I feel truly blessed to have them in my life. They believe that humanity can make the world a better place, and they have inspired me to work toward that goal. I am grateful for the support of my brilliant sister, Madelyn, her equally amazing husband, Mike, and the most creative couple I know, my brother Steve and his wife, Shira. Susan Dole is my Other Mother—some might call her my mother-in-law but that sounds much too mechanical, for she is a part of our family in heart and soul; my gratitude to Susan and to John.

I am grateful to Betsy and Peter, my aunt and uncle, who have offered invaluable input and have graciously taught me about what it means to be an effective leader. My aunt Margaret has helped me to understand the deeper dimensions of existence that seem to so easily slip us by if we are unaware of them.

No words can describe the depth of gratitude I feel toward my wife and children for all their love and support. I often have turned to my boys to learn from the purity of their perspectives. They naturally see the simple truths behind theoretical complexity, and some of their insights have made it into this book. So thank you, Noah, Zachary, and Liam. Your daddy loves you more than infinity times infinity. Finally, deepest thanks to my wife, Mia. I appreciate every moment of every day with you, and am ever grateful for your many sacrifices to help make this book a reality. I have learned more from you than from anyone on this planet. Our differences are our strength, our similarities are enduring, and my love for you is nonnegotiable.

Appendix I

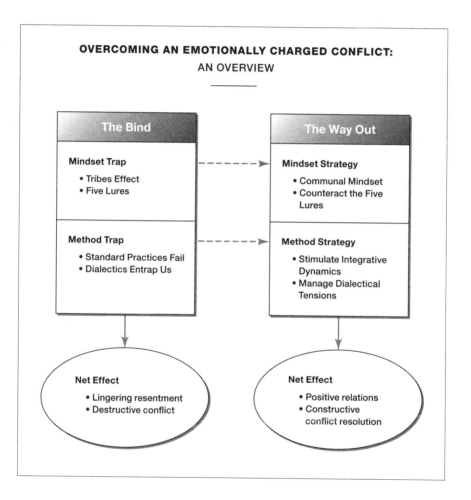

OVERCOMING AN EMOTIONALLY CHARGED CONFLICT:
AN OVERVIEW

The Bind

Mindset Trap
- Tribes Effect
- Five Lures

Method Trap
- Standard Practices Fail
- Dialectics Entrap Us

Net Effect
- Lingering resentment
- Destructive conflict

The Way Out

Mindset Strategy
- Communal Mindset
- Counteract the Five Lures

Method Strategy
- Stimulate Integrative Dynamics
- Manage Dialectical Tensions

Net Effect
- Positive relations
- Constructive conflict resolution

Appendix II: The Ladder of Being

The Ladder of Being is a conceptual tool I developed to expand awareness of the interconnectedness of people. Because conflict narrows our conscious awareness of such connections, a material framework can help direct our attention to the depth and breadth of those connections, reminding us of the expansiveness of our relational consciousness.

For example, during my family's annual vacation to Rhode Island, my wife and I ritually sit on the porch and watch the sun set. We feel a transcendent connection with each other. In contrast, when we get into an argument, we shore up the walls of identity, see each other as distinct and "dangerous," and defend against attack. At these moments of high tension, our transcendent connection fades into the background. It still exists, but we no longer notice it. Conflict creates the illusion of separation.

The Ladder of Being originates with an insight from the German existential philosopher Martin Heidegger that humans are not things but ways of being in the world. We do not exist as a separate entity from the world in which we live but are intrinsically connected to it. The world does not exist without our consciousness, just as our consciousness does not exist without the world.

Accordingly, the Ladder of Being calls attention to five levels of self-awareness. No level is more "real" than another, just as the outer layer of an onion is no more authentic than its core.

In a conflict, it can be helpful to identify your level of being and then consider to what level you aspire.

Level I: Pure Being

At this level you perceive the world through the perspective of the *I*, of pure consciousness. Like an infant new to the world, you experience no boundary between self and others, between the inner and outer worlds. Your identity is void of a censor. During the heat of conflict—as in the heat of passion—you enter a flow so powerful that you lose your sense of the *me*, the story you tell yourself about yourself.

You do experience conflict at this level, even if you are not aware of it. Without a structure of self and other, you experience no blame, no anger, no shame—only need and satisfaction. If a mother fails to feed her newborn, the baby cries not in anger but out of need.

Level II: Being-in-Relation

At this level your *I* is joined by the *me*: You construct a single master narrative about who you are, who the other is, and how you connect. Because you are cognizant of only a single story about yourself—a solitary *me*—you guard it intensely against any perceived threat.

Level III: Being-in-Relations

By this stage, you become aware of your repertoire of constituent entities. You may be a businessperson, parent, friend, and peacemaker. Each part of your identity has its own narrative with its own emotional undertone, equipping you with a variety of scripts to relate to others and yourself. At any point in time, you may accentuate and "live in" one subidentity or another.

Level IV: Being-in-the-World

This level recognizes that you hold multiple worldviews and have subidentities within each worldview. Each worldview frames how you make meaning of a particular set of subidentities, providing them with a cohesive philosophy of being.

For example, I have a Korean American childhood friend. His parents emigrated to the United States before he was born, but his entire home life was based on traditional Korean norms. He learned two distinct worldviews—Korean and American—and built a set of subidentities to relate to people in each setting. The way he acted, reacted, and thought about himself when he was at home with his family was strikingly different from his behavior and thinking at school with his friends.

Level V: Transcendent Being

The most expansive form of relational consciousness is the recognition that your worldviews are held together through a *singular connection of common humanity.* You and others are not separate beings—floating spheres of identity—but essentially interconnected through your shared humanity. You transcend your shell of being, maintaining your self at the same time that it exists within a transcendent plane of universal coexistence.

To attain a transcendent mindset, recognize that your identity in a conflict exists within an expansive network of interconnection. Emotionally charged conflicts push you down the Ladder of Being, toward more egoistic understandings of your self in the world. To resolve such situations, fight this tendency. Seek to understand at what level of being you are currently standing and consciously climb up the ladder to become increasingly aware of the expansiveness of your being.

Paradoxically, level V and level I are fundamentally alike. The experience of full transcendence is the same as the experience of pure consciousness. Each results in an undifferentiated experience of being in the world. Thus the Ladder of Being might be better viewed as the "Circle of Being," for the deeper our experience of being, the more we return to its original state.

LADDER OF BEING

Level	What's It Look Like?
I. Pure Being	I
II. Being-in-Relation	I ME
III. Being-in-Relations	I ME I ME
IV. Being-in-the-World	I ME I ME I ME I ME
V. Transcendent Being	I ME I ME I ME I ME I ME I ME I ME I ME

Notes

Introduction: Why This Book?

xi **in Yugoslavia and in the United States:** My personal stories in this book are based upon real situations, though I have at points changed some of the facts to protect the identity of involved parties. I led the workshop in Serbia with cofacilitators and good friends Jennifer Delmuth and Melissa Agocs.

xvi **I share these insights with you:** Integrative dynamics moves us beyond problem solving to joint meaning making, trying to make sense of who we are in relation to one another and how we can best work and live together. It is as much a theory of mind as a theory of practice, presenting a psychologically focused method to transform identity from an obstacle into an asset.

Traditionally the field of negotiation has focused on discrete elements of negotiation. Central to this approach has been the work of my mentor Professor Roger Fisher, founding director of the Harvard Negotiation Project, who developed the Seven Elements of Negotiation, critical factors for understanding the negotiation landscape. The Seven Elements are interests, options, legitimacy, commitments, alternatives, relationship, and communication. If one were to compare negotiation theory with the human body, the seven elements would be the organs, and integrative dynamics (a method I introduce in this book) would be the interactive dynamism among these organs. An emotionally charged conflict is built upon dynamism, as evidenced by the seismic pushes and pulls overriding the Davos leaders' rational thinking. Integrative dynamics accounts for these powerful forces stimulating rational people to act in seemingly irrational ways, calling attention to each party's relational identity. Even when one side's core identity appears irreconcilable with the other's core identity, there may be ways to change the system of relations, thus reducing conflict and improving cooperation.

Chapter 1: The Hidden Power of Identity

3 **all our lives:** I adapted parts of this chapter from an article I published, "Relational Identity Theory: A Systematic Approach for Transforming the Emotional Dimension of Conflict," in *American Psychologist* (Shapiro 2010).

3 **"continuity of tribes"**: Ibid. I define a tribe as any group whose members view themselves as (1) *like-kinded*, (2) *kinlike* in their relational connection, and (3) *emotionally invested* in their group's enhancement. As I describe in the article, all three elements are necessary for a group to be considered a tribe:

   Being of like kind denotes that group members identify themselves as part of a common identity group. Ethnopolitical groups—such as Palestinian Arabs and Israeli Jews, Catholics and Protestants of Northern Ireland—may be tribes, but tribes often are *not* built on ethnic or blood ties. Rather, tribes are socially and psychologically constructed. They can emerge whenever individuals share a common identity, whether as members of a neighborhood community, religious sect, corporation, nation, or international political organization.

   A tribe, however, is more than just a loose affiliation or a coalition joined for purely instrumental purposes. *Kinlike connection* specifies the relational nature of the identity group, because tribe members subjectively define one another as "of the same stock." This connection may be based on literally any shared characteristic, such as a physical trait, ideology, language, geographical "home," organizational mission, or religious conviction. As a result of the kinlike connection, members intensify their identification with the tribe and, consequently, intensify the emotional significance they place on their relationships with fellow tribe members.

   Members feel *emotionally invested* in the existence and enhancement of their tribe. They become so emotionally invested in the survival and enhancement of the tribe that they are willing—and group norms often require them—to put aside self-interest in order to protect and defend one another and advance group causes. This investment, at its most potent, can lead tribe members to sacrifice their own lives or those of their children.

6 **a handful of times:** I facilitate the Tribes Exercise as a classroom exercise, not a controlled experiment. I adapt the questions in the exercise to each group; redesign the room to make it feel closed, dark, and cramped; broadcast intense drum music to keep the emotional environment electric and tense; and otherwise take liberty in shaping the context to increase the likelihood of the Tribes Effect. But I also make sure that tribes have an opportunity to save the world. On the rare occasion when the world is saved, tribes tend to take the exercise lightly and fail to assume ownership of their newly devised tribal identity: They view the exercise as just a game. But when groups emotionally enter the marginal world of fantasy/reality, the world almost inevitably explodes.

7 **resolve emotionally charged conflicts:** I refrain from using the label "identity-based conflicts" for two reasons. First, *every* conflict implicates your identity to a greater or lesser degree. The emotional charge of a conflict derives from *your* frustrated needs, *your* frustrated values, *your* frustrated beliefs. Your identity defines what you consider meaningful and calibrates the intensity of your emotional response, so it makes little sense to designate only some conflicts as identity-based. Second, identity is never the sole

basis of conflict. To label a conflict identity-based is to presume the blanket superiority of identity and to discount other potential roots, ranging from neurobiological proclivities to macroeconomic forces, sociological structures to political motivations.

7 **(Footnote) emotionally charged conflict:** To reach sustainably harmonious relations, conflict resolution necessitates addressing three dimensions. First, you need to *settle* your substantive differences, such as those over distribution of land or money. Second, you need to *transform* the emotional nature of your relationship, turning each other from adversaries to allies. Third, you need to *internalize* your revised relationship. Thus, conflict resolution includes settlement, transformation, and reconciliation, each addressing a vital dimension of conflict resolution: interests, emotion, and identity. See Kelman 1956 and Rouhana 2004.

7 **neuroscience suggests they interrelate:** For example, see Damasio 1994. He focuses specifically on the interrelations among emotion, cognition, and decision making.

8 **conflict resolution: emotions:** See Lerner et al. 2015 and Shapiro 2004.

8 **ended in deadlock:** Because this book focuses on *emotionally* charged conflict, it is important to distinguish between (1) *positive and negative emotions*, which describe how we feel, such as uplifted or depressed, and (2) *helpful and problematic emotions*, which describe the behavioral impact of our feelings. Similar to my latter distinction is the Dalai Lama's distinguishing between "afflictive" and "nonafflictive" emotions. Should fear stir you to kill your neighbor, the emotion is negative and afflictive (problematic). Should fear stir you to save the life of your child, the emotion is negative and nonafflictive (helpful). See Dalai Lama 2005, 27–28.

9 **shapes their relationship:** Marital researchers Harville Hendrix and Helen LaKelly Hunt make a similar point in the context of marital relations; see Hendrix and Hunt 2013, 54. Psychologist Ruthellen Josselson (1992) discusses the space between.

10 **the more you know:** Charles Horton Cooley (1902) coined the term "looking-glass self" to describe his theory that a person's self emerges through understanding of how others perceive him or her.

Chapter 2: The Dual Nature of Identity

11 **"times since then":** See Lewis Carroll's *Alice's Adventures in Wonderland* (New York: Macmillan & Co., 1865), 60.

11 **fluid *and* fixed:** Political scientists have long debated whether ethnic identity is *primordial* (fundamentally existing) or *constructed* (arising out of human interaction). In other words, is there an innate quality to it, or is it constructed through social interaction? I believe that identity is constructed within the constraints of social structures, political forces, cultural assumptions, and biological givens, implying that we all have some—but not full—freedom to create our identities. Society presents us with what I call *identity templates*, social scripts from which to conceive of

ourselves, and we have autonomy to choose from among those templates. As Kempny and Jawlowska (2002, 4) note, "identities are embedded in coherent and integrative social practices."

Thus cultural identities can transfer across generations, giving them the appearance of primordialism, though they can and often do change. David Laitin (1983) offers a compelling case study illustrating that cultural identifications such as national identity are not immutable; conflict itself can change the identity of a group. For other important perspectives on the primordialism/constructivism debate, see the work of scholars Samuel Huntington, Clifford Geertz, Alexander Wendt, and Robert Hislope.

12 **easier to change than others:** Marcia (1988) proposes two dimensions for constructing identity: exploration and commitment. Exploration is a process of sorting through multiple ways of being, while commitment represents the adoption of a set of ideals. Once you commit to a set of ideals, you gain a sense of continuity, purpose, and fidelity—antidotes to identity confusion. See also Schwartz 2001, 11.

12 *characteristics that define you:* While political scientists, psychologists, and sociologists have produced hundreds of definitions of identity, there is of course no perfect way to parse this complex topic; the parsing I have done in this chapter is designed to introduce important concepts to help you better deal with conflict in your own life. I have tried to create an inclusive definition of identity, in response to the fact that identity scholars often conceptualize identity through the landscape of their narrow field of inquiry. Social psychologists, for example, tend to see identity as a social marker but neglect its physical and spiritual qualities.

My definition of identity is loose and imperfect but pragmatic. It is narrow enough to focus your attention on the characteristics that clash in a conflict and broad enough to capture the full breadth of attributes that define you. You have a physical body with organs, blood pumping, moving parts, and interconnected tissue. You have stable and changing memories about people, places, and things. You have an evolving personality with many subsystems that govern a great portion of your behavior. You have a panorama of beliefs, some strongly held and others weaker, along with fleeting thoughts, variable moods, and automatic mental processes for perceiving reality. You play a variety of roles, such as child, parent, and colleague. Indeed, this list could stretch on ad infinitum, which suggests why identity is so troublesome in a conflict. There are a lot of interconnected parts.

12 **"tell yourself about yourself":** See Stone, Patton, and Heen 1999.

12 **person telling it:** See the appendix for details. I propose that there are multiple levels to identity that bring it its dynamic complexity.

13 **your embodied experience the *I*:** See William James (1890) and G. H. Mead (1934), whose use of the *I* and *me* was central to his sociological theory called symbolic interactionism.

13 **spiritual beliefs and cultural practices:** Three aspects of your *core identity* are important to note. First, your core identity is "core" because it is fairly stable across situations and relationships. For example, your family name is part of your core identity; you do not change your name every time you

interact with a different person. Second, your core identity houses more than just your deepest beliefs; it includes any stable characteristics about you, whether central *or* peripheral to your life. The fact that you like the color yellow over blue is part of your core identity, though it may have minimal personal meaning as compared with your allegiance to your parents. Third, your core identity is more than just the story you tell yourself about yourself. It includes unconscious and biological characteristics—mind and body—that maintain continuity across interactions. Professor Jonathan Turner has a similar definition of "core identity," defining it as "the conceptions and emotions that individuals have about themselves as persons that they carry to most encounters" (Turner 2012, 350).

14 **identities to prioritize:** See Amartya Sen (2006, 30).

14 **met certain death:** See L. Mlodinow, *Subliminal: How Your Unconscious Mind Rules Your Behavior* (New York: Vintage Books, 2012), 153. For additional resources, see (1) H. T. Himmelweit, "Obituary: Henri Tajfel, FBPsS," *Bulletin of the British Psychological Society* 35 (1982): 288–89; (2) William Peter Robinson, ed., *Social Groups and Identities: Developing the Legacy of Henri Tajfel* (Oxford: Butterworth-Heinemann, 1996), 3–5; and (3) Henri Tajfel, *Human Groups and Social Categories* (Cambridge: Cambridge University Press, 1981).

15 *meaning in life:* In support of my proposition that the purpose of identity is to seek significance, Frederic Bartlett noted years ago that one can "speak of every human cognitive reaction—perceiving, imagining, remembering, thinking and reasoning—as an *effort after meaning*" (Bartlett 1932, 44). As we interact with ourselves and the world around us, we use mental schemas—narratives—to make meaning of our experiences. We have an instinct to make meaning. In this sense, the whole of psychological life may be viewed as the building and application of narratives to make personal meaning.

16 **also can change:** I differentiate between nominal and semantic identity. Your *nominal identity* is how you and others label one another, whether as American, German, teacher, or friend. Your *semantic identity* is the meaning you bring to that label: What does it *mean* to be American, German, a teacher, or a friend? Similarly, social anthropologist Fredrik Barth (1981) differentiates between *nominal identity* and *virtual membership*.

16 **what it means to be "in":** Your social self is not entirely fixed. See Barth 1969.

17 *person or group:* Relational identity theory suggests you are defined through your relations with others, a concept that resonated with French philosopher Jean-Paul Sartre, who once quipped, "If the Jew did not exist, the anti-Semite would invent him" (Sartre 1965, 13).

Relational identity theory has crucial utility for policy makers working to avoid large-scale violent conflict in multiethnic societies. Policy makers trying to understand the vulnerability of a society to violent conflict would be well advised to examine the following: (1) Affiliation: Does a specific group feel excluded from major political, social, economic, and cultural platforms? (2) Autonomy: Does a specific group feel constrained in its freedom to affect decision-making processes around relevant political, social, economic, and cultural dimensions? The greater the number and intensity of threats to a group's perceived affiliation and autonomy, the more likely that group will be to combat the frustration of its needs.

In line with relational identity theory, studies by Professor Frances Stewart of Oxford University suggest that a major reason for the manifestation of violent conflict in multiethnic societies is not differences in equality among individuals ("horizontal inequality") but perceived inequities between ethnopolitical groups ("vertical inequality"). Stewart and Brown (2007, 222) propose that when cultural differences (whether based on ethnopolitical, religious, gender, age, or other lines) coincide with economic and political differences between groups, deep resentment can arise and lead to violent struggle.

17 **as you really are?:** The human mind is constantly appraising the social environment for threats to physical and psychological survival. Social survival requires us to scan unconsciously for threats to autonomy and affiliation. The amygdala may contribute to this appraisal process, acting as a "relevance detector" to a broad range of events including but not limited to threats to our social and physical well-being. See Sander et al. 2003.

17 **meaning in *coexistence*:** I have developed relational identity theory to address the practical needs of conflict resolution. This theory is rooted in the scholarship of such intellectual giants as William James, Henri Tajfel, Erik Erikson, and Jean Baker Miller. While relational identity theory draws on psychoanalytic insights, it is also a reaction to them. The originator of psychoanalysis, Sigmund Freud, theorized that humans are driven by the pleasure principle: We seek pleasure and avoid pain. He saw humans as driven to satisfy their libidinal drives. Psychoanalyst Ronald Fairbairn radically departed from this assumption, arguing that we are not pleasure seeking but object seeking. In psychoanalytic jargon, an "object" is the internal representation of a person or group with whom we are relating. So Fairbairn was saying that we do not relate to people to fulfill our libidinal drives, but just the opposite: We seek pleasure to relate to others. We are driven to relate.

Fairbairn's empirical research underscores the instinct to relate. He found that abused children preferred to return home than stay in a safe haven. In other words, rather than rejection making children feel less attached to their mothers, it made them feel *more* attached. The unmet need for connection could be met only by the mother. See Celani 1994, 29. Similarly, psychoanalyst D. W. Winnicott (1952, 99) emphasized the systemic importance of relationship in human experience, observing that in the mother-child unit "the centre of gravity of the being does not start off in the individual. It is in the total set-up."

17 **power to shape it:** See Barth 1969. Terrell Northrup (1989, 81) analyzes the dynamics of identity conflicts and concludes that the most effective strategy for resolution "would appear to be one that begins . . . with the nature of the relationship, because pressure for change at this level would be less threatening than at the level of the identities of the parties."

18 **"is withering away"**: Relational identity is less about characteristics you
    have than relations you *construct*. In fact, relational identity may be defined
    as *perspectivized relationality*: You define your identity on the basis of how
    you perceive your relations with others.

18 **affiliation and autonomy**: Scholars across disciplines have converged
    around autonomy and affiliation as fundamental motivational forces driv-
    ing social behavior. Some examples:

    Mervin Freedman, Timothy Leary, Abel Ossorio, and Hubert Coffey
    (1951) distinguish between dominance/submission and affiliation/hostility.

    Carol Gilligan (1982) differentiates between justice and care.

    Ervin Staub (1993) contrasts autonomous/individualistic identities
    and relational/collectivistic identities.

    Deborah Kolb and Judith Williams (2000) illuminate the impor-
    tance of advocacy and connection.

    Robert Mnookin, Scott Peppet, and Andrew Tulumello (1996)
    emphasize the tension between assertiveness and empathy.

    Erich Fromm (1941, 39–55) contrasts separate identity and oneness
    with the world.

    Edward Deci, Richard Ryan, and colleagues illuminate the impact of
    self-determination on emotions and behavior. See Deci 1980 and Deci and
    Ryan 2000.

    Lorna Benjamin (1984) codifies the tension between autonomy and
    affiliation with the Structural Analysis of Social Behavior (SASB), a derivative
    of H. Murray's work on "personology"; SASB is a system to classify social inter-
    actions in terms of focus, affiliation, and interdependence (i.e., autonomy),
    allowing for a sharper understanding of how people perceive the meaning of
    a social event.

    Jerry Wiggins (1991) reviews research on autonomy and affiliation
    and their conceptual correlates.

    David Bakan (1996) presents a deep, compelling rationale for the fun-
    damental importance of agency and communion. He reveals, "I have
    adopted the terms 'agency' and 'communion' to characterize two funda-
    mental modalities in the existence of living forms, agency for the existence
    of an organism as an individual, and communion for the participation of
    the individual in some larger organism of which the individual is a part.
    Agency manifests itself in self-protection, self-assertion, and self-expansion;
    communion manifests itself in the sense of being at one with other organ-
    isms. Agency manifests itself in the formation of separations; communion
    in the lack of separations. Agency manifests itself in isolation, alienation,
    and aloneness; communion in contact, openness, and union. Agency man-
    ifests itself in the urge to master; communion in noncontractual coopera-
    tion" (pp. 14–15).

18 **cooperative relations in a conflict**: Autonomy and affiliation are not *com-
    pletely* fluid: Your relationships gain structural continuity through *roles* you
    play and *statuses* you hold. These structures are packaged forms of autonomy
    and affiliation. For example, participants in the Tribes Exercise in Cairo
    quickly donned the role of adversaries. Once this role was established, they

knew what to expect out of their relationship: adverse affiliation and disregard for one another's autonomy.

Roles provide expectations about the scope of your affiliation and autonomy. If I visit my doctor for an annual checkup and he tells me to take off my shirt, I readily comply. In the role of patient, I grant him autonomy to check my physical health and expect he will maintain a professional distance in our affiliation. On the other hand, if I am walking down the street and a stranger demands that I remove my shirt, I will quickly walk away. The role of stranger does not confer the same expectations with respect to autonomy and affiliation.

Your relationships also gain continuity through status—your standing relative to others in some hierarchy. In a company, for example, the higher your formal position, the more autonomy you *consistently have* to authorize decisions. But informal status also structures your relations. On a project team, employees know who has formal decision-making authority but also tacitly understand whom to turn to for project advice, emotional support, or a fun conversation.

Though roles and status are fairly stable, you can redefine them to help resolve a conflict. See Fisher and Shapiro 2005 for details.

If you establish *positive* structural relations, reconciliation becomes more likely. In fact, the goal of reconciliation is to *internalize* positive structural relations. This was the case in one of the few times the world was saved in the Tribes Exercise. It happened in the Middle East during a workshop for a government leadership group. Four tribal spokesmen met in the center of the room to negotiate. Within minutes they came to a full and final agreement. I was surprised. How did this happen? By chance, three of the four negotiators were uniformed military officers, and as they negotiated, their allegiance to their newly created tribe paled in comparison to their shared role as members of the military. This common role established positive affiliation and mutual respect for autonomy. The highest-ranking officer proposed an agreement, the other officers deferred, and the lone nonmilitary leader fell in line with group consensus. The common role and predictable status hierarchy constituted a clear relational structure.

The relational context establishes expectations about the limits of autonomy and affiliation as well as liabilities for a breach of the implicit relational contract. These expectations are manifest in the roles we play and the statuses we hold. For details, see McCall and Simmons 1978, Stets 2006, and Stryker 2004.

18 **in times of war:** Neuroscience provides insight into the neurochemical basis of affiliation. A neuropeptide called oxytocin promotes trusting relations, just as trusting relations produce oxytocin. In one study Zak and colleagues (2005) discovered that negotiators who felt their counterpart demonstrated trustworthiness experienced the release of oxytocin. In another study Kosfield and colleagues (2005) administered oxytocin to participants, who then were much more likely to trust their counterparts and to invest more money with them in an investment game that used real

money. In a third line of study, Ditzen and colleagues (2009) found that intranasal oxytocin increases positive communication and reduces cortisol levels between couples who are in conflict.

Scholars from other disciplines also have converged around the importance of affiliation. R. Baumeister and M. Leary (2000) conducted a comprehensive review of the empirical evidence for the need to belong and concluded that "human beings are fundamentally and pervasively motivated by a need to belong, that is, by a strong desire to form and maintain enduring interpersonal attachments. People seek frequent, affectively positive interactions within a context of long-term, caring relationships." See Baumeister and Leary 2000.

Social scientist Donald T. Campbell (1971, 105) observed that "elements close together are more likely to be perceived as parts of the same organization." Campbell's observation is extremely insightful. If we clump people as "close" along some characteristic—whether religious beliefs, hair color, or any other attribute—we are more likely to see them as sharing an identity. A single characteristic motivates us to see them as adjoined.

18 **with the Iraqi people:** Shapiro 2008.
18 **culturally respectful questions:** Packer 2006.
19 **processes physical pain:** See Eisenberger et al. 2003.
19 **far more difficult:** See Herman 1992, 51.
19 **to bite back:** Edward Deci (1980) has illuminated the impact of self-determination on emotions and behavior. If your perceived scope of freedom feels unduly imposed upon, you react negatively and may forgo "rational" interests for the sake of satisfying your yearning for self-determination.
20 **"our diverse heritage":** These perspectives derive from conversations between me and leaders on each side of the conflict. Additionally, my word choice about the name of the land is based upon the official usage of the U.S. Department of State. Yet by referring to the Republic of Macedonia as such, I may unintentionally offend the autonomy of some Greeks who feel that they should be the sole arbiters of usage of the name "Macedonia."
21 **paramount to harmonious relations:** Conflict over autonomy and affiliation often happens at a symbolic level. A striking example comes from Czech author Milan Kundera's book *Ignorance*. The book's main character, Irena, returns home to Czech Republic after spending twenty years in France; her circle of friends express no interest in her time abroad, as though they have amputated those years from her life. By shutting out critical parts of Irena's core identity—aspects of her *me*—they wall off her autonomy to be as she wants to be. Irena is distressed over affiliation: *What parts of me will my friends accept? What parts will they reject? Can I bear rejection—or should I cease these friendships?* As in real life, these relational issues manifest indirectly, through symbolic messages, such as when the Czech friends demonstrate no interest in drinking Irena's French wine (Kundera 2002).
22 **good of all:** This Confucian account is drawn from Wiggins (1991), whose source is Hackett (1979, 27–28). The notion of original oneness can be found

even in Darwinian evolutionary theory, which was founded on the assumption that human lineage originates with the interconnectedness of all living beings. In that sense the striving for transcendent unity is no more than the ambition to return to our original state of oneness. The Dalai Lama (2005) makes a similar point.

22 **wishes and fears:** I describe various "structures" of identity—the architecture—but subscribe to the insight of psychoanalyst Harry Stack Sullivan that intrapsychic structures are a fiction: In reality these structures are not material elements but patterns of energy transformation. See Greenberg and Mitchell 1983, 91.

Chapter 3: A Way Forward

23 **a seemingly insurmountable one:** What generates the us-versus-them mindset of the Tribes Effect? *Relational identity theory* suggests that when there is a threat to important aspects of autonomy and affiliation, the Tribes Effect is triggered. *Realistic conflict theory* proposes that threats to a group's military, political, social, or financial resources will generate in-group identity and ethnocentrism. *Social identity theory* proposes that *mere identification with a group* is sufficient to cause conflict: Individuals identify with the group and aspire to positive distinctiveness. For more on realistic conflict theory, see Sherif et al. 1961, 155–84, and Campbell 1965. For more on social identity theory, see Tajfel and Turner 1979.

23 *us versus them:* Technically, I define the Tribes Effect as a divisive rigidification of our relational identity vis-à-vis another person or group.

23 **resistant to change:** While the Tribes Effect may be resistant to change, its function is protective. In this mindset, we aim to protect the people and principles most important to our identity. In fact, evolutionary biologists have worked to quantify the degree to which we protect our own kin and kind from external threat. Indian biologist J. B. S. Haldane investigated the mathematics of kin selection and quipped, "I would risk my life for two brothers or eight cousins." His observation set the scene for *Hamilton's rule*, which quantifies the nature of kin selection: $br - c > 0$. In the equation b is the "beneficial impact on the Darwinian fitness of the recipient of any social act, c is the Darwinian cost to the individual performing the social act, and r is the coefficient of relatedness between the two parties. The resulting inequality specifies the conditions under which natural selection should favor acts of apparent altruism" (Mock 2004, 20). When the rule's inequality is satisfied, we behave altruistically; when it is not satisfied, we behave in self-interest.

24 **prospects for collaboration diminish:** In an article in *American Psychologist* I describe several qualities of tribal dynamics that can prove helpful for the tribe but that can also make intergroup reconciliation more difficult:

    (a) Loyalty to the tribe takes priority. Tribes are heavily emotional entities, the members of which are likely to make greater sacrifice for those to whom they are more closely related.

    (b) Tribal norms reinforce loyalty. Indeed, the *fundamental taboo of the tribe* is to engage in any behavior that undercuts the legitimacy of the tribe and the relations binding everyone together. The tribe itself may be perceived as sacred, and sustaining its existence can become a holy mission. Disloyalty to the tribe's identity narrative can lead to shame, humiliation, ostracism, and death.

    (c) Tribal loyalty tends to be strongest when members share a collective identity narrative that I term the *myth of common bloodlines*. This shared narrative binds people together through the belief that they are of the same stock, linked by a common lineage and destiny. A threatened group can turn quickly into a tribe the moment its members feel connected through a myth of common bloodlines. While a multinational company in a conflict can become a tribe, the more cohesive tribes—the ones for which people are willing to sacrifice the most—tend to be based on spiritual or actual bloodlines. Members are more likely to be fortified by righteousness when fighting to fulfill God's destiny than when fighting for a company's vision.

    (d) The myth of common bloodlines is resistant to change. Tribes build a narrative based upon their perceived history of victories, losses, trauma, and victimization, and this narrative is surprisingly resistant to political and social transitions (Volkan 1998). In many ways, the preservation of a tribe's historical narrative is an exercise in establishing its autonomy as an insoluble entity (Shapiro 2010).

24 **self-righteous, closed mindset:** The Tribes Effect is a fundamental aspect of intense conflict and is reminiscent of the characterization of conflict proposed by Coser (1956) in his classic book *Functions of Social Conflict*: The more intense a conflict, the more the conflict will generate (1) clear-cut boundaries for each party, (2) centralized decision-making structures, (3) structural and ideological solidarity, and (4) suppression of dissent and deviance, a dynamic I refer to as taboos.

24 **us and minimizing similarities:** Strong emotion can intensify the Tribes Effect. Experimental research demonstrates that emotional arousal reduces the cognitive complexity of social perception, resulting in polarized evaluations of the other party (Paulhus and Lim 1994). For individuals or communities living in a constant state of fear and threat, polarization may become the norm. In fact, experiments demonstrate that people confronted with their own mortality will heighten the perceived significance of their own group and depreciate the out-group (Greenberg et al. 1990).

24 **to defend it:** Hans Magnus Enzensberger (1994), an eminent German political and literary critic, suggests that the problem of intergroup conflict is not fragmentation but *autism*: Groups insulate themselves in their own circle of self-righteous victimhood and can't listen, can't hear, can't learn from anybody outside themselves. What they are missing is *empathy* and its consequential power to learn from others' perspectives.

24 **"described as criminals":** Maalouf 2001, 31.

25 **our own identity:** The closed characteristic of the Tribes Effect may stem in part from neurobiological barriers to empathy that establish upon your

categorizing the other side as different. A key part of your brain that kicks in when you think about your own thoughts and feelings is called the ventral medial prefrontal cortex (vMPFC). Strikingly, it becomes active when you listen to the perspective of someone you perceive to be *similar* to you but *less so* when you listen to the perspective of someone you view as *different* from you. Empathy appears biased toward your own kin and kind (Jenkins et al. 2007). This is consistent with my belief that in a conflict situation, we need to almost "force" ourselves to empathize with the other side. Empathy for an adversary does not come naturally in the throes of the Tribes Effect.

25 **a** *threat response:* Kelly Lambert and Craig Howard Kinsley (2010) discuss a similar anxiety response when we face a real or imagined threat. Conflict resolution scholar Terrell Northrup (1989) describes four stages of conflict escalation that implicate identity, the first being threat, followed by distortion of social reality to avoid invalidation, rigidification of interpretation of the world, and collusion in prolonging the conflictual relationship.

25 **mind and spirit:** A threat to your identity makes you fear disintegration of your identity. Divisive dynamics, therefore, shield your identity from harm by building a wall of defenses that can incite hostility and, ironically, create the conditions for existential conflict.

25 *narcissism of minor differences:* Psychoanalyst Vamık Volkan (1996) describes two types of identity: Your *personal identity* is like a garment only you wear; it protects you from dangers in the environment around you. Your *social identity* is like a "large canvas tent" that protects you and all those under it. As long as the tent stays strong and the leader upholds it, your social identity is not a matter of urgent concern. But should someone shake the tent, everyone underneath it worries for their collective security and tries to shore it up again. From the perspective of social identity theory, the Tribes Effect impacts intergroup division because it illuminates each party's social identity, which suppresses positive relations with other groups and solidifies intragroup relations. Conflict creates the perception of *us* and *them* (Korostelina 2007, 44).

But does a strong identity fuel conflict or protect us from it? On the one hand, a strong social identity may lead us to enhance our self-esteem by devaluing outside groups, increasing the likelihood of intergroup conflict. On the other hand, Erik Erikson (1956, 1968) suggests that with a strong ego identity we are *less* prone to volatile conflict. We are confident in who we are and therefore do not need to prove our superiority through conflict. For nuanced perspectives, see Marilyn Brewer's chapter in Ashmore et al. 2001 and Gibson 2006.

Finally, it is not only the aggressive impulse that ignites the Tribes Effect. Sometimes people are simply bored, and so they start a fight to keep life exciting. I call this the *ennui syndrome,* and I think it plays a bigger part in conflict escalation than people often assume. If young siblings get bored, for example, one may start to tease the other and ignite the Tribes Effect. In my Tribes Exercise as well, I find that people sometimes pick a fight or take a strong stance to make the exercise more engaging, more thrilling. Their intention at first is to make the exercise more engaging, but egos quickly get hooked, and the Tribes Effect takes over.

25 **threatened by minor differences:** The narcissism of minor differences may have evolutionary roots. Darwin discussed the "struggle for existence," which is not competition between species but competition *among near relations for some hereditary innovation* that allows their subflock to survive through the generations. Species-level survival tends to be most compromised by rivalries not between species but within a species. See Lorenz 1966.

25 **takes on outsized importance:** As our world becomes increasingly interconnected through the Internet and related technologies, there is more opportunity for the narcissism of minor differences to play out. The social field for comparing ourselves with others vastly opens, and we need to work harder to defend the psychological boundaries of our identity to maintain our sense of distinctiveness.

25 **produces harmonious relations:** The relational matrix is a simplified representation of the subjective field of human relations, for autonomy and affiliation are each multidimensional. For example, a religious man who submits his loyalty to the divine sacrifices his autonomy to the divine; yet by that same act he simultaneously *expands* his autonomy through affiliation with a power he believes will bring him everlasting equanimity. As another example, quarreling lovers may feel great love for each other while simultaneously feeling resentful; they may feel autonomous around some issues yet constrained on others.

25 **self-protection trumps collaboration:** Suzanne Retzinger and Thomas Scheff (2000) contend that the root of protracted conflicts rests in "bimodal alienation": isolation between groups and engulfment within each group. This is consistent with the Tribes Effect, in which we distance from other tribes and fuse with "our own kind."

We also can experience the Tribes Effect within ourselves. For example, imagine I get into an argument with my wife. I know that I should empathize and validate her perspectives. But in my mind there is all-out tribal warfare between different "parts" of me. Psychologist Dick Schwartz (1995) calls the interaction among these parts an "internal family system": I have a whole family of parts, and any part may dominate, submit, accommodate, or rebel. So in my mind my "mother" urges me to listen and reconcile; my "father" tells me to just resolve the issue and be done with it; my "pride" tells me that *my wife* should empathize with me before I empathize with her; and my "conflict resolution expert" strives to resolve the issue amicably and efficiently. These parts battle it out within my mind, with pride feeling enraged that I'm not heard while mother tells me to calm down and extend an olive branch.

26 **Five Lures of the Tribal Mind:** Tension is a core component of many theories of human motivation. Religious scriptures depict tension between good and evil, light and dark. Psychologists have articulated constructive and destructive forces of conflict, all the way back to the seminal work of Sigmund Freud, who postulated a fundamental tension between a death

force (*thanatos*) and a life force (*eros*). In a famous letter to Albert Einstein, he expressed pessimism about humans ever suppressing their aggressive instincts, instead suggesting that "what we may try is to divert it into a channel other than that of warfare. . . . If the propensity for war be due to the destructive instinct, we have always its counter-agent, Eros. . . . All that produces ties of sentiment between man and man must serve us as war's antidote" (Freud 1932).

Forty years later Professor Morton Deutsch (1973) of Columbia University differentiated between constructive and destructive conflict, shedding light on the forces that bring us toward mutual gains or loss. Psychologist Steven Pinker (2011) argues that violent conflict is stimulated by five "inner demons" (predatory or instrumental violence, dominance, revenge, sadism, and ideology) while four "better angels" (empathy, self-control, moral sense, and reason) promote peaceful coexistence.

In relational identity theory, I view the struggle between these so-called inner demons and better angels as dynamic; thus I call the inner demons the *Five Lures of the Tribal Mind* and articulate the opposing force as *integrative dynamics*, which can be stimulated through the four-step method described in this book. While Pinker's theory raises important insights, his demons and angels are predominantly discrete, static concepts. My theory builds on his insights in emphasizing that conflict resolution is dynamic and pragmatic; it requires *practical processes* for disputants to enact in order to reach a state of sustained harmonious coexistence.

27 **prospects for collaboration:** The Five Lures may be seen as internal processes used to exile negatively charged feelings from consciousness. Should someone step on a taboo, demean the sacred, or replay old patterns (and, in Paul Russell's conceptualization, "not feel"), we are able to tolerate the intolerable through psychological banishment. Freud developed a structural scheme of resistance and repression to show how the "banishment of the incompatible idea to the unconscious and the consequent blockage of its affective charge from the most expeditious release enables the idea to exercise its pathogenic effect" (Greenberg and Mitchell 1983, 33).

The Five Lures can reduce prospects for collaboration. Religion, for example, may not factor greatly into an interfaith couple's marriage until they get a divorce and need to decide what religion to raise their child; suddenly each becomes a religious zealot. An assault on the sacred has lured them into the Tribes Effect, and it becomes hard for them to get out.

28 **closer through integrative dynamics:** According to the Dalai Lama, seventh-century Buddhist philosopher Dharmakirti proposed the psychological law that two opposing states cannot coexist without one undermining the other. He argued that if one state is stronger, the opposing state is weaker. If you are hot, you are not cold. If you are happy, you are not sad. The Dalai Lama (2005, 146) conjectures that "the cultivation of loving-kindness can over a period diminish the force of hate in the mind." This would suggest that, rather than expending too much energy on neutralizing the Five Lures, one might strive to build crosscutting connections that

invigorate positive emotions. If your emotional wounds are potent, however, healing them is often a prerequisite to building positive relations.

Chapter 4: Vertigo

32 *your emotional energies:* I conceived of the vertigo concept in a paper called "Vertigo: The Disorienting Effects of Strong Emotions on Negotiation," a working paper of the Harvard Negotiation Project. I applied the concept to postconflict contexts in a subsequent paper with Vanessa Liu, "The Psychology of a Stable Peace" (Shapiro and Liu 2005).

Vertigo warps our sense of time and place and therefore shares characteristics with the unusual condition known as synesthesia, in which the senses intertwine. The Russian journalist S. V. Shereshevskii suffered from this condition and described his experience to psychologist Alexander Luria: "If I read when I eat, I have a hard time understanding what I'm reading—the taste of the food drowns out the sense" (Foer 2006, 9). Vertigo induces in us that same general experience, wherein our adversarial feelings drown out the feelings of others; the emotional world we enter fills us with strong sensations and feelings that affect how we see, hear, and feel in our relationship with the other.

32 **to win it:** Vertigo proves difficult to alleviate, because the more intensely we experience it, the greater is our emotional momentum to maintain it— and the greater our resistance to changing course. It is like a person who drinks too much alcohol—the more drunk he gets, the more he wants to keep drinking and resists calls to stop.

32 **experience a spinning sensation:** Modern medicine uses the term "vertigo" as a diagnostic marker for such conditions as "positional vertigo" and "ringing vertigo," each describing a type of spinning sensation. Years back, William James studied vertigo—possibly because he suffered from seasickness. He found that of 200 Harvard students sitting on a rapidly unwinding swing rope, only one did not experience dizziness; of 519 deaf children, a majority reported little dizziness. This underscored the importance of the inner ear to vertigo. It also raises the notion that in a conflict situation, some people may have greater susceptibility than others to fall into a state of vertigo. I conjecture that people who have a stronger ego identity, and who are particularly self-aware, will be less likely to fall into this state of being. For more on James's research on vertigo, see James 1882 and Milar 2012.

32 **state of adversarial relations:** Two points about vertigo. First, it is not necessarily bad. Two teenagers who fall head over heels in love are in the dizzying grasp of positive vertigo; nothing can jolt them out of it. Even phrases that describe such an experience—*growing* fond, *falling* in love, *sweeping* you off your feet—depict the dynamic nature of vertigo. Of course, vertigo also has its darker side. It galvanized the couple at the mall to fall from grace into the clutches of the Tribes Effect. Just as you can fall in love, you can fall in hate. While falling in love is an ego-enhancing experience,

falling in hate is a self-threatening experience, motivating self-protection to avoid harm to our identity. In this book, I use the term "vertigo" to describe its negative side, though I believe the optimal negotiation process involves disputants who enter an intense positive flow, a positive vertigo.

Second, vertigo is distinct from an *amygdala hijacking*, a term coined by Daniel Goleman in his seminal book *Emotional Intelligence*. In an amygdala hijacking, your emotional brain overtakes your rational one, resulting in a short-lived burst of anger. Vertigo can coexist with an amygdala hijacking, but it is more of a relational mindset than a short-lived emotional response. You get consumed by vertigo, and it can stay with you for days or months. The professor and his wife may have resolved their conflict in the mall yet continued to feel consumed with mutual animosity; similarly, two ethnopolitical groups may live and breathe hatred for decades after a peace accord is signed.

32 **state of vertigo:** While Aristotle maintained that there are five senses—vision, hearing, smell, taste, and touch—there is a sixth: balance. Vertigo spins you into an all-consuming state of relational consumption in which you lose your sense of emotional equilibrium.

32 **frenzy of their squabble:** If you stand up and spin in circles, then stop, you will see a very warped vision of reality that is a better representation of your mind than the world around you. It is the same with vertigo.

33 **inciting you to fight:** All five senses can escalate the sensation of vertigo. Take sound, for example. The drumbeat of war excites people to come together to fight a common enemy. In the Tribes Exercise, I typically play frenzied drum music to rouse participants, who become so focused on asserting their tribe's superiority that they often are unaware of the tremendous impact of the sound on their emotional frenzy and aggressive behavior.

33 **noticing it altogether:** While we habituate to vertigo, we do not habituate to an amygdala hijacking. A divorcing couple may experience the relational consumption of vertigo for months as they figure out the painful details of their divorce, yet they only confront an amygdala hijacking during their periodic fights.

33 **striking consequences result:** Vertigo changes our relational perspective in two fundamental ways. We become (1) *self-absorbed*, retreating within ourselves for safety and confirmation of our self-righteousness, and (2) *other-objectifying*, viewing the other as not a subject but an object. The stronger our case of vertigo, the greater our decreased ability to perceive the other's subjectivity. In short, the more subject I am, the more object you are.

34 **guilt or shame:** Vertigo shares phenomenological similarities with the experience of copulation. The more intense each experience, the more you lose awareness of everything beyond the relational experience consuming you.

34 **readily apparent factors:** See Fiske and Neuberg 1990.

34 **your stereotypic perceptions:** Social psychologist Gordon Allport (1954, 9) wisely notes that "prejudgments become prejudices only if they are not reversible when exposed to new knowledge."

35 **would challenge it:** As parties categorize each other as adversaries, they focus increasingly on their own pain and suffer from a reduced capacity to appreciate each other's humanity. Social psychologists Susan Fiske and Stephen Neuberg's (1990) *continuum model of impression formation* suggests that when you initially perceive a person, you categorize him or her in terms of age, gender, and race; this is fast and easy to do. You are likely to hold to your categorization of the person if (1) what you observe is consistent with your initial categorization and (2) you are not motivated to learn more about the person. The latter creates a tension between speed and accuracy; the more accurate your perception, the longer it takes and the more effort you need to exert. You may try to, in Gordon Allport's (1954) terminology, "re-fence" your categorization ("Some of my best friends are Jews, but . . . "). Fiske and Neuberg (1990) have found that task interdependence tends to encourage appreciation of the other's unique attributes. This happens whether you are working on a team task at work, competing with someone else in a chess game, or trying to better understand your boss; all those activities require task interdependence.

35 **were dismissed automatically:** Because vertigo dramatically reduces your ability to self-reflect, it creates what I call a *bind of nonrecognition.* In a tense conflict, the only way out appears to be the *other side* acknowledging your pain and perspective. But neither side in vertigo is likely to recognize the other's pain, especially given mutual objectification. You each are in a bind of nonrecognition, and conflict escalation can seem like the only way forward.

35 **this is happening:** Vertigo affects your perception of time, which is much more flexible than clock time. Geologist Michel Siffre (1964) speculated that there are three levels of time: biological time (your body rhythm), perceived time (your sense of the passage of time), and objective time (what the clock says). At the age of twenty-three he spent two months in total isolation in a subterranean glacial cavern, where he studied geological patterns and his own perceptions of the passage of time. When he reemerged two months later on September 14, he thought it was August 20. Perceived time was warped. But remarkably, as he phoned daily to check in with his assistants, who tracked the reported time he awoke, ate, and slept, there was a clear biological pattern. The conclusion: Biological time tends to be quite regimented, while perceived time is much more fluid and context dependent.

Vertigo evokes outward-focused emotions—you do not bask in shame but revel in anger—and this affects your perception of the passage of time. By focusing on the other, you lose your own sense of the passage of time, truncating its passing. On the other hand, self-conscious emotions such as boredom, shame, or depression slow down your sense of time. William James (1890) suggested that in such contexts time drags because you "grow attentive to the passage of time itself," just as you do when you close your eyes for a minute; it can feel much longer. According to Claudia Hammond (2012, 34), "experiments confirm that people with depression give time estimations that are on average twice as long as those who are not depressed. In other words time is going at half its normal speed." In one devious study, researchers primed some participants to feel rejected and others to feel popular. A researcher then took each participant to a private room, started her stopwatch, stopped it after 40 seconds, and asked how much time had passed. Those subjects who felt well liked estimated the passing of time as 42.5 seconds on average, whereas the rejected individuals gauged it on average as 63.6 seconds (Twenge et al. 2003).

35 **passage of time:** In vertigo clock time passed more quickly than the quarreling couple thought. In other words, clock time was longer than perceived time, as depicted here:

Clock Time Passed:————————————————— (20 min)

Perceived Time Passed:———— (5 min)

35 **you are right side up:** Vertigo distorts your usual sense of the flow of time. Time has an inherent asymmetry to it: It is biased in terms of moving from past to future. Vertigo can break this rule of asymmetry, shifting your attention to incidents from the past, then forward into the feared future, then perhaps back again, and sometimes seemingly freezing in an emotional moment of distress. For more on time asymmetry see Davies 1974.

Vertigo appears to disorient what neuroscientist Antonio Damasio calls *mind time.* Similar to the time theory of geologist Michel Siffre is Damasio's (2002, 66–73) description of how human beings experience time in two distinct ways: body time and mind time. Body time governs your biological clock, which is set to the alternating rhythms of darkness and light (your circadian rhythm); it is located in the hypothalamus. Mind time relates to "the passage of time and how we organize chronology," capturing the way in which, as the clock ticks, our experience of time can seem fast or slow, short or long. Mind time is constantly active, helping us to perceive everything from the length of silence between two musical notes to the span of time since we last saw a friend. Damasio has observed that people suffering from amnesia have intact body time but dysfunctional mind time.

Based on studies of patients with brain damage, it appears that three regions are particularly important to perceive the passage of time:

(1) The hippocampus, which helps us form new memories. When it is impaired, people experience *anterograde amnesia*: They cannot hold new memories for long periods of time.

(2) The temporal lobe, which is critical to forming and recalling memories that bear a time stamp. Damage to the temporal lobe appears to be associated with *retrograde amnesia,* an impairment of the ability to recollect personal events that happened in a particular time, place, and context.

(3) The basal forebrain, which plays a key role in identifying the chronology of past events. If you injure your basal forebrain, you will remember events but not the chronology of their occurrence.

35 **thrill of the moment:** When our survival feels at stake, emotions can slow down our perception of time. "One minute becomes elastic and can feel like fifteen," notes Claudia Hammond (2002, 25). Novice skydivers, for example, underestimate the duration of other skydivers' falls but overestimate the time they spend in the sky. When our survival is at stake, perceived time slows down (p. 27). That helps to explain why people in war

zones and traumatic living conditions may feel like they have lived endless lives of suffering.

35 **sound and image:** This relationship between fear and time dilation has been borne out in experiments. In one study, neuroscientist David Eagleman invited his subjects to an amusement park, where they climbed a 150-foot tower before free-falling—upside down, with no harness—into a net below, landing roughly three seconds after taking their leap. Not surprisingly, this experience generated substantial fear in participants, who were asked one question upon their return to terra firma: How long did the plummet take you? Then, after watching someone else take the fall, they were asked another question: How long did the fall take that person? On average the subjects estimated that their own fall took 36 percent longer than the falls they observed from the ground. In the midst of their plummet, the subjects' fear had made it seem as though time were slowing, expanding.

More generally, there is fascinating literature on the malleability of time. Some articles for starters: Gardner 1967; Whitrow 1972; McTaggart 1908; Dennett and Kinsbourne 1992; Johnson and Nishida 2001; Angrilli et al. 1997.

36 **her watch suggests:** Almost any emotion can warp your sense of time and space—even love. Richard Wiseman (2009) spent a day in London's King's Cross railway station, approaching individuals as well as couples embracing and asking them, "Excuse me, do you mind taking part in a psychology experiment? How many seconds have passed since I just said the words 'Excuse me'?" Wiseman found that the embracing couples significantly underestimated the amount of time that had passed.

36 *Is it over already?:* We can understand the dynamics of vertigo through visual depiction of relational identity:

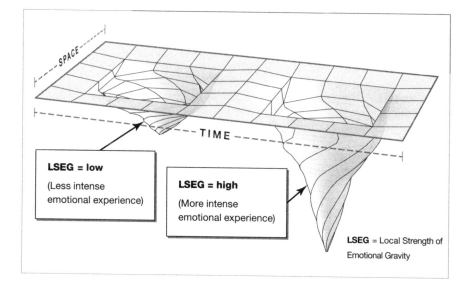

Your relational identity exists in a relational field, which represents your experience of space and time within an interaction. Your location within this field is always relative to that of others. In a conflict you will experience time and space from your vantage point, just as your counterpart will experience it from theirs. You may experience time moving fast while they may experience it moving slowly, depending upon your perceived positions in that field.

Every relational field has time-space warps. Should you fall into one, you enter the disorienting time and space of vertigo.

The intensity of your fall depends upon what I call the "local strength of emotional gravity." Sacred pillars of identity are located in specific regions of your relational field; the local strength of emotional gravity is high in these regions. Should someone offend any such pillar, they should expect a strong emotional response, for you are likely to fall quickly into this warped region of time and space. Because of the intensity of emotional gravity, these conflicts will feel emotionally heavy, and mind time will feel much faster than clock time.

Insubstantial aspects of your identity lie in other regions of your relational field. The local strength of emotional gravity in these regions is low. So even if any such region is warped, you will not fall as quickly, nor with as much intensity, and consequently your conflict will not feel as emotionally heavy. You are likely to experience little difference between the passage of mind time and clock time.

When you are in a region where emotional gravity is high, you are much more resistant to changing your ways. You feel "stuck" in your ways, pulled downward by gravity. When sensitive issues arise and you feel threatened, you are in a region of the relational field in which the local strength of emotional gravity is high.

36 **guide your behavior:** Professor David Eagleman has conducted studies showing that repeated stimuli appear briefer in duration than novel stimuli of equal duration, suggesting that novel learning may slow our internal sense of time (Eagleman and Pariyadath 2009).

36 **time has passed:** *Within* a state of vertigo you may experience fleeting moments of dilated time.

37 **nothing to diminish:** See Sebenius and Curran 2001.

37 **from the past:** Ibid.

38 **the distant past:** See Volkan (2004).

38 **"1941, 1841, or 1441":** Ignatieff 1997.

38 **cannot be trusted:** My notion of *memories of the future* is based upon the way memory works in the brain. Though most humans experience life in a past-present-future chronology, there is no reason why the brain should necessarily *catalog* these experiences in chronological order. Indeed, the brain catalogs experience in many different ways; some memories gain more accessibility based upon emotional meaning, traumatic impact, or the mere fact of repetition and familiarity. And there are other factors that distort chronological storing of information. Consider *source amnesia*, the inability to recall when, where, or how you acquired specific memories; a

variety of mechanisms may cause this amnesia, ranging from Alzheimer's disease or frontal-lobe damage to the futility of trying to store *every* stimulus you perceive. Furthermore, Professor Elizabeth Loftus (2005) has shown that memory is malleable: Misinformation can easily be implanted into our minds, causing us to "remember" a false incident as real.

Consequently, you can form certainty about an outcome that has not happened and might never happen. Such a memory of the future is perhaps more pernicious than a past memory, because it can threaten, in no uncertain terms, the fundamental fabric of your existence, driving you to take preemptive action that fuels conflict. Thus, mathematically, a memory of a future event makes that future event more probable. The event is seen and felt as though it is a fait accompli. While a future event is never as predictable as a past event, an entrenched memory of a feared future boosts the likelihood of that event actually happening. In that sense the past may not be the best predictor of the future; our memories of the future may better indicate conflictual behavior patterns. When we perceive ourselves to be under imminent threat, memories of a feared future motivate us to action.

40 **the other party:** Just as an electrical jolt changes your experience of consciousness, a relational jolt changes your experience of relational consciousness. This is necessary, for vertigo boxes you into an emotional system that is dynamically static: You fall deeper and deeper into conflict and see no way out. Thus, a jolt to the relationship is a tactic to switch to a metaframe, to expand your vision of your own subjectivity. Jolting the relationship is a practical way to enact what Kurt Lewin (1948), the grandfather of social psychology, proposed as essential to conflict resolution: to "unfreeze" a difficult system. Leadership scholar Ronnie Heifetz (1994) and negotiation expert William Ury (1991) both suggest another tactic for switching to a metaframe: Envision yourself on a balcony observing yourself in conflict.

42 **the two countries:** There are risks to using surprise in a negotiation. Though Sadat's trip to Jerusalem constructively jolted Israeli-Egyptian relations, his actions had huge consequences for Egypt and the Arab World, with political ramifications for Cairo and also a sense in some communities of Arab unity being undermined.

43 **an imprecise will:** This case is adapted from a real-life situation; details have been changed to protect stakeholders.

43 **"things [were] spiraling":** This quote is from Dennis Ross (2002), U.S. Middle East envoy at the time, who more fully stated, "What I was always concerned about in a case like this, where you have a cycle that takes on a life of its own, you have to find a way to give people a reason to take a step back, to pause, to think, so that things don't continue to spiral out of control. That's what was happening then, so that's why we basically came up with the thought that we would bring them here."

44 **of those senses:** Breaking free from vertigo requires us to experience the fullness of our subjective reactions in the conflict while also taking a third party perspective to our conflict, coming to see the conflict from what I call

a *meta-perspective*. To straddle these two worlds usually necessitates a *transitional environment*, a space and time in which we can explore what is keeping us enveloped in vertigo and how it might feel to overcome it. For related ideas, see Pizer 1998. A transitional environment does more than simply contain toxic emotions (Bion 1967). It creates the foundation for trusting relations. That is why it is important to build a transitional environment that is founded upon mutual safety and deemed legitimate by each of the stakeholders.

45 **the *overview effect*:** See White (1998).

47 **"tell the truth":** See Wilde and Ellmann 1969, 389.

47 **driving your conflict:** A good example of externalizing the negative comes from Rosamund Stone Zander, a psychotherapist, who was conducting therapy with a couple on the verge of separation. The wife was enraged at her husband's habit of withdrawing and accused him of not loving her. Rosamund blurted, "Who *could* love you when you act like this?" Feeling terrified at what she just said, she continued: "But it's not you speaking . . . it's something else. Revenge. Revenge is speaking in your voice. It's a creature, sitting on your shoulder, and it's going to get him no matter what, even if it has to destroy you in the process." Rosamund noted that the wife now "saw the vicious circle in which she [the wife] would have to blame her husband for her outrageous behavior just to keep her sanity, while the Revenge Creature celebrated its victory" (Zander and Zander 2000, 189).

Chapter 5: Repetition Compulsion

50 *"creatures of the repetition compulsion"*: Adapted from Burroughs 1993.

50 **go about his business:** From the Chaplin movie *Modern Times* (1936). I was introduced to this movie clip through a journal article on the repetition compulsion by David Kitron (2003).

50 **time and again:** See Freud 1920.

51 **result in "unpleasure"?:** Freud (1920, 16) highlighted the power of the repetition compulsion in "people all of whose human relationships have the same outcome: such as the benefactor who is abandoned in anger after a time by each of his protégés, however much they may otherwise differ from one another . . . or the man whose friendships all end in betrayal by his friend; or the man who time after time in the course of his life raises someone else into a position of great private or public authority and then after a certain interval, himself upsets that authority and replaces him with a new one; or, again, the lover each of whose love affairs with a woman passes through the same phases and reaches the same conclusion."

51 **"which it overrides":** Freud (1920) saw the compulsion to repeat dysfunctional behavior as driven by the desire to seek release. It is reminiscent of Jacob Moreno's concept of "act hunger," in which a person suffering from mental illness feels compelled during psychodrama to reenact a particular scene from the past (Moreno and Moreno 1946).

51 **a desired response:** I propose three major reasons why we resist changing our conflictual behavior: habit, utility, and identification.

(1) Habit. This is the first source of resistance to change. Every time a husband criticizes his wife, she may bite back with a critical retort. The couple need not think about this interaction. It just happens. A habit is a mere association of stimulus and response. This habit may produce animosity in both husband and wife, but the habit does not care. It is not out to please you, reward you, or punish you. It merely binds stimulus (the husband's criticism) and response (the wife's retort). The more you do it, the more solidified it becomes. We resist changing our behavior, thoughts, or feelings simply because we are acting as "we always do."

A habit can be beneficial or harmful. Brushing your teeth is good; smoking is bad. Your full trail of habits binds you to the life you lead, just as it binds society together. William James (1917, 142) observed that a habit is society's "most conservative agent," keeping us "within the bounds of ordinance." He went on to note that a habit "saves the children of fortune from the envious uprisings of the poor. It alone prevents the hardest and most repulsive walks of life from being deserted by those brought up to tread therein. It keeps the fisherman and the deck-hand at sea through the winter; it holds the miner in his darkness, and nails the countryman to his log cabin and his lonely farm through all the months of snow; it protects us from invasion by the natives of the desert and the frozen zone."

(2) Utility. We also resist change if we reap utility from our current pattern of behavior. Why should my grandmother have quit smoking if it relieved her of deep anxiety about dying? Why should a political renegade stop killing what he sees as "dirty insects" if his current behavior sustains his political power? Utility means that we get something of tangible, personal benefit out of the repetition of behavior, feelings, or thoughts. There may be good moral or health reasons to cease these behaviors, but that is not the concern of the utilitarian, whose calculations are based on amoral cost-benefit analysis. Myopic utilitarians—many of us in an emotionally charged conflict—do not even consider weighing the costs and benefits of our current behavioral pattern against an alternative, potentially more constructive behavioral pattern. The question we ask ourselves is not "Should I continue fighting or negotiate?" Rather, it is "Are the benefits of fighting outweighing the costs?" If so, we keep fighting.

Psychologists use the term "functional analysis" to describe the search for the personal benefits afforded a person by repeating a pattern of behaviors, thoughts, or feelings. In essence, a functional analysis assesses the personal benefits we may get out of behaviors that may appear dysfunctional at first glance. Why might a couple repeatedly argue about trivialities, day in and day out? Perhaps Cupid's arrow accidentally paired them together, but perhaps their conflict serves a deeper, functional purpose: Every time they fight, they air their frustrations and feel closer afterward. It may be that for some couples intense conflict serves a greater rational utility.

(3) Identification. Our deepest resistance—that which fuels the repetition compulsion—comes from perceived pressure to change a part of who we are. The repetition compulsion may be egged on by habit and utility, but its

core is identification with a particular way of interacting with others. A threat to your identity drives you to repeat a behavioral pattern that has protected you in the past. You *act out* this pattern, an emotion-driven story, again and again in a typically unconscious effort to protect your identity from hurt or annihilation, no matter how awful the behaviors' effect might be on your actual survival.

51 **would rather not:** See Russell 2006. Also see Denise Shull (2003), who provides evidence in support of the neurobiology of the repetition compulsion. She contends that childhood experiences influence brain tissues and chemistry—ranging from placement of synapses to fundamental procedural memories—creating filters for subsequent learning, perception, and behavior. We may repeat earlier patterns of behavior based upon the resulting relationships between brain mechanisms and structures such as the amygdala, supported by adrenaline, dopamine, and oxytocin.

52 **of present circumstance:** See LaPlanche and Pontalis, 1973, p. 78, who observe that "at the level of concrete psychopathology, the compulsion to repeat is an ungovernable process originating in the unconscious. As a result of its action, the subject deliberately places himself in distressing situations, thereby repeating an old experience, but he does not recall this prototype; on the contrary, he has the strong impression that the situation is fully determined by the circumstances of the moment."

   Note a key difference between impulsive and compulsive behavior. We typically enact an *impulsive* behavior to gain a short-term reward, giving little thought to the consequences of our behavior. The impulsive overeater, for example, does not realize he is eating a lot of cake until it is gone. The impulsive behavior is ego-syntonic: he enacts the behavior because he likes how it feels. Conversely, we tend to enact a *compulsive behavior* to relieve ourselves of anxiety and distress, as when we are excluded from a friend's party, feel abandoned, and compelled to call up the friend and yell at him. The compulsion is ego-dystonic: we do not like the feeling and take action to get rid of it.

52 **directly with them:** Paul Russell (1998, 45) notes that "trauma to the psyche, like trauma to the body, creates damage that requires repair. The bonds of connectedness, of attachment, must be created anew."

53 **of her situation:** Our brains house what neuroscientists call "autoassociative neural networks," templates of memories within our brains which allow us to create a full picture of something from a small snippet of information. Let's suppose I am in conflict with my neighbor over the legal border between our properties. We sit down to "talk it out," and as we do, my mind unconsciously draws on an age-old relational template of my relations with the angry, arrogant football star of my high school. This template—an autoassociative neural network—produces two powerful effects. First, I automatically fill in any ambiguities about my neighbor using this archaic template. Whether or not my neighbor is an angry guy, I immediately attribute negative intentions and arrogance to his every word or action. If he starts off the meeting by saying, "I'm happy we could meet," I might think, *He's obviously saying that to get me in a good mood so he can manipulate me.* Second—and here's where our psychology gets really

twisted—I ignore realistic differences as "noise." Once the autoassociative neural network is flipped on, I literally do not see exceptions to the template in my mind. My neighbor may accede to my demands and empathize with my grievances, but I am blind to his intentions. I simply see his arrogant behavior and, as I treat him with insolence, he *becomes* insolent. I create the adversary I perceive him to be.

Freud (1920) postulated that the repetition compulsion may derive not from an instinct to live but from a countervailing instinct to die, "an urge in organic life to restore an earlier state of things." The purpose of the repetition is thus to master the destructive death instinct.

53 **the healing process:** See Russell 1998.

54 **own repetition compulsions:** A student of mine noted that the Bible calls attention to this phenomenon. Matthew 7:3 states: "Why do you look at the speck of sawdust in your brother's eye and pay no attention to the plank in your own eye?"

54 *Compulsion Feels Education-Resistant:* Paul Russell (1998, 2) notes that the repetition compulsion "feels spooky. . . . There is some powerful resistance that appears to operate against all efforts at learning to anticipate, to avoid, or to alter the painful repetition. The repetition compulsion is education-resistant."

55 *by present circumstances:* This is consistent with Paul Russell's (1998, 46) theory about the repetition compulsion. The response to emotional injury (trauma) is the repetition compulsion. Trauma confronts us with two paths. We can (1) grow and master our injured emotions or (2) avoid learning new ways of being, staying stuck in the repetition compulsion. The repetition compulsion, with its affective correlates, "sculpts out exactly the problem of relatedness that has not yet been solved"—such as feelings of abandonment, incompetence, or worthlessness.

55 **full emotional presence:** Paul Russell (2006, 41) states that the repetition compulsion is experienced "with the complete conviction on the part of the person that it is a new event occurring in, and totally determined by, the present."

55 **"drawn to some fatal flame":** See Russell 1998.

55 **their familiar patterns:** Freud conceived of the repetition as a defense mechanism, a way to protect against feelings of inadequacy, disappointment, and neglect. We repeatedly try to change ourselves to fix this felt inadequacy.

56 **compulsion's key difficulties:** Breaking free of the repetition compulsion requires a difficult internal negotiation. Paul Russell (1998, 111) states that "the only thing that works [to transform the repetition compulsion] is negotiation, namely a negotiation around whether things have to happen the same way this time." In other words, will you repeat the past—with all its costs—or strive toward a more desirable future? Resolving this dilemma requires a difficult internal negotiation.

57 **("the TCI method"):** As Russell (1998, 20) notes, "The repetition compulsion is an invitation to a crisis. The repetition can occur alone, but the crisis cannot." My TCI model has strong parallels to Albert Ellis's ABC Model of Cognitive Behavioral Therapy, which helps people dealing with emotional distress to identify the activating event, behavior, and consequence. A major difference is that Ellis's model focuses on discrete behaviors, whereas the TCI model focuses on a cycle of discord.

58 **calls "somatic markers"**: For more on somatic markers, see Damasio 1994.

59 **of potential danger**: A key strategy to break free of the repetition compulsion is to *catch the spark before the flame*: Become aware of your behavioral intentions that precede the repetition compulsion. There is a window of time between the behavioral pattern manifesting in your behavior and your ability to inhibit its performance. This is a variation of what I call the space between, and this is where you hold power to break unconscious repetitive patterns. In a well-known study, neuroscientist Benjamin Libet asked subjects to look at a clock and move their own hand whenever they wanted to—and then to document the precise moment in time they decide to move their hand. The subjects were also connected to an EEG measuring the electrical activity in the brain. Libet reliably found that deflections of the EEG traces happened approximately one half second *prior* to the reported moment the subjects noted they decided to move their hands.

60 **giving in to it**: The repetition compulsion is an emotional force that resists change. To counteract it, you need to resist your resistance to change, which can feel unnatural.

60 **how to ski**: This example and subsection draw from Russell 2006, 39. The skiing example is adapted from his paper.

60 **"forces the issue"**: Ibid.

61 **anger, or shame**: You need ego strength to acknowledge the lure of the compulsion without succumbing to it. The paradoxical aim is to change while remaining the same; you escape the repetition compulsion but do not change your core identity. See Russell 1998, 12, on the importance of ego strength to tolerate this paradox.

62 **three powerful questions**: These questions are adapted from Russell 2006, 39.

66 **"aid you know"**: See James (1899).

66 **the Unguarded Moment**: Similarly, Father Joseph C. Martin, an expert on alcoholism, warned: "Be on guard against the unguarded moment." (See his video *Relapse*, produced by Kelly Productions, Inc., 1985.)

67 **toward constructive dialogue**: Professor Ronald Fisher describes a similar experience in facilitating intergroup dialogue around the Cyprus conflict. Turkish Cypriots resisted moving toward peace building out of fear that the traumatic events of the past would be repeated. Fisher and colleague Herbert Kelman facilitated a discussion in which each side acknowledged the other's traumatic history and made assurances that such behavior would never be repeated. Then participants moved into discussion on cooperative activities (Fisher 2010).

Chapter 6: Taboos

71 **that public rejection**: See Sobelman 2010.

71 **community deems unacceptable**: A community can range in size from a dyad (such as a married couple) to a large social group (such as a society).

71 **or broader society**: Radcliffe-Brown (1939) clarifies the concept of taboo: "In the languages of Polynesia the word means simply 'to forbid,' 'forbidden,' and can be applied to any sort of prohibition. A rule of etiquette, an

order issued by a chief, an injunction to children not to meddle with the possessions of their elders, may all be expressed by use of the word tabu."

R. D. Laing (1969, 77) further delineates the social dilemmas of taboos, though he does not explicitly reference the word "taboo." He describes how families make certain matters taboo; to even talk about the taboo is taboo, resulting in a double bind around matters that drive the family dynamic: "There is concerted family resistance to discovering what is going on, and there are complicated stratagems to keep everyone in the dark, and in the dark they are in the dark. We would know more of what is going on if we were not forbidden to do so, and forbidden to realize that we are forbidden to do so."

71 **a social construction:** Taboos are socially constructed and contextually defined. In other words, the boundaries between what is taboo and what is not vary across types of relations and the nature of the issue at hand. Fiske and Tetlock identify four types of relations (communal sharing, market exchange, authority ranking, and equality matching) and hypothesize that "people will regard trade-offs as natural and intelligible only up to the limit of the socially meaningful relations and operations defined under the relevant relational structure." Beyond that limit the trade-off will feel taboo. They provide the example of a lover saying, "I want more kisses. I'll hug you twice as much if you'll kiss me twice as much." They suggest that this trade-off seems wrong, for it treats a relationship based on communal sharing like one based on market exchange. The norms for what is taboo vary across these types of relationships.

Fiske and Tetlock argue that conflicts between relationships of different types—such as an obligation to community versus one to authority—are particularly stressful: "Should you go visit your dying mother if the trip would require you to desert your wartime post and dishonor your military unit? Should you report your mother's treason to the authorities if you discover that she is spying for the enemy in wartime? Should you commit a mortal sin to protect your best friend, who once did the same for you?"

Fiske and Tetlock's (1997) dilemmas are emotionally provocative, because they challenge what I call the *fundamental taboo of the tribe*: to betray your own identity group. These dilemmas force you to define your loyalties—and your level of sacrifice to those loyalties. Ultimately these questions confront you with decisions regarding what you hold most sacred.

72 **on its restriction:** Eminent social psychologists Lee Ross and Richard Nisbett (2011, 9) underscore a key insight of Kurt Lewin, the grandfather of social psychology: "When trying to get people to change familiar ways of doing things, social pressures and constraints exerted by the informal peer group represent the most potent restraining force that must be overcome and, at the same time, the most powerful inducing force that can be exploited to achieve success."

72 **punishment for violation:** I conjecture that the emotional guardians of taboos are fear and shame. We fear the political, social, physical, or economic consequences of breaking a taboo, and we fear the shame of social rejection.

72 **or get hanged:** Professor Stanley Schachter (1951) found that groups can tolerate a degree of deviance with respect to important issues, beyond which the group will socially reject or expel the deviant.

72 **members within it:** Taboos are a conservative social mechanism. Nobody likes to feel shamed or alienated from their own community, so taboos establish societal limits on acceptable behavior. If you overstep the taboo line, you risk shame or alienation. Yet taboos do not always preserve values that serve the common good. During a visit to the U.S. State Department on October 7, 2009, I was part of a leadership group that met with Ambassador Luis deBaca, who talked about how taboos often hide the core meaning in our communication and distance us from truth. He noted that society uses the term "sexual violence" rather than "rape," "trafficking" rather than "slavery," and "domestic violence" rather than "murder." He advocated for the importance of confronting and owning taboo language.

73 **in a conflict:** Psychoanalyst R. D. Laing (1970, 1) depicts taboos through his description of "knots" people get themselves into: "They are playing a game. They are playing at not playing a game. If I show them I see they are, I shall break the rules and they will punish me. I must play their game, of not seeing I see the game." It is useful to disentangle the emotional knots promoting destructive conflict.

74 **of moral unease:** Tetlock (2000) calls this the "mere contemplation effect." The theory posits that the longer people believe you contemplate a taboo trade-off, the more moral outrage they will feel toward you. See Tetlock et al. 2000.

76 **or even death:** This is true in Afghanistan, Somalia, and Pakistan. See "Riots Over US Koran Desecration," BBC, May 11, 2005.

77 **taboo on association:** Kim Jong-un, leader of North Korea, first met Dennis Rodman during a basketball exhibition in North Korea; they built a quick rapport, and Rodman later called Kim Jong-un a "friend for life." See Silverman 2013. Many Americans heard about Rodman's comment and thought, *Is Rodman a fool? He must be! How can anyone befriend this irrational tyrant of the North?* Even CNN posted an article titled "North Korea: Reality vs. The World According to Dennis Rodman" (Levs 2013). But that all speaks precisely to my point. Taboos constrain our thinking, limiting what we view as possible to say or do in a conflict. Also see Blake 2013.

77 **high in triumph:** Substantial portions of this story are drawn from the article "Balkans' Idolatry Delights Movie Fans and Pigeons," by Dan Bilefsky, in the *New York Times*, November 11, 2007.

77 **anything but clear-cut:** In the *New York Times* article (ibid.), Bojan Marceta, a twenty-eight-year-old local cameraman who raised the funds to commission the statue, said, "Nobody from the wars of the 1990s or from the former Yugoslavia deserves a monument, because all our leaders did was to prevent us from progressing. . . . My generation can't find role models, so we have to look elsewhere. Hollywood can provide an answer."

77 **"never gives up":** See "Rocky to Knock Out Disaster News," *Metro*, February 7, 2007.

79 **clear your conscience:** The notion of purifying oneself after making contact with the taboo dates back at least to Captain Cook's voyage to the Pacific. He notes, "When the *taboo* is incurred, by paying obeisance to a great personage, it is thus easily washed off" (Cook 1785). Indeed, many

religions have rituals of purification, such as the Christian confession to a priest, which results in absolution of sin on behalf of God. For psychological insights into the process of purification, see Tetlock et al. 2000.

81 **"said but didn't?"**: These questions are adapted from Stanford psychotherapist Irvin Yalom's work (1985, 147).

82 **pathways to change**: Professor Kurt Lewin (1948) highlights the importance of "gatekeepers" in his chapter in Maccoby et al. Gatekeepers hold substantial power. For example, if you want to influence a decision to be made by the president of an organization, you might be wise to discuss the matter with his or her most trusted confidant.

83 **"people from fear"**: Mandela 1999.

84 **system for decades**: Ibid.

84 **all human beings**: What makes a historic agreement historic? It breaks taboos. Mandela proved that point. He exercised the courage to break long-standing taboos against the promotion of racial equality—and he changed history. Without the breaking of taboos, the repetition compulsion is likely to win out.

84 **of your decision**: Harvard social psychologist Daniel Gilbert's (2005) research on affective forecasting suggests that we are not great at predicting our future level of happiness. One way to gain greater perspective on the impact of breaking a taboo is to solicit the input of a trusted friend or colleague.

85 **against destructive behavior**: This section is based in part on the work of economist Kenneth Boulding (1978, 16–17), who calls these tacit agreements "negative social contracts."

85 **acts extremely infrequent**: Boulding proposes that the difference between war and peace boils down to taboos. During times of peace, the United States could bomb an ally with whom it has a dispute but refrains from doing so *because it is taboo*: "What is the essential difference between a warring party and a non-warring party? The basic answer to this question would seem to be found in the nature of the taboo system of the parties involved. . . . From the point of view of the warring party the transition from peace to war is largely a transition in the position of the taboo line. There is a whole range of actions which are taboo in peace but which are not taboo in war."

Boulding goes on to note that each party's self-image is of the utmost importance: "The Ford Motor Company might be experiencing severe competition from General Motors but, if it ever occurred to the directors of Ford Motor Company to assassinate the directors of General Motors and blow up their plant, it is very doubtful whether that thought would even have been expressed in a board meeting, simply because the self-image of the Ford Motor Company would not permit that kind of behavior even if it were physically possible" (ibid.). He concludes with a caveat: "Self-images, of course, change under stress, and they likewise erode and change under a lack of stress" (ibid., pp. 15–16).

Similarly, should the president of the United States disagree with the pope on major policies, taboos make it inconceivable that the United States would bomb the Vatican. Unfortunately, acts of tragic violence—such as the mass murder of children in a school or the use of chemical weapons in war—can stretch the taboo line in a negative direction, neutralizing a taboo and making such behavior within the realm of possibility for the unstable few. One antidote is to reassert constructive taboo lines ("We will not stand for this inhumane behavior"), enforce those lines to the extent possible, and legitimize those revised taboo lines via gatekeepers within the perpetrators' community of influence. Indeed, evidence from anthropology documents the critical importance of taboos against violence for cultivating peaceful societies. See Fry 2006.

86 **forestall aggressive behavior:** Taboos often gain their strength from people or groups who hold structural power within a community; the prohibitions deter behaviors that threaten the community's power structure.

86 **"our psychological barrier":** See Boulding (1978, 16–17).

87 **against these behaviors:** Even the stability of international relations depends upon taboos. International law, for example, has no ultimate enforcement mechanism—as there is no single global government—which means that taboos against violating international law, along with resulting social alienation within the global community, arguably become critical enforcement mechanisms.

Taboos are also a tool in identity politics. If the president of a country declares any questioning of its military intervention "unpatriotic," the taboo has been planted. Of course, a grassroots organization could wage a counter-campaign declaring the military intervention itself "unpatriotic." Now there is a conflict over what should be deemed taboo: the military intervention or the questioning of it.

See the World Economic Forum's *Report on the Middle East Summit 2008*, Geneva, Switzerland. A description of my session ("Building Peace, Breaking Taboos") can be found at http://www.weforum.org/pdf/SummitReports/middleeast08/workspace.htm "Building Peace, Breaking Taboos."

88 **stalemate and peace:** Ibid.

Chapter 7: Assault on the Sacred

91 **withstand the blow:** Philosopher Mircea Eliade contends that the sacred holds special importance because it contains all "reality": The sacred holds the source of our values. If we confront a moral dilemma, we rely on sacred values to decide our path forward. Should someone assault what we hold sacred, they threaten the foundation of our reality.

An assault on the sacred is the most severe impingement on autonomy. For example, political psychiatrist Robert Jay Lifton (2001) discusses how, soon after the 9/11 attacks on the World Trade Center, strong anti-American sentiment in the Middle East stemmed in part from U.S. soldiers "put in various sacred places" in the Middle East, including Saudi Arabia.

91 *with divine significance:* Tetlock and colleagues (2000, 853) define a sacred value as "any value that a moral community implicitly or explicitly treats as possessing infinite or transcendental significance that precludes comparisons, trade-offs, or indeed any other mingling with founded or secular

values." Similarly to my theory, they note that sacred values have infinite utility and thus cannot be traded or compromised.

The sacred has a unique impact on our experience of being. Rudolf Otto (1917, 40) describes the spiritual experience of revering the sacred, calling it "numinous consciousness." This is a "non-rational, non-sensory experience or feeling whose primary and immediate object is outside the self." This consciousness has contrasting feelings of *mysterium fascinans*, a fascination that attracts you to the sanctified object, and *mysterium tremendum*, a powerful fear of the object's regal authority.

What is the function of the sacred? Consider several possibilities:

On a psychological level, we may have an innate reservoir—a basic need—for experiencing transcendent emotions. The sacred awakens these emotions, allowing us to transcend the boundaries of ordinary existence and to recognize our humbleness in relation to a higher power, a deeply significant relationship, or a connection to whatever we consider divine. Similarly, the sacred may furnish believers with an unconscious belief in omnipotence; a subjective and intersubjective sense of identity, continuity, and cohesion; and comfort and security for persons and communities during periods of anxiety. See LaMothe 1998.

On a sociological level, the sacred may derive from the unexplainable spirit of group fervor—what Durkheim called *effervescence*.

On a theological level, influential theologian Paul Tillich theorized that the sacred (religion specifically) quells humankind's deep-rooted anxiety over loss and extinction. He argued that no therapy can calm those fears.

91 **specifically religious entity:** Durkheim (1912, 52) postulated, "By sacred things one must not understand simply those personal beings which are called gods or spirits; a rock, a tree, a pebble, a piece of wood, a house, in a word anything can be sacred." He saw the power of the sacred as deriving not from any intrinsic holy essence, but from its social separation from the profane.

91 **or cherished event:** Anything can be deemed sacred: It is a matter of what the believer believes. Scholars have taken this principle to heart and looked at political conflicts involving decisions traditionally considered rational in nature. For example, see Professor Dehghani and colleagues' (2009) analysis of negotiations over the Iranian nuclear program.

91 **departed spouse's ashes:** There is an old Upanishads saying about the divine: "When before the beauty of the sunset or of a mountain you pause and exclaim, 'Ah,' you are participating in divinity" (Campbell and Moyers 1988, 258).

92 **the offended party:** The sacred is about indivisibility of the totality, no matter the consequences. Yet the sacred is not totally indivisible per se. The human capacity to reinvent meaning and reconcile contradiction is remarkable. A spiritual leader, for example, may reinterpret sacred text and thus redefine the community's understanding of the inviolable.

92 **"apart and forbidden":** Émile Durkheim (1912) contrasts two worlds: the profane, which is the mundane experience of everyday life, and the sacred, which includes things set apart and forbidden. Religion, he believed, is what holds these two worlds as separate.

93 **"martyr, Allah Willing"**: See the *Iran Data Portal* (2015) at Princeton University. Website: https://www.princeton.edu/irandataportal/laws/supreme -leader/khomeini/rushdie-fatwa/.

93 **on literary freedom:** A *New York Times* reporter asked Rushdie if he had any advice for other writers under similar threat. His response: "Don't compromise. It's a question of . . . knowing who you are and why you did what you did." See "Life During Fatwa: Hiding in a World Newly Broken," *New York Times*, September 18, 2002. In this article Charles McGrath interviews Salman Rushdie.

94 **now expressed remorse:** When one party infuses a conflict with sacred meaning, there is a tendency for the other side to do likewise. For example, terrorists framed the September 11 attacks on the World Trade Center in the language of the sacred—including Osama bin Laden's declaration of a holy war on the United States—and American leaders framed their response in terms of sacred values of life, freedom, and American institutions (Mahoney et al. 2002).

94 **"bottle of wine"**: This example derives from a classic *New Yorker* cartoon by Mike Twohy, published on May 31, 1999, in which a couple enters a party, hands the host cash, and says, "We didn't have time to pick up a bottle of wine, but this is what we would have spent."

95 **address these conflicts:** Baron and Spranca were some of the earliest researchers to investigate the role of sacred values in human decision making. They refer to sacred values as "protected values" and conceptualize them as resistant to trade-off with economic values. They uncovered five properties that correlate with trade-off resistance: quantity insensitivity, agent relativity, moral obligation, anger at the thought of making the trade-off, and denial of the need for trade-offs through wishful thinking. Their notion of "quantity insensitivity" relates to my point earlier in this chapter that even a small offense to a sacred value can have a big emotional impact. See Baron and Spranca (1997) and Scott Atran and Robert Axelrod (2008), who illustrate the sacred's quantity insensitivity in noting that armies often risk the lives of many soldiers to save a few as a matter of sacred duty.

Philip Tetlock has shown that conflict over sacred values is more likely to lead to hard bargaining and impasse. Tetlock and colleagues (2000) provide empirical evidence that a threat to a sacred value incites moral outrage and cognitive rigidity. Hard bargaining strategies become more likely. By reframing the conflict as not over sacred values but about "costs and benefits," one may be able to transform or mask the emotion-laden nature of a taboo trade-off.

Why is the sacred resistant to resolution? One reason is that you cannot use conventional cost-benefit models of decision making to measure satisfaction in a conflict over sacred values. Satisfaction is measured over time, but in the world of the sacred time is infinite. There is no concept of short-term or long-term utility—but merely infinite value forever. Because the sacred is seen as eternally of infinite value, an assault on the sacred tends to instigate a relentless and seemingly disproportionate reaction.

96 **respect those boundaries:** A totem is that which we deem sacred, whether a book, object, or holy text. Listen carefully to discover what the other side holds as a totem, thus providing you with insight into what they may value in the conflict.

97 **they are going:** The story of how you came to be is what I term your *mythos of origin*, for it roots your identity through a connection to the past. The story of your life purpose is what I term your *prophecy mythos*, because it roots your identity through a connection to the future.

97 **trust only kin:** Consider the question of whether evolutionary theory should be taught in the school system. One camp of dissenters holds to a mythos of origin that the world was created through an all-powerful deity; to teach alternative—or even complementary—narratives threatens that core identity. Another camp views its mythos of origin as based on the notion that humans did not necessarily appear on this earth in full-fledged form through divine intervention but have evolved into their current structure and function over time in response to heritable physical and behavioral traits and survival of the fittest.

97 **stirs moral outrage:** I coined the term "sanctuaries of identity" to describe the sacred spaces that serve as a physical manifestation of our most cherished beliefs and values.

97 **for sanctified activities:** Professor Abraham Joshua Heschel proposes the Jewish Sabbath as the sanctification of time, noting that the "Sabbaths are our great cathedrals."

98 **under some conditions:** Bazerman, Tenbrunsel, and Wade-Benzoni (2008) propose that when a negotiator appeals to the sacred, three scenarios are possible: (a) *The issue is truly sacred.* The authors claim this issue is not open to discussion or compromise. However, in this chapter I suggest that even these issues are negotiable, for you can appeal to hermeneutics in an attempt to reinterpret the conception of the sacred. You also can speak in the language of the sacred and attempt to tailor your message to the other side's sphere of identity. (b) *The issue is not sacred but is framed so as a tactic, a means to an end.* (c) *The issue is "pseudosacred"*—sacred under some but not all conditions.

    In follow-up research, Tensbrunsel and colleagues (2009) present evidence that people in a dispute are more likely to fight for sacred values when they have a strong walk-away alternative. In such situations they can "afford" to act on principle. This relationship between sacred values and the walk-away alternative's strength is exhibited whether participants hold moderate or extreme views on the issues at stake. These findings suggest that context matters in terms of how strongly people frame a situation as involving sacred values, though there are likely to be some issues that are, in my terms, *sacred sacred*, impervious to context.

99 **held intrinsic value:** Eliade (1958, 7) believed that the sacred is not constructed; it reveals itself to us. He referred to this manifestation of the sacred as *hierophany*. A flag is no more than an interweaving to everyone but the nationalist, who experiences it as sacred. The same is true of myths: To the believer they are not just stories but hierophanies.

99 **a secular one:** Philip Tetlock and colleagues (2009) propose three types of
    trade-offs:
    > *routine trade-off:* secular value vs. secular value;
    > *taboo trade-off:* secular value vs. sacred value; and
    > *tragic trade-off:* sacred value vs. sacred value.

    In a fascinating article, Tetlock (2003, 323) examines ways to avoid
    compromising moral boundaries in order to reach a negotiated settlement
    when faced with a taboo trade-off. For example, he notes that "efficiency
    experts on toxic clean-up can escape blame for a taboo trade-off if they ear-
    mark the surplus not for general revenue but for saving lives in other ways."
    Thus the taboo trade-off transforms into a tragic trade-off. Tetlock also notes
    that not everything is open to rhetorical reframing: "Some taboos—abortion
    rights, racism, or the sacred soil of Jerusalem or Kashmir—become so
    entrenched at certain historical junctures that to propose compromise is to
    open oneself to irreversible vilification."

    Symbolic concessions (such as an unreserved, sincere apology) can
    improve the chances of compromise when sacred issues are at stake. Pro-
    fessors Jeremy Ginges, Scott Atran, Douglas Medlin, and Khalil Shikaki
    (2007) conducted a study showing that people who negotiate a sacred issue
    increase their resistance to compromise when offered material incentives,
    whereas they *decrease* their opposition to compromise when offered sym-
    bolic compromise. The study focused on the Israeli-Palestinian conflict
    and used subjects who were directly affected by the conflict.

    Atran and Axelrod (2008) provide strategies to address a dispute
    implicating sacred values, such as acknowledging the other side's sacred
    values. For example, after World War II anthropologists Ruth Benedict and
    Margaret Mead argued to the U.S. government that it should signal respect
    for the Japanese emperor, thus reducing the likelihood that the Japanese,
    who revered him, would fight to the death to save him.

99 **termed "constitutive incommensurability":** See Raz 1986.

99 **to commit sacrilege:** When conflicts focus on sacred issues, people tend
    not to apply instrumental, cost-benefit analyses but instead apply moral
    rules and intuition. This crucial distinction is expanded upon in Ginges
    et al. 2007. Additionally, the researchers discovered that symbolic conces-
    sions decrease moral absolutists' opposition to peace deals.

100 **truly at stake:** Consider two more examples of how a taboo trade-off can
    be converted into a tragic trade-off. Lecturer Lily Kong (1993) discusses
    how the Singaporean government acquired and often demolished reli-
    gious centers (sacred institutions) to make room for public housing, indus-
    trial estates, and urban renewal (secular concerns). The government
    quelled local resistance by reframing this taboo trade-off (sacred concern
    vs. secular concern) as a tragic trade-off (sacred building vs. sacred public
    good), arguing that the communal value of the religious acquisitions and
    infrastructural changes superseded the value of the sacred buildings them-
    selves. For example, Kong interviewed "a Methodist [who] argued that if a
    religious building had to give way so that a road could be widened to ease
    traffic congestion it was for the benefit of all and, as a Christian testimony,

'we should do something good for the country and not think of ourselves first.'"

A second example focuses on Ariel Sharon, former prime minister of Israel, who wanted to vacate Israeli settlements in Gaza to return control to the Palestinians. A senior member of the National Security Council later noted his strategy: "On the settlers [who were to be removed from Gaza], Sharon realized too late that he shouldn't have berated them about wasting Israel's money and endangering soldiers' lives. Sharon told me that he realized now that he should have made a symbolic concession and called them Zionist heroes making yet another sacrifice" (Atran et al., 24 August 2007, 1040).

101 **for its subject:** William James views the sacred as a property of the individual, whereas Durkheim views it as "a social imperative that affirms society and binds the individual to it" (Coleman and White 2006). In other words, James focuses on that aspect of the sacred "which lives itself out within the private breast," whereas Durkheim views it—and religion more broadly—as serving a *social function*, creating a powerful bond that motivates people to enact communal values that preserve social continuity.

According to my relational-identity theory, a shared sacred belief can become a source of affiliation, linking both of you together. This is in line with Durkheim's theory on the communal function of the sacred. Yet a belief in the sacred paradoxically enhances and reduces your autonomy: As you submit to the sacred, you limit your autonomy to question the sanctity of the sacred but simultaneously expand your autonomy through connection to the infinite value of the sacred.

103 **beliefs, values, or family:** Robert Jay Lifton (1979) coined the term "symbolic immortality" and proposes we achieve a sense of it in five ways: *biological immortality* (my bloodline outlasts my mortal self); *creative immortality* (my works outlast my mortal self); *theological immortality* (my spirit outlasts my mortal self); *natural immortality* (nature outlasts my mortal self: "from dust you come and to dust you shall return"); and *experiential transcendence* (my experiences take me outside my mortal self).

103 **to be sacred:** For details on the process of sanctification, see Pargament and Mahoney 2002. People also commonly create sacred meaning by engaging in ritual, pilgrimages, etc.

103 **Camp David Peace Accords:** See Sadat 1978.

103 **from their marriage:** See Mahoney et al. 1999.

104 **have proven ineffective:** The same holds true in contemporary global society, where financial inducements are often not enough to dissuade religious extremists from committing violent acts. What is needed, in part, are global platforms for religious leaders—seen as legitimate in the eyes of extremists—to denounce violence as an effective means for dealing with values-based differences.

104 **outside your control:** According to Ben Dupré (2009, 72–75), the concept of fundamentalism derives from American Christian fundamentalism, a movement that arose in the early twentieth century in reaction to the "reforming tendencies of 'liberal' theologians. . . . A unifying theme of different religious fundamentalism is the conviction that there is a single,

authoritative set of teachings that contain the essential and fundamental truth about God (or gods) and his (or their) relationship to mankind. The sacred text is the literal word of the deity and emphatically not open to interpretation and criticism. In the same way, the moral injunctions and codes contained within the text are to be followed to the letter."

The sphere of identity that I call "fundamentalist" relates to what Scott Atran calls the "devoted actors" model of conflict resolution, which, in contrast to the rational-actor model, depicts those who are willing to make extreme sacrifices that are independent of, or seem out of all proportion to, likely prospects of success. This notion of devotion to a group helps to explain the otherwise irrational behavior of participants in my Tribes Exercise, who would rather die for their newly established kin than save the world. For details on the devoted-actor model, see Atran 2003. Tetlock and colleagues (2000) propose a similar conception of sacred decision making, the *intuitive moralist-theologian*.

104 **who you are:** Strikingly, both religious zealots and strict biological determinists occupy this fundamentalist sphere of identity, for both believe that their identity develops through forces outside their control. Religious zealots believe that a divine power determines the parameters of their identity; biological determinists believe identity is established through biology, structures of DNA, and the like. You are who you are because of either the template of divine ordinance or your body's preestablished biogenetic codes.

In fact, we *all* may be fundamentalists. The constructivist *fundamentally believes* in his or her view of identity, much as the religious zealot cannot be convinced otherwise. In fact, neuropsychological evidence suggests that you cannot argue individuals out of their commitment to what they conceive of as vital to their own identity. Researchers discovered that, whether one evaluates objective assertions (2+2=4) or subjective assertions (God is real), each gets its stamp of belief or disbelief in primal locations of the brain associated with emotion, taste, and odor. See Harris et al. 2008.

105 **but no essence:** I am using the term "anattist" quite narrowly. In a conversation with religious scholar Professor Richard Oxenberg (e-mail communication on July 20, 2015), he noted, "Buddhist doctrine of *anatta* is more a functional than a metaphysical doctrine; it is designed to get the adept to cease to see himself as an isolated entity separate from, and in opposition to, all else. But the person of nirvanic consciousness does not come to see himself as having no identity, but as being (in some sense) identified with everything. It is an expansion of identity, not an elimination of it. It is a sense of being 'at one' with all. Thus it is an overcoming of the dualistic consciousness associated with the sense of being an I (isolated self) standing in opposition to, and threatened by, a world of not-I. It is just in this sense that Thich Nhat Hanh says that the person of nirvanic consciousness transcends the dread of death, because he comes to see himself as a continuation of all that preceded 'him' and will survive 'him.'"

The Dalai Lama (2005, 46–50) invokes the Buddhist theory of emptiness, which posits that "things and events are 'empty' in that they do not possess any immutable essence, intrinsic reality, or absolute 'being' that affords independence. This fundamental truth of 'the way things really are' is described in the Buddhist writings as 'emptiness,' or *shunyata* in Sanskrit." The Dalai Lama states that "if on the quantum level, matter is revealed to be less solid and definable than it appears, then it seems to me that science is coming closer to the Buddhist contemplative insights of emptiness and interdependence."

The Dalai Lama references Buddhist philosopher Nagarjuna's distinction between two truths: (1) *conventional truth*, which is reality as we experience it, including core identities, and (2) *ultimate truth*, which is the ontological, deeper level of reality (p. 67). The Dalai Lama (p. 51) implies that assuming that objects are discrete entities has ethical dangers: "I once asked my physicist friend David Bohm this question: From the perspective of modern science . . . what is wrong with the belief in the independent existence of things? . . . He said that if we examine the various ideologies that tend to divide humanity, such as racism, extreme nationalism, and the Marxist class struggle, one of the key factors of their origin is the tendency to perceive things as inherently divided and disconnected. From this misconception springs the belief that each of these divisions is essentially independent and self-existent."

For additional insights into Buddhist philosophy on thinking and feeling, see *Thoughts without a Thinker: Psychotherapy from a Buddhist Perspective*, by Mark Epstein (New York: Basic Books, 1995).

107 **possibility of reinterpretation:** I am grateful to Dr. Steve Nisenbaum, instructor in psychiatry at Harvard Medical School, who highlighted this point in a personal e-mail communication.

107 **known as *hermeneutics*:** Hermeneutics is the study of the interpretation of text. Dialogue can be seen as living text open to interpretation. The philosopher Martin Heidegger (1962) gives a good account of hermeneutics as a way to understand the inextricable link between self and culture—what he calls *being-in-the-world*. The craftsman, he illustrates, is an individual not separate from his trade—his tools, wood, and workshop—but wholly connected to it. Heidegger notes that the craftsman is not "set over and against the world" but an engaged participant in activities imbued with cultural meaning; they are integrated parts of a broader whole. In other words, culture and self are not independent but intrinsically interconnected, which means that, in terms of conflict resolution, one can change cultural understanding to change self-perception, just as one can change self-perception to transform the cultural framing of an event.

109 **resolution requires sacrifice:** Social psychologist Kurt Lewin notes that making a sacrifice for an organization increases loyalty to it. I believe that in any conflict we make sacrifices to fight for "our" side, thus increasing our loyalty to our side. But this same power of sacrifice can be used to mutual benefit: If disputants on both sides of a conflict jointly make a sacrifice of

equal perceived magnitude for the sake of agreement, it can help bind them together.

Chapter 8: Identity Politics

112 **thousand years ago:** Aristotle believed that the state is a product of nature; to exist in the state, humans are by nature "political animals." This notion relates directly to my theory of the Tribes Effect. Aristotle noted that "he who by nature and not by accident is without a state, is either above humanity, or below it; he is the 'Tribeless, lawless, heartless one,' whom Homer denounces—the outcast who is a lover of war; he may be compared to a bird which flies alone." This individual is fully autonomous, with no care for affiliations, placing him or her outside the moral order, liable to pursue any means necessary to satisfy internal needs. This is a strong argument for the positive value of tribes. While the Tribes Effect can lead to aggression, its function is to protect those with whom we affiliate. Without a tribal connection, we risk becoming the "heartless one."

112 **"when, and how":** Harold Laswell, *Politics: Who Gets What, When, How* (New York: Whittlesey House, 1936).

112 *a political purpose:* I use the term "identity politics" to refer to a neutral psychological mechanism of influence. This is in contrast to the traditional, often liberalist political use of the term, which refers to oppressed minorities fighting for increased political power, as in the civil rights and feminist movements; these "identity groups" advocate for change to a political system to expand their social and legal rights.

113 **privilege or paucity:** Foucault (1984) argues that identity is not a "thing" we have but an emergent property of human interaction. Accordingly, identity becomes a tool for defining power relations, as when a government prioritizes resources for "these people" over "those people." See Gagnon 1994.

113 **us and others:** Do ethnic divisions create conflict, or do politics create ethnic divisions? According to Professor Banton, politics raises the salience of ethnic divisions, leading traditionally peaceful ethnic groups to suffer periods of violence. For Hutus and Tutsis in Burundi and Rwanda, social change preceded the violence and increased salience of ethnic identity. Professor Banton (1997, 76) concluded that "the recent history of Rwanda and Burundi shows that ethnic consciousness did not create conflict, but, to the contrary, the conflict has done much to increase the ethnic consciousness." Professor Martha Minow (1998, 119), dean of Harvard Law School, argues a similar sentiment: "The alternations of forgetting and remembering itself etches the path of power." In other words, politics shapes power dynamics, which shape ethnic relations.

113–14 **the other side:** The Machiavellian leader can use history as a tool for political manipulation. Threatened groups are prone to what Vamık Volkan (2001) calls *chosen traumas* and *chosen glories:* "These are shared mental representations of past catastrophes or triumphs that have become markers of a group's identity. . . . In the case of chosen traumas, they involve humiliation and losses that have not been properly mourned, and although the actual event may be centuries old, the mental representation of it is embedded in the group's sense of identity and may, when reactivated, provide fuel for aggression or a sense of victimhood in the present day." Volkan asserts that many leaders intuitively know how to stimulate chosen traumas and glories as a tool for political influence.

115 **webs of influence:** See de Waal 1982, 207.

116 **"anything without insult":** *Utani* is the tie between tribes or villages; the individuals who are tied together refer to one another as *watani*—people tied together through *utani*. *Utani* institutionalizes friendship and insulates against political violence through good humor, financial generosity, and support during difficult times, such as cooking and cleaning at the funeral of a member of an *utani* tribe. See Tsuruta 2006.

117 **means they can:** See Brubaker 2004, 13.

117 **political pressures (level 2):** See Putnam 1988 and Walton and McKersie 1965, who debunk the unitary actor assumption within the context of organizational negotiations. Also see Lax and Sebenius 2006, who provide a useful framework for dissecting these various internal and external forces influencing the decision-making process.

121 **perpetrators of the tragedy:** Fortunately my neighbor was not injured at the marathon.

122 **on this idea:** My notion to have Northern Ireland focus on building a positive identity was an idea that clearly some other political leaders had already realized and were pursuing.

122 **British and Irish identities:** Leadership from the United Kingdom and the Republic of Ireland sought on many occasions to paint identities in the positive. For example, in May 2011 Queen Elizabeth made the first-ever visit by a British monarch to the Republic of Ireland, and Irish President Mary McAleese noted that Ireland and Britain were "forging a new future, a future very, very different from the past, on very different terms from the past." (See "McAleese Hails 'Extraordinary Moment,'" *Irish Times*, May 16, 2011.) When Queen Elizabeth recalled her visit several years later, she noted, "We now cooperate across the full range of public business; indeed, there is today no closer working relationship for my Government than that with Ireland." (See "The Queen's Banquet Speech for the State Visit of Irish President Michael Higgins: In Full," *Belfast Telegraph*, August 4, 2014.) In 2014 Irish President Michael Higgins made a state visit to the United Kingdom, at which time Queen Elizabeth stated, "We, who inhabit these islands, should live together as neighbors and friends. Respectful of each other's nationhood, sovereignty, and traditions. Cooperating to our mutual benefit. At ease in each other's company." (See "Queen Says Ireland, Britain Should Live as Friends," *Irish Times*, April 9, 2014.) During that visit, the Irish president noted, "As both our islands enter periods of important centenaries, we can and must reflect on the ethical importance of respecting different, but deeply interwoven, narratives. Such reflection offers an opportunity to craft a bright future on the extensive common ground we share and, where we differ in matters of interpretation, to have respectful empathy for each other's perspectives." (See "Irish President

Talks of Lasting Reconciliation in Historic Speech," *The Guardian*, April 8, 2014.)

122 **will reignite hostility:** This section has benefited from the keen perspectives of John Kennedy of Insight Strategies, who has worked tirelessly to promote peace within Northern Ireland.

123 **the ECNI method:** See Fisher and Shapiro 2005. The ECNI method is a revised version of the Bucket System, developed by Mark Gordon, a senior adviser to the Harvard Negotiation Project. For similar approaches to deciding how to decide, see Vroom and Yetton 1976 and Bradford and Allan Cohen 1998.

124 **Harvard Law School:** See Sebenius and Green 2014.

126 **then in his midthirties:** This group was led by Madam Ruth Sando Perry, former president of Liberia. According to Diop, the international community supported the inter-Congolese dialogue to end the crisis, and their team of female African leaders contributed to this goal.

127 **things done (cooperation):** Mary Parker Follett, a pioneer in the field of conflict resolution, distinguished power over (coercion) from power with (coaction).

127 **over tribal identity:** A fundamental principle of Nyerere's ruling party was "to fight tribalism and any other factors which would hinder the development of unity among Africans." See M. H. Abdulaziz, "The Ecology of Tanzanian National Language Policy," in *Language in Tanzania*, eds. Edgar C. Polome and C. P. Hill (Oxford: Oxford University Press, 1980).

127 **his leadership abilities:** This perspective on the leadership of President Nyerere derives from a conversation with a Tanzanian diplomat at the World Economic Forum Summit on Africa in Dar es Salaam, Tanzania, on May 6, 2010.

Chapter 9: Integrative Dynamics—a Four-Step Method

131 **relations with others:** Transcendent unity is the ultimate aim of reconciliation. Professors Erin Daly and Jeremy Sarkin (2007) describe reconciliation as "the coming together of things that once were united but have been torn asunder—a return to or recreation of the status quo ante, whether real or imagined."

Reconciliation can happen *within ourselves*; we can resolve tension between conflicting emotions. Professor Bakan (1966, 45) draws upon Freudian psychoanalytic theory to describe the transformation of neurosis into emotional reconciliation: (1) We *separate* what we like from what we do not like and repress the latter; (2) we try to *master* our emotional situation; (3) we *deny* the repressed feelings; and (4) we behold the feelings that have been denied. Thus the ultimate task of psychoanalysis is to discover "the inner unity which is behind separation and repression" (48). As with integrative dynamics, we aim to look beneath division for transcendent unity.

One way to spot repression is through a concept Sigmund Freud (1925, 235) called *negation*. A patient says to Freud: "You ask who this person in the dream can be. It's *not* my mother." Upon hearing these words,

Freud is confident the person *is* the mother: "With the help of negation only one consequence of the process of repression is undone—the fact, namely, of the ideational content of what is repressed not reaching consciousness. The outcome of this is a kind of intellectual acceptance of the repressed, while at the same time what is essential to the repression persists" (236).

133 **those deeper motivations:** See Fisher and Ury 1981.

133 **field of negotiation:** The orange example derives from Fisher and Ury, 1981. I first articulated this section's critique of the example in my dissertation presentation in 1999 at the University of Massachusetts, Amherst. In addition to an empirically based dissertation, I presented my committee with a self-drawn cartoon of two girls fighting over an orange, dividing orange from peel, and then arguing moments later about an unrelated issue.

133 **forestall a new conflict:** Collaborative problem solving becomes extremely difficult in the face of strong negative emotions. I refer the reader to research showing that when we assume someone is similar to us, we introspect about their mental characteristics as we would about our own but that we fail to do so for people deemed dissimilar. See Jenkins et al. 2008.

Disgust may further obscure our efforts to problem solve. I suspect that as the Tribes Effect takes hold, we feel a sense of disgust toward the other side for their perspective and for not empathizing with our perspective. Disgust evokes a tendency to dispose of that which we view as disgusting, a strong negative reaction that can override rational considerations. See Han et al. 2010.

134 **us versus them:** Professor Joseph Campbell describes transcendence as "an essential experience of any mystical realization. You die to your flesh and are born into your spirit. You identify yourself with the consciousness and life of which your body is but the vehicle" (Campbell and Moyers 1988, 134).

134 **adversarial to collegial:** Pioneering peace researcher John Paul Lederach (1997) describes the *identity dilemma*: Disputants in a protracted conflict may resist peace because their adversarial identities are familiar to them.

134 **enmity to amity:** In *The Varieties of Religious Experience,* William James (1958, 165) discusses the psychology of religious conversion and introduces the concept of a *habitual centre of emotional energies.* This section draws on his insights.

134 **extend beyond self-interest:** The neurochemical serotonin has been shown to enhance harm aversion. See Crockett et al. 2010.

137 **strictly accurate description:** Professor Peter Coleman of Columbia University has pioneered Dynamical Systems Theory, which helps disputants better understand the complex causes of conflict and ways forward. Professor Coleman and J. K. Lowe (2007) identify four key variables useful for resolving protracted conflict: (1) *cognitive complexity:* understanding the complex narratives of each party, (2) *tolerance of contradiction:* tolerating information that contradicts your narrative and resisting simplification of issues or solutions, (3) *openness and uncertainty:* seeking contradictory information, and (4) *emotional resilience:* engaging in emotional coping strategies to channel feelings into constructive action.

Reconciling ethnopolitical conflict is especially complex, involving victims and offenders as well as multiple methods for healing and exercising justice, truth seeking, and reparation. For an excellent resource on intergroup reconciliation, see Bloomfield 2003.

137 **are both important:** Professor John Brewer (2010, 127) argues that "peace processes require an envisioning of the future as much as an emotional packaging of the past."

137 **a better future:** Professors Erin Daley and Jeremy Sarkin (2007, 134) note that a critical question about the past is "For what purpose do we remember the past? It might be for purposes of keeping alive the fire of anger or revenge or to vindicate the victims."

138 **of your relations:** The ability to understand trauma—and, by extension, conflict resolution—requires political support. As Harvard trauma expert Judith Herman (1992, 9) notes, "In the absence of strong political movements for human rights, the active process of bearing witness inevitably gives way to the active process of forgetting."

Chapter 10: Uncover Your Mythos of Identity

139 **to your identity:** Professor Jerome Bruner (2002, 89) argues that narrative is our "preferred, perhaps even obligatory medium for expressing human aspirations and their vicissitudes, our own and those of others. Our stories also impose a structure, a compelling reality on what we experience, even a philosophical stance." Bruner (1990, 77) asserts that a narrative involves a necessary perspective on experience; it cannot be "voiceless."

139 **as the villain:** A story is an exposition with a plot. A narrative provides perspective to the story. One might imagine the story as a building, while the narrative is your interpretation of that building. Ten people can look at the same building and all have different interpretations. In a conflict, the story is the unfolding drama, while narrative is each person's perspective on that drama. A narrative can exist without story. When I listen to blues music, for example, I experience an unfolding personal narrative, but it lacks the plot of a story. The aim of integrative dynamics is to help parties uncover and acknowledge each other's defining narratives—the mythos of identity—which exposes the diverging perspectives forming an overarching story of conflict.

139 **behavior becomes understandable:** "If we could read the secret history of our enemies, we would find sorrow and suffering enough to dispel all hostility," observed Henry Wadsworth Longfellow. See Henry Wadsworth Longfellow, *Prose Works of Henry Wadsworth Longfellow*, vol. 1 (Boston: James R. Osgood and Company, 1873), 452.

139 **most explosive conflict:** At a small gathering of academics at Harvard Business School organized by Professor Michael Wheeler on February 15, 2007, emotions researcher Paul Ekman commented, "For many it will be irresistible to tell you their story if they think you will understand. Very few people don't want to be understood. It's not about how they view my story but *why* I've done what I've done with my life. The only reason to

block that desire to tell you my story is contempt—my contempt for you."
By understanding each side's mythos, we understand why we live the story
we live.

141 **thought to do so:** The elites could have drawn on the work of philosopher
John Rawls to produce a morally sound plan for resource distribution.
Rawls proposed that parties deciding societal principles for allocation
of resources or rights should approach their decision from behind a "veil
of ignorance"—that is, without knowing what their own circumstances
would be in that society. This method minimizes personal biases and
prejudices, for it treats all members of the society with equal moral value.
Should the elites have decided resource allocation behind a veil of ignorance, they might also have announced to the broader group their method
of decision making, which could have quelled at least some of the lower
classes' anger.

141 *as in Biography:* This particular distinction draws from Joseph Campbell's
(1988, 60–61) discussion of Jungian archetypes and their role in the time-
lessness of mythology. Campbell inspired several key concepts in this
chapter, particularly in relation to the power and purpose of mythology in
everyday life.

141 **biologically based component:** See Jung 1936.

142 **of personal experience:** Jung theorized that your unconscious consists of
two main components: the personal unconscious and the collective unconscious. Your *personal unconscious* is home to hidden feelings, secret fantasies, and repressed trauma. Your *collective unconscious*, in contrast, houses
ideas and images formed independently of your personal experience and
shared by all human beings. As mentioned, archetypes are the content of
your collective unconscious.

142 **characteristics of humanity:** Technically, Jung (1968, 5–6) differentiated
between the *archetype* (which is lodged forever in the collective unconscious) and the *archetypal image* (which intrudes into consciousness and
frames our intuitive understanding of the world). I am using the term
"archetype" to refer to the archetypal image. We can never see the archetype itself; we see its manifest form through an archetypal image. In Jung's
own words, "The term 'archetype' thus applies only indirectly to the 'representations collectives,' since it designates only those psychic contents
which have not yet been submitted to conscious elaboration and are therefore an immediate datum of psychic experience. In this sense there is a
considerable difference between the archetype and the historical formula
that has evolved. Especially on the higher levels of esoteric teaching the
archetypes appear in a form that reveals quite unmistakably the critical
and evaluating influence of conscious elaboration. Their immediate manifestation, as we encounter it in dreams and visions, is much more individual, less understandable, and more naïve than in myths, for example. The
archetype is essentially an unconscious content that is altered by becoming conscious and by being perceived, and it takes its colour from the individual consciousness in which it happens to appear. . . . Primitive man is
not much interested in objective explanations of the obvious, but he has

an imperative need—or rather, his unconscious psyche has an irresistible urge—to assimilate all outer sense experiences to inner, psychic events."

142 **the social world:** It is extremely difficult to "prove" that archetypes are primordial and not socially constructed. How should a scientist go about validating the reality of a latent archetype if it is not yet fully formed nor visible? Indeed, where does an archetype exist in the mind? For purposes of conflict resolution, there is no need to obsess over the reality of archetypes. Conflicts transpire in the form of a narrative, and any narrative has fundamental themes. The search for archetypes is ultimately a search for core relational themes that motivate emotion, cognition, and behavior in a conflict.

142 **communicating its content:** See Chomsky 1972 and Cook et al. 2007.

142 **your current conflict:** This requires "active imagination," a term coined by C. G. Jung, who depicted it as a technique to unveil unconscious content in a waking state (Stevens 1990).

143 **an *eternal return*:** See Eliade 1958.

143 **each side's mythos:** Creative introspection is a process for uncovering each disputant's archetypal relational identity vis-à-vis the other side.

144 **and reconsider perspectives:** Brian Arao and Kristi Clemens developed the concept of a "brave space" and discussed the critique of "agreeing to disagree." See Brian Arao and Kristi Clemens, "From Safe Spaces to Brave Spaces," in L. Landreman, ed., *The Art of Effective Facilitation: Stories and Reflections from Social Justice Educators* (Sterling, VA: Stylus, 2013), 135–50. Many of the ideas I present on brave spaces are drawn from their excellent book chapter. Additionally, see R. Boostrom, "Safe Spaces: Reflections on an Educational Metaphor," *Journal of Curriculum Studies* 30, no. 4 (1998): 397–408.

145 **illusion of safety:** See Arao and Clemens (ibid.).

145 **can easily unravel:** Professor Vamık Volkan (1999) elucidates a useful set of emotional dynamics to look out for in a conflict:

1. *Displacement onto a mini conflict*: Parties enact a mini crisis during their dialogue, which provides a condensed, symbolically rich illumination of major concerns fueling tension.

2. *The echo phenomenon*: Parties echo recent external events implicating their opposing identities.

3. *Competition to express chosen traumas and glories*: Parties compete over whose historical grievances are worse, refusing to empathize with the other's pain and suffering.

4. *The accordion phenomenon*: Each party gets closer to the other, then withdraws, in a repetitive pattern.

5. *Projections*: Parties cast unpleasant aspects of their identity onto others.

6. *Time collapse and transgenerational transmission of trauma*: Parties fuse past trauma with present experience, reviving feelings associated with the trauma.

7. *Narcissism of minor differences*: Parties assign large importance to small differences in identity, marking the border between their side's core identity and the other's and protecting it from damage or erosion.

145 **fundamental relational needs:** Emotions researcher N. H. Fridja (1988) defines a concern as a "more or less enduring disposition to prefer particular states of the world."

145 **status, and role:** See Fisher and Shapiro 2005.

146 **interests behind them:** Fisher et al. 1991.

147 **in the conflict:** My concept of comparative questioning can be traced in part to the theoretical insights of C. Sluzki (1992, 2), who suggests that stories are "self-regulated, semantic systems that contain a plot (what), characters (who), and setting (where and when). These narrative components, in turn, are held together, regulated by, and in turn regulating, the moral order (meaning or overall theme) of the story, effectively sealing off alternative interpretations. To shift the nature of a story, one useful technique is to shift labels into behavior, asking questions such as "Under what circumstances do you feel . . . ?"

148 **the same questions:** Most of these questions are drawn from an article by Professor Sara Cobb (2003), who calls this form of inquiry "circular questioning," a technique developed in the 1980s in Milan, Italy, by systemic family therapists; circular questioning frames questions that invite comparisons across time, conflicting parties, or relationships.

149 **in the conflict:** Sometimes a mediator or facilitator may need to help each side truly hear the other side's mythos. Retzinger and Scheff (2000, 76) contend, "Perhaps the biggest block to progress in negotiating stuck conflicts is that one or both parties feel that their stories have not been told or, if told, not heard. When both parties feel deeply heard, the mood may change to the point that negotiation can begin. The mediator's task in such cases is to help the parties to formulate their stories in a way that does not ignore the emotions and to be sure that when they are told, they are acknowledged."

150 **your own emotions:** As Philip Wilkinson and Neil Philip (2007, 15) note, "myths, like poems, work through metaphor. They fold the world over on itself, until points that were distant and distinct from each other touch and merge, and these equivalences show us who we really are."

151 **contextualize your conflict:** To understand a person's mythos, you must understand the personal impact of the conflict *as well as contextual factors* such as political, social, or economic influences. Kurt Lewin (1997, 337), the grandfather of social psychology, postulated a conceptually similar formula to predict behavior: Behavior (B) is a function of the Person (P) and his or her Environment (E). In short, B=f(P,E). He explained, "To understand or to predict behavior, the person and his environment have to be considered as *one* constellation of interdependent factors" (338). This has implications for reconciliation. A mythos is a product not simply of the individual *or* the environment but of the *combined result*.

151 **a primal drama:** Historian Joseph Campbell proposes that myths allow us to contact parts of us beyond our own consciousness.

152 **an unproductive argument:** This workshop was held in May 2013 in Istanbul, Turkey, in conjunction with the World Economic Forum Middle East Summit.

153 **"as understandably cautious":** See Neu and Volkan 1999.

154 **revise your mythos:** Symbolic representation of the human experience can help us see beyond secular analysis to the deeper spiritual drivers of behavior. Analyzing ritual, for example, can focus attention on the symbolic practices feeding the hunger for spiritual meaning.

158 **other side's power:** These sources of power are adapted from B. H. Raven, "A Power Interaction Model on Interpersonal Influence: French and Raven Thirty Years Later," *Journal of Social Behavior and Personality* 7, no. 2 (1992): 217–44. Raven added a sixth base of power—information—in 1965. See B. H. Raven, "Social Influence and Power," in *Current Studies in Social Psychology,* eds. I. D. Steiner and M. Fishbein (New York: Holt, Rinehart, Winston, 1965), 371–82.

160 **source of power:** In a conflict with asymmetric power dynamics, *each* party may resist storytelling. Those who perceive themselves as more powerful may resist sharing their narrative for fear of losing power. Those who perceive themselves as *less* powerful may resist sharing their narrative for fear of retribution.

   Yet even if only one side shares its narrative, both sides can benefit. Consider the work of eminent social psychologist Ervin Staub, who conducted an intervention in Rwanda to promote postgenocidal healing between Hutus and Tutsis. The conflict had left more than one million people dead, mostly as a result of extremist Hutus killing Tutsis and moderate Hutus. When Staub was in Rwanda, the Tutsis were now in power; but he worked with a mixed group of Hutus and Tutsis. Though the Hutus refrained from sharing stories, he observed that having them hear the Tutsis' stories promoted empathy and contributed to the reconciliation process. See Staub and Pearlman 2001, 203.

Chapter 11: Work Through Emotional Pain

163 **"a better grace":** See Joseph Glatthaar 2008, 151.

163 **necessity to avenge:** Retaliation may be a useful strategic move—but nevertheless it should be the result of a conscious decision, not a knee-jerk response. Consider relations between twelve-year-old Nick and his younger brother Joe. If Nick steals Joe's prized book, Joe may retaliate by stealing Nick's favorite book, in effect sending the message: *Don't mess with me.* But if Joe comes back and slugs Nick in the face, the original retaliation may not have had its intended effect. The purpose of working through emotional pain is to ensure that you are pursuing an optimal strategy, rather than simply retaliating blindly for a perceived offense.

164 **all your might:** Helen Lewis (1971) notes that most of us would rather turn the world upside down than turn ourselves inside out.

165 **deciphering its meaning:** I propose that, as a general rule, healing needs to occur at the same level of identity as the pain: personal, social, or spiritual. If the New England Patriots football team suffers a humiliating loss (pain to fans' social identity), the collective psyche of New Englanders will feel hurt, and individual psychotherapy will be much less curative than

the team's win the following week. In contrast, an emotional wound that results from a fight with your sibling is unlikely to heal without a heart-to-heart conversation with that person. One must foster healing at the same level as the pain.

165 **you feel hurt:** Ensure that disputants take ownership for the full scope of their emotions. Social psychologist James Averill (1982) observed that we assume altruistic emotions as our own but tend to abdicate responsibility for anger and related afflictive emotions. The philanthropist does not apologize for a generous donation made on a whim but will seek to excuse his ranting at someone who criticizes his business practices.

165 **and talk back:** This approach is similar to cognitive behavioral therapy, which advises people to notice negative self-talk and respond in defense of themselves. Indian philosopher Krishnamurti (1991, 215) believed in journaling to catch those thoughts: "This whirling machinery must slow itself down to be observed, so writing every thought-feeling may be of help. As in a slow motion picture, you are able to see every movement, so in slowing down the rapidity of the mind, you are then able to observe every thought, trivial and important."

166 **is necessarily painful:** Sharing painful emotions can foster self-consciousness. We may fear being judged and then feel shame about our shame. Scheff (1988) calls this the "shame spiral." In such a circumstance we may become acutely sensitive to our image in the eyes of others, as suggested by Charles Horton Cooley's (1902, 179–85) theory on the "looking-glass self." He observed that "in imagination we perceive in another's mind some thought of our appearance, manners, aims, deeds . . . and are variously affected by it. A self-idea of this sort seems to have three principal elements: the imagination of his appearance to the other person; the imagination of his judgment of that appearance; and some sort of self-feeling such as pride or mortification" (p. 184). Shame tends to be among the most difficult emotions to acknowledge and work through. Whereas anger is about what you or someone else did, shame is about *who you are.*

167 **each other's pain:** See Brian Arao and Kristi Clemens, "From Safe Spaces to Brave Spaces," in L. Landreman, ed., *The Art of Effective Facilitation: Stories and Reflections from Social Justice Educators* (Sterling, VA: Stylus, 2013), 135–50.

167 **or professional mediator:** A mediator can be particularly useful in helping disputants work through shame and humiliation. These emotions are typically hidden; to talk about them can raise more shame. While traditional approaches to conflict resolution encourage us to "vent" our emotions, this can shame our counterpart and damage bonds; but the vulnerability inherent in direct dialogue can also lead each side to feel shame. Thus in an emotionally charged conflict a mediator can establish a brave space and safely help clients acknowledge each other's mythos and feelings of rejection, alienation, and humiliation. See the work of Professor James Gilligan (1996) for more on the power of shame in conflict escalation.

168 **you have incurred:** Lifton (1979) argues that we cannot move beyond loss without mourning. Volkan (1981) proposes that to promote collective

mourning, such as after a communal conflict, groups can create objects to link present circumstance with past loss; monuments, holidays, and other rituals can serve this purpose.

168 **metabolizing of loss:** Freud believed that making the unconscious conscious is essential to mental healing. In his article "Remembering, Repeating, and Working-Through," he discusses two pathways to deal with traumatic memories: (1) *acting out,* whereby we unconsciously remember and act out traumatic memories, replicating dysfunctional patterns of behavior, and (2) *working through* the trauma by consciously remembering and coming to terms with it. See *The Standard Edition of the Complete Psychological Works of Sigmund Freud,* vol. 12, 1950 (originally published in 1914), 145–56. In *Mourning and Melancholia,* Freud argues that there are two responses to loss: (1) *Melancholia* is an unconscious response to loss, a pathological fixation on the lost object that emotionally consumes us, while (2) *mourning* is a conscious process of grieving for the loss; we come to accept and emotionally detach from the lost object or person and recast our emotions elsewhere. See *The Standard Edition of the Complete Psychological Works of Sigmund Freud,* vol. 14, 1950 (originally published in 1917), 237–58.

169 **wholly nonverbal impression:** See Herman 1997 and Van der Kolk 1988.

169 **into the air:** I am grateful to Polly Hamlen, of the Program on Negotiation at Harvard Law School, for her insights into the connection between ritual and the basic elements of our planet.

171 **"impossible to sink":** See C. S. Lewis, *Letters to Malcolm Chiefly on Prayer: Reflections on the Intimate Dialogue Between Man and God* (New York: Harvest Book, 1963), 106.

171 **"the human community":** See Gobodo-Madikizela 2003, 117.

171 **clarity will emerge:** South African Archbishop Desmond Tutu and his daughter, Mpho Tutu, emphasize that you need to decide whether to renew or release a relationship. To *renew* the relationship is to forgive and move on *within* the relationship; to *release* the relationship is to walk away from it. The authors emphasize that "the preference is always toward renewal or reconciliation, except in cases where safety is an issue. . . . Renewing our relationships is how we harvest the fruits that forgiveness has planted. . . . It is possible to build a new relationship regardless of the realities of the old relationship. It is even possible to renew a relationship born out of violence" (Tutu and Tutu 2014, 148).

173 **even forgave the perpetrators:** Professor Jonathan Cohen (1999) wrote an excellent article on the legal dimensions of apology. He contends that "lawyers should discuss apology more often with their clients because often doing so would make *their clients* better off. . . . In many cases, the potential benefits of apology are great, and when care is taken in how the apology is made—within a 'safe' legal mechanism like mediation, and with attention to nuances such as admitting fault without assuming liability if insurance coverage is at issue—the risks of apology are small" (p. 1068).

173 **remorse and defensiveness:** Enright and Coyle (1988) differentiate forgiveness from pardoning, condoning, excusing, forgetting, denying, and reconciling.

Chapter 12: Build Crosscutting Connections

175 **multiracial, democratic state:** See the video *Five Skills for Getting to Yes* (1996) with Roger Fisher.

176 **its armed struggle:** This story derives from three sources: (1) personal conversation with Roelf Meyer in Tanzania at the World Economic Forum's Africa Summit; (2) his presentation at Harvard Law School's Program on Negotiation on April 11, 2014; and (3) a videotaped interview by Professor Roger Fisher of Cyril Ramaphosa and Roelf Meyer about their fishing experience and its impact on the negotiation process to end apartheid (see Fisher's video (ibid.).

176 **stronger your relationship:** According to Harvard professor Gordon Allport's (1954, 267) *contact hypothesis*, merely assembling two groups together is not enough to improve intergroup relations. The nature of the contact affects the nature of relations. He observes that "prejudice . . . may be reduced by equal status contact between majority and minority groups in the pursuit of common goals. The effect is greatly enhanced if this contact is sanctioned by institutional supports (i.e., laws, custom, or local atmosphere), and if it is of a sort that leads to the perception of common interests and common humanity between members of the two groups."

177 **turmoil of conflict:** See Josselson 1992 for a related model that conceptualizes dimensions of human connection.

177 **of the world:** Affiliation is a core variable at play. Just as inclusion feels good, exclusion feels bad—and registers in the same areas of the brain where we experience physical pain. Researchers from the University of California examined the brains of participants lying in an fMRI scanner while playing a computerized ball-tossing game. The participants thought they were playing the game with two other players; the latter two were actually computerized confederates. At first everyone tossed the ball back and forth. Then the two confederates systematically excluded the participant. It turns out that exclusion activated the dorsal anterior cingulate cortex (dACC), a key region of the brain that activates when we feel physical pain. They found that even when participants were aware that the computer program was preset to exclude them, they *still* felt rejected (Eisenberger et al. 2003).

Neural circuitry exists to mitigate the pain of rejection. In one study, researchers administered Tylenol for three weeks to half the participants while the other half received a placebo pill. Neither group knew what pill they were ingesting. Every night participants completed a questionnaire about their felt experience of exclusion. By the ninth day in the study, the Tylenol-taking group reported feeling less social pain than the placebo group. With each passing day the difference in feelings of social pain widened. In a follow-up study, participants who had taken Tylenol for three weeks did not feel rejected in a computerized ball-tossing game, even when no one tossed the ball in their direction (DeWall et al. 2010). These studies confirm common sense—that rejection hurts and that its pain can be soothed—but raise the hairy question of *how to mitigate the pain.* Telling two nations at war to simply take Tylenol misses the point.

178 **from diplomatic discussions:** Someone may ignore you as a way to gain leverage over you. A powerful nation, for example, may refuse to politically recognize a rebel group in order to avoid legitimizing that group.

178 **attaches to it:** See Iacoboni 2009.

178 **of their pain:** Professor Tania Singer and colleagues (2004) performed the landmark study showing mirroring of empathic experience and made two important discoveries. First, whether you or your partner gets zapped, the same parts of your brain's pain matrix activate, including the bilateral anterior insula, rostral anterior cingulate cortex, brain stem, and cerebellum. In other words, when you empathize with your partner's pain, *your neural networks activate* so that you literally feel your partner's pain. Second, you do not feel your partner's pain in its experiential fullness. Empathy replicates the *affective tone* of your partner's pain, but typically without the full sensory experience. You may feel your partner's anxiety, but without a knot in your stomach or tightness in your chest. Also see de Vignemont and Singer 2006.

     Follow-up studies suggest that, within a variety of conditions, pain-related empathy extends to a partner you do not know. Watch a video of a needle stinging the back of a stranger's hand and, unsurprisingly, you cringe in pain yourself. You cannot, however, feel everyone's pain or joy, for there would be no emotional space left in your brain to feel your own emotions. Emotional empathy tends to activate in those relationships deemed emotionally significant or salient for you. For example, see Morrison et al. 2004.

178 **an enduring bond:** My definition of attachment is consistent with a classic definition provided by psychologist Mary Ainsworth (Ainsworth and Bell, 1970, 50), a pioneer in attachment theory, who defined attachment as "an affectional tie that one person or animal forms between himself and another specific one—a tie that binds them together in space and endures over time." John Bowlby (1969/1982, 194), another pioneer in attachment theory, defined attachment as a "lasting psychological connectedness between human beings."

179 **"white and the non-white":** See Malcolm X., *The Autobiography of Malcolm X: As Told to Alex Haley* (New York: Ballantine Books, 1964), 346–47.

181 **realistic, but inevitable:** Technically, I call this a *memory of an inevitable future*, because disputants want to create a mental image of the future so vivid and tangible that one cannot even imagine the reality of an alternative future.

181 **in the future:** This workshop was held in Sharm El-Sheikh, Egypt, in 2008; I have used this same approach in subsequent workshops in the Middle East.

184 **each other's space:** A key benefit of crosscutting connections is that *each stakeholder* builds an emotional investment in the relationship. One could look at this like a marriage: The *principle of least interest* suggests that the one with the least interest in the relationship has the most power in it. If both sides hold relatively equal investment in the relationship, they each will have relatively equal commitment to stay in it (Waller 1938).

186 **"is in order"**: Srđa Popović shared this technique with me during a conversation at Harvard Business School on November 29, 2012.

187 **conversation and decision making:** Matthew Lieberman (2013) discovered that by the time we are ten years old, our brains have spent ten thousand hours learning to make sense of people and groups. Even when our brains are on break, we are likely to be thinking about the social world.

187 **respond to them:** Professor John Gottman (2002, 229) coined the phrase "bid for connection."

188 **repeated and meaningful:** This section on ritual draws heavily on ideas in Gottman 2002, 229.

189 **heads and hearts:** See Allport 1958.

190 **of this network:** M. Crystal, "The Siege on Bethlehem" (lecture presented at the Program on Negotiation at Harvard Law School, Cambridge, MA, September 20, 2007).

190 **"bound up in yours":** Archbishop Tutu shared this insight on human connection during the Closing Plenary of the World Economic Forum's Annual Meeting in Davos, Switzerland, in 2012.

Chapter 13: Reconfigure the Relationship

192 **"will you facilitate?":** The Park51 situation is based on fact. I fictionalize parts to illuminate key points in this chapter. For example, in the real situation Mayor Bloomberg strongly supported Park51's right to keep the location of the community center and mosque. Additionally, as of the writing of this book, there has been no definitive solution to the situation. I was not involved in the negotiation processes surrounding Park51.

194 **conversation about identity:** In the United States, national debate about race relations has often been triggered by a single episode of gross racial injustice, which serves as the stimulus for broader dialogue about the issues.

195 **separation, assimilation, and synthesis:** Professor Donald Horowitz (1985, 64–65) elucidates several processes for ethnic fission and fusion: amalgamation, incorporation, division, and proliferation (in which groups produce additional groups within their ranks). Also see Byman 2000.

196 **leaders he met:** Conformity has its costs: Some people criticized President Obama for following a misguided protocol that belittled the stature of the United States ("Obama Draws Fire for Bow to Japanese Emperor" 2009).

196 **not by force:** According to William James (1958, 165), conversion results when you shift a cluster of ideas peripheral to your being to the "habitual centre of personal energy."

196 **and theirs coexist:** Some methods for promoting intergroup relations may appear synthetic but ultimately are not. Multiculturalism without an overarching umbrella of shared governance and connection is arguably no more than a charade of synthesis. The melting-pot theory is arguably a method not of synthesis but of accommodation by all to a common group identity. Synthesis requires each tribe to preserve its independent identity while affiliating to other tribes through a common group identity, thus

building a community of tribes. In other words, the aim is to optimize both autonomy and affiliation. For more on common in-group identity, see Gaertner et al. 1993.

196 **identifying as American:** Social psychologist Karina Korostelina (2007) describes how the king of Morocco synthesized clashing identities of Arab Istiqlal and Berber tribes. The Berbers had suffered political and social exclusion, including from 1956 to 1958, when the Istiqlal Party mandated that all political posts be held by Arabs and prohibited Berber-language broadcasts. King Mohammed recognized that a synthesized identity was the only way to ensure peace and security. According to Korostelina, "The King of Morocco invented the concept of 'Arabized Berbers' and satisfied the most important concerns of Arabs (such as teaching Arabic in all schools) and Berbers (recognition of their political party) within the framework of a unified nation."

Political scientist Donald Horowitz (1985, 598) provides a variety of structural arrangements to promote synthesis: (1) disperse the conflict by proliferating the points of power so as to take the heat off a single focal point, such as by scattering power among institutions at the center, as in the U.S. system; (2) emphasize intraethnic differences, which casts attention away from interethnic differences; (3) create policies that incentivize interethnic cooperation; (4) create policies that encourage alignment of interests rather than ethnicity; and (5) reduce disparities between groups.

196 **occupation of Korea:** See Dunbar 2012 and Hong 2014.

196 **a new city hall:** Hong 2014, 284.

197 **history deserved acknowledgment:** Ibid.

197 **over its predecessor:** See Metropolitan Government 2012.

197 **and radiant present:** This outcome did not please everyone. One criticism, for example, was that the wave over the old city hall was an insult to Japan, which had recently suffered a typhoon (Baseel 2013).

197 **Synthesize, Assimilate, Separate:** See Haslam (2004, 128) for a related model depicting category-based solutions to intergroup conflict.

198 **to *keeping* it:** Social identity theory complicates Robert Frost's assertion that "good fences make good neighbors." While fences separate, they also demarcate *us* from *them*, laying the groundwork for social comparison and potential discrimination. See Tajfel and Turner 1979.

199 **the peace accord:** See Pogatchnik 2008.

199 **an integrated society:** Another consideration to separation is the challenge of reintegration. How, for example, should the government remove the peace walls? The obvious response: "Just tear them down!" But this process imposes the government's will upon communities, which may not be ready for change. To force change is to risk triggering the Tribes Effect. An alternative approach, laid out by David Ford, former justice minister of Northern Ireland, is to tear down peace walls only with community consent. While this may better address local emotional sentiments, it also takes time, coordination, and resources.

200 **powerless prefer synthesis:** For example, a study of universities—one predominantly white and another predominantly black—found that the

majority group preferred assimilationist policies, whereas the minority group preferred pluralistic policies (Hehman et al. 2012).

200 **"enemies—mostly Germany":** See Rodriguez-Vila 2009, 27.

200 **"twenty years earlier":** Ibid.

202 **"killed on 9/11":** See J. Shapiro, *Bill Clinton Endorses Muslim Center Near Ground Zero*, in DNAinfo, September 21, 2010, http://www.dnainfo.com/new-york/20100921/downtown/bill-clinton-endorses-muslim-center-near-ground-zero.

Chapter 14: Managing Dialectics

208 **a step further:** Philosopher Georg Wilhelm Friedrich Hegel credited Kant with forming the thesis-antithesis-synthesis model; Johann Fichte refined and popularized it (Buytendijk 2010, 11).

208 **dialectic to completion:** Hegel conceptualized the purpose of dialectics as "to study things in their own being and movement and thus to demonstrate the finitude of the partial categories of understanding" (Hegel 187, 149).

208 **concrete synthesis emerges:** Hegel's dialectic method inspired Karl Marx and Friedrich Engels to create "dialectical materialism," a philosophy of science and nature foundational to the communist system of the Soviet Union. Marx argued that the dialectic struggle between the bourgeoisie (capitalists and landowners) and the proletariat (manual laborers) produces a predictable cycle of revolutions. In other words, the people making all the money enjoy their wealth (thesis), while the manual laborers work physically straining jobs for relatively small compensation (antithesis). The manual laborers understandably get frustrated and revolt. As new elites take the reins and new revolts burst out, the political system moves closer and closer to its final synthesis—communism—a classless, stateless society based on common ownership and satisfaction based on need, not materialistic desire.

209 *a Bundle of Contradictions:* The phrase "a bundle of contradictions" is used by Anne Frank in *The Diary of a Young Girl*.

211 **"is an incapable":** James 1926, 393–94.

211 **worthy of criticism:** See Beck 1999. Also see Burns 1980.

213 **have of retaliation:** Greek mythology includes three avenging spirits known in Latin as the Furies: Alecto (unceasing anger), Tisiphone (revenge), and Megaera (grudge). According to Bob Bailey Mucker (2014, 16), "the ancient Greeks were so afraid to offend them that they rarely mentioned them by name." In a conflict these three relational experiences—anger, revenge, and grudge—drive a great deal of destructive dynamics.

214 **"even the score":** If we feel that another party has intentionally inflicted suffering upon us, we tend to experience the desire to inflict suffering upon them to at least the same degree we feel we have suffered. This is the classic "eye for an eye." To the outsider it may be hard to understand how the scale of our retaliation is appropriate to what they might perceive as a small slight. But the insider may have experienced the same action as a major attack on identity, justifying the intense retaliation. Similarly, in *Inferno*, fourteenth-century

Italian poet Dante Alighieri describes how, as payback for people's sins on earth, their souls suffer commensurate punishment in hell. For example, the souls of adulterers, which he calls the "carnal malefactors," endure the heavy winds of violent storms, a fitting punishment for their poor carnal judgment based upon lust. Indeed, if we feel victimized, we may experience a Dante-esque yearning for the other to be punished *contrapasso*—that is, in a way either resembling or contrasting with the sin itself.

214 **humiliation and shame:** The concept of catharsis has a storied intellectual history. Aristotle originally used it as a metaphor to illustrate the emotional force behind tragic plays. In *Romeo and Juliet*, star-crossed lovers commit suicide as a sacrifice for their love, and catharsis appears as the lovers' families reconcile a long-standing fight. Centuries later the Austrian physician Josef Breuer introduced the concept of catharsis into psychology. He hypnotized traumatized patients and encouraged them to express repressed emotions around the trauma, claiming to cure them of their symptoms. Sigmund Freud (1925), Breuer's protégé, incorporated catharsis into psychoanalysis, arguing that emotions build up within us, much like steam in a kettle, pressuring us to either release them or "blow up." This is known as the hydraulic model of emotion.

214 **nicotine or cocaine:** See de Quervain et al. 2004.

215 **about the offender:** See Carlsmith et al. 2008. In this study, subjects who punished "free riders" in an economic exchange game forecast they would feel better after their act of revenge, but actually felt worse.

216 **desire for revenge:** See C. Tavris, *Anger: The Misunderstood Emotion* (New York: Touchstone, 1989, rev. ed.).

216 **an emotional frenzy:** The "cognitive neoassociation theory of anger and aggression" helps to explain why thinking angry thoughts makes you angrier. See Berkowitz 1993.

216 **underscores this point:** See Bushman 2002.

216 **were equally aggressive:** Participants who hit the bag while ruminating about their offensive counterpart were more aggressive than those who punched the bag and thought about physical fitness, though this difference was not statistically significant.

217 **resides within everyone:** If one is capable of compassion, one is capable of redemption. There is solid evidence that compassion is innate; Professor Dacher Keltner (2010) of the University of California at Berkeley proposed that humans have a *compassionate instinct*, which can be observed even in young children. Children who are prelinguistic or just linguistic "quite readily help others to achieve their goals in a variety of different situations" (Warneken and Tomasello 2006).

217 **to relieve it:** See Batson (1998), who refers to compassion as "empathic concern."

218 **spent only one:** P. Valdesolo and D. A. DeSteno. "Synchrony and the Social Tuning of Compassion." *Emotion*, 11 no. 2 (2011): 262–66.

219 **to empathic sensitivity:** See Lutz et al. 2008. These researchers have linked the regular practice of LKM—that is, the ritual cultivation of positive

emotions toward self and others through contemplative practice—to brain circuitry associated with empathy and perspective taking.

219 **"good physical health"**: See Fredrickson et al. 2008. Meditating on compassion generates increased brain activity in areas responsible for empathy and planned movement, suggesting that meditation may prepare the brain *and body* to relieve the suffering of others. See Lutz et al. 2008.

219 **compassion to them**: See Sharon Salzberg, *Lovingkindness: The Revolutionary Art of Happiness* (Boston, MA: Shambhala, 2002).

219–20 **of their relationship**: A social covenant represents a deeper agreement than a social contract. A social contract implies an instrumental contract defining people's rights and responsibilities. A social covenant is a moral agreement, which can build positive relations between groups for whom trust has ruptured, whether government and citizens, management and the workforce, or parents and children. The World Economic Forum's Global Agenda Council on Values, of which I am a member, has devised an initiative to encourage business and government leaders to create their own social covenants to promote values-based leadership. Building a social covenant confronts you with tough questions about the defining features of who you are and who you want to be. Values do not give you a precise path forward but rather provide fundamental principles upon which to base decisions.

220 **"with their humanity"**: Personal conversation with Robert Jay Lifton, June 2010.

221 **"I have no regrets"**: See Lifton 2011, 276–77.

222 **the third dialectic**: Baxter and Montgomery (1996) highlight the dialectical nature of autonomy and dependency, pointing out some of the dynamics that arise as a couple feels the desire to both unite and maintain some autonomy.

Chapter 15: Fostering the Spirit of Reconciliation

226 **calls a "possibilitarian"**: Norman Vincent Peale stated: "Become a possibilitarian. No matter how dark things seem to be or actually are, raise your sights and see possibilities—always see them, for they're always there." See http://www.quotes.net/quote/4490.

226 **the *positive possible***: The possibilitarian can use imagination for good or evil. The Nazis spent years sharpening technologies for mass killing, starting with firing squads at close range, then realizing the efficiency of gas chambers and crematoriums; the Auschwitz concentration camp cremated approximately 4,400 people per day. But there are also innumerable examples of individuals using their imaginations to improve the human condition.

226 **what *can be***: Michelangelo described his process of sculpting *David* as an effort to rid the sculpture of its superfluous material. Similarly, I believe that the challenge of constructive conflict resolution is to help people chip away the superfluous material of their relations to discover their shared humanity.

Select Bibliography

Ainsworth, M., and S. Bell. "Attachment, Exploration and Separation: Illustrated by the Behavior of One-Year-Olds in a Strange Situation." *Child Development* 41 (1970): 49–67.

Allport, G. *The Nature of Prejudice*. Cambridge, MA: Addison-Wesley, 1954.

Angrilli, A., P. Cherubini, A. Pavese, and S. Manfredini. "The Influence of Affective Factors on Time Perception." *Perception and Psychophysics* 59, no. 6 (1997): 972–82.

Atran, S. "Genesis of Suicide Terrorism." *Science* 299 (2003): 1534–39.

———, and R. Axelrod. "Reframing Sacred Values." *Negotiation Journal* 24 (2008): 221–46.

———, and R. Davis. "Sacred Barriers to Conflict Resolution." *Science* 317 (2007): 1039–40.

Bailey-Mucker, B. *Classical Mythology: Little Books About Big Things*. New York: Fall River Press, 2014.

Bakan, D. *The Duality of Human Existence: An Essay on Psychology and Religion*. Chicago: Rand McNally, 1966.

Banton, M. *Ethnic and Racial Consciousness* 2nd ed. London: Longman, 1997.

Baron, J., and M. Spranca. "Protected Values." *Organizational Behavior and Human Decision Processes* 70, no. 1 (1997): 1–16.

Barth, F. *Ethnic Groups and Boundaries: The Social Organization of Culture Difference*. Oslo: Universitetsforlaget, 1969.

———. *Guided and Guarded: German War-Corporal Turns to Mormonism*. Salt Lake City: Barth Associates, 1981.

Bartlett, F. *Remembering: A Study in Experimental and Social Psychology*. New York: Macmillan, 1932.

Baseel, C. "The Unfortunate Implications of Seoul's Tsunami-Shaped City Hall." *Rocket News* 24, November 7, 2013.

Bateson, G., D. Jackson, J. Haley, and J. Weakland. "Toward a Theory of Schizophrenia." *Behavioral Science* 1, no. 4 (1956): 251–64.

Batson, C. "Altruism and Prosocial Behavior." In *The Handbook of Social Psychology*, edited by D. Gilbert, S. Fiske, and G. Lindzey, New York: McGraw-Hill, 1998, 282–316.

Baumeister, R., and M. Leary. "The Need to Belong: Desire for Interpersonal Attachments as a Fundamental Human Motivation." In *Motivational Science: Social and Personality Perspectives,* edited by E. Higgins and A. Kruglanski, 24–49. Philadelphia: Psychology Press, 2000.

Baxter, L., and B. Montgomery. *Relating: Dialogues and Dialectics.* New York: Guilford, 1996.

Bazerman, M., A. Tenbrunsel, and K. Wade-Benzoni. "When 'Sacred' Issues Are at Stake." *Negotiation Journal* 24, no. 1 (2008).

Beck, A. *Prisoners of Hate: The Cognitive Basis of Anger, Hostility, and Violence.* New York: HarperCollins, 1999.

Benjamin, L. "Principles of Prediction Using Structural Analysis of Social Behavior." In *Personality and the Prediction of Behavior,* edited by A. Zucker, J. Aranoff, and J. Rubin, New York: Academic Press, 1984, 121–73.

Berkowitz, L. *Aggression: Its Causes, Consequences, and Control.* New York: McGraw-Hill, 1993.

Berreby, D. *Us and Them: Understanding Your Tribal Mind.* New York: Little, Brown, 2005.

Bilefsky, D. "Balkans' Idolatry Delights Movie Fans and Pigeons." *New York Times,* November 11, 2007.

Blake, A. "Dennis Rodman: Kim Jong-Eun Is My 'Friend.'" *Washington Post,* March 13, 2013.

Blakeslee, S. "Cells That Read Minds." *New York Times,* January 10, 2006.

Bloomfield, D. *Reconciliation After Violent Conflict: A Handbook.* Stockholm: International IDEA, 2003.

Boulding, K. *Stable Peace.* Austin, TX: University of Texas Press, 1978.

Bowlby, J. *Attachment and Loss.* Vol. 1, *Attachment.* New York: Basic Books, 1971.

———. *Separation: Anxiety and Anger.* New York: Basic Books, 1973.

Bradford, D., and A. Cohen. *Power Up.* John Wiley & Sons, 1998.

Brewer, J. *Peace Processes: A Sociological Approach.* Cambridge: Polity Press, 2010.

Brewer, M. "Ingroup Identification and Intergroup Conflict: When Does Ingroup Love Become Outgroup Hate?" In *Social Identity, Intergroup Conflict, and Conflict Reduction,* edited by R. Ashmore, L. Jussim, and D. Wilder, Oxford: Oxford University Press, 2001, 17–41.

———. "The Social Self: On Being the Same and Different at the Same Time." *Personality and Social Psychology Bulletin* 17 (1991): 475–82.

Brubaker, R. *Ethnicity Without Groups.* Cambridge, MA: Harvard University Press, 2004.

Bruner, J. *Acts of Meaning.* Cambridge, MA: Harvard University Press, 1990.

———. *Making Stories: Law, Literature, Life.* New York: Farrar, Straus and Giroux, 2002.

Burns, D. *Feeling Good: The New Mood Therapy.* New York: Morrow, 1980.

Burroughs, E. *The Beasts of Tarzan.* Charlottesville, VA: University of Virginia Library, 1993.

Bushman, B. "Does Venting Anger Feed or Extinguish the Flame? Catharsis, Rumination, Distraction, Anger, and Aggressive Responding." *Personality and Social Psychology Bulletin* 28, no. 6 (2002): 724–31.

Buytendijk, F. *Dealing with Dilemmas: Where Business Analytics Fall Short.* New York: John Wiley & Sons, 2010.

Byman, D. "Forever Enemies? The Manipulation of Ethnic Identities to End Ethnic Wars." *Security Studies* 9, no. 3 (2000): 149–90.

Campbell, D. "Ethnocentric and Other Altruistic Motives." In *Nebraska Symposium on Motivation, 1965, Current Theory and Research on Motivation*, vol. 13, edited by D. Levine, Lincoln: University of Nebraska Press, 1965, 283–311.

Campbell, J., and B. Moyers. *The Power of Myth.* New York: Doubleday, 1988.

Carlsmith, K., T. Wilson, and D. Gilbert. "The Paradoxical Consequences of Revenge." *Journal of Personality and Social Psychology* 95 (2008): 1316–24.

Celani, D. *The Illusion of Love: Why the Battered Woman Returns to Her Abuser.* New York: Columbia University Press, 1994.

Chomsky, N. *Studies on Semantics in Generative Grammar.* The Hague: Mouton, 1972.

Cobb, S. "Fostering Coexistence Within Identity-Based Conflicts: Toward a Narrative Approach." In *Imagine Coexistence: Restoring Humanity After Violent Ethnic Conflict*, edited by A. Chayes, San Francisco: Jossey-Bass, 2003, 294–310.

Cohen, J. "Advising Clients to Apologize." *Southern California Law Review* 72, no. 4 (1999), 1009–69.

Coleman, E., and K. White. "Stretching the Sacred." In *Negotiating the Sacred: Blasphemy and Sacrilege in a Multicultural Society*, edited by E. Coleman and K. White. Canberra: ANU E Press, 2006.

Coleman, P., and J. Lowe. "Conflict, Identity, and Resilience: Negotiating Collective Identities Within the Israeli and Palestinian Diasporas." *Conflict Resolution Quarterly* 24, no. 4 (2007): 377–412.

Cook, J. *A Voyage to the Pacific Ocean.* London: H. Hughes, 1785.

Cook, V., and M. Newson. *Chomsky's Universal Grammar.* 3rd ed. Malden: Wiley-Blackwell, 2007.

Cooley, C. *Human Nature and the Social Order.* New York: Scribner's, 1902.

Coser, L. *The Functions of Social Conflict.* Glencoe, IL: Free Press, 1956.

Crockett, M., L. Clark, M. Hauser, and T. Robbins. "Serotonin Selectively Influences Moral Judgment and Behavior Through Effects on Harm Aversion." *Proceedings of the National Academy of Sciences* 107, no. 40 (2010): 17433–38.

Dalai Lama. *The Universe in a Single Atom: The Convergence of Science and Spirituality.* New York: Morgan Road Books, 2005.

Daly, E., and J. Hughes. *Reconciliation in Divided Societies: Finding Common Ground.* Philadelphia: University of Pennsylvania Press, 2007.

Damasio, A. *Descartes' Error: Emotion, Reason, and the Human Brain.* New York: Putnam, 1994.

———. "Remembering When." *Scientific American*, September 1, 2002, 66–73.

Darley, J., and C. Batson. "'From Jerusalem to Jericho': A Study of Situational and Dispositional Variables in Helping Behavior." *Journal of Personality and Social Psychology* 27, no. 1 (1973): 100–108.

Davies, P. *The Physics of Time Asymmetry.* Berkeley: University of California Press, 1974.

Deci, E. *The Psychology of Self-Determination.* Lexington, MA: Lexington Books, 1980.

———, and R. Ryan. "The 'What' and 'Why' of Goal Pursuits: Human Needs and the Self-Determination of Behavior." *Psychological Inquiry* 11, no. 4 (2000): 227–68.

Dehghani, M., R. Iliev, S. Sachdeva, S. Atran, J. Ginges, and D. Medin. "Emerging Sacred Values: Iran's Nuclear Program." *Judgment and Decision Making* 4, no. 7 (2009): 930–33.

Dennett, D., and M. Kinsbourne. "Time and the Observer: The Where and When of Consciousness in the Brain." *Behavioral and Brain Sciences* 15, no. 2 (1992): 183–247.

de Quervain, D., U. Fischbacher, V. Treyer, M. Schellhammer, U. Schnyder, A. Buck, and E. Fehr. "The Neural Basis of Altruistic Punishment." *Science* 305 (2004): 1254–58.

Deutsch, M. *The Resolution of Conflict: Constructive and Destructive Processes.* New Haven, CT: Yale University Press, 1973.

de Vignemont, F., and T. Singer. "The Empathic Brain: How, When and Why?" *Trends in Cognitive Sciences* 10, no. 10 (2006): 435–41.

de Waal, F. *Chimpanzee Politics: Power and Sex Among Apes.* London: Cape, 1982.

DeWall, C., G. MacDonald, G. Webster, C. Masten, R. Baumeister, C. Powell, D. Combs, D. Schurtz, T. Stillman, D. Tice, and N. Eisenberger. "Acetaminophen Reduces Social Pain: Behavioral and Neural Evidence." *Psychological Science* 21 (2010): 931–37.

Ditzen, B., M. Schaer, B. Gabriel, G. Bodenmann, U. Ehlert, and M. Heinrichs. "Intranasal Oxytocin Increases Positive Communication and Reduces Cortisol Levels During Couple Conflict." *Biological Psychiatry* 65, no. 9 (2009): 728–31.

Dunbar, J. "Seoul City Hall's Metamorphosis Pleases Book Lovers." Korea.net, October 25, 2012.

Dupré, B. *50 Big Ideas You Really Need to Know.* London: Quercus, 2009.

Durkheim, E. *The Elementary Forms of Religious Life.* New York: Free Press, 1912.

Eagleman, D., and V. Pariyadath. "Is Subjective Duration a Signature of Coding Efficiency?" *Philosophical Transactions of the Royal Society B: Biological Sciences* 364, no. 1525 (2009): 1841–51.

Eisenberger, N., M. Lieberman, and K. Williams. "Does Rejection Hurt? An FMRI Study of Social Exclusion." *Science* 302 (2003): 290–92.

Eliade, M. *The Sacred and the Profane: The Nature of Religion.* New York: Harvest Book, 1959.

Enright, R., and C. Coyle. "Researching the Process Model of Forgiveness Within Psychological Interventions." In *Dimensions of Forgiveness: Psychological Research and Theological Perspectives*, edited by E. Worthington, Philadelphia: Templeton Foundation Press, 1988, 139–61.

Enzensberger, H. *Civil Wars: From L.A. to Bosnia*. New York: New Press, 1994.

Erikson, E. *Identity, Youth, and Crisis*. New York: W. W. Norton, 1968.

———. "The Problem of Ego Identity." *Journal of the American Psychoanalytic Association* 4 (1956): 56–121.

Fisher, Roger. *Five Skills for Getting to Yes*. Video. 1996. Produced in association with CMI Concord Group, Inc., Wellesley, MA.

———, and D. Shapiro. *Beyond Reason: Using Emotions as You Negotiate*. New York: Viking, 2005.

———, and W. Ury. *Getting to YES: Negotiating Agreement Without Giving In*. Boston: Houghton Mifflin, 1981.

Fisher, Ronald. "Commentary on Herbert Kelman's Contribution to Interactive Problem Solving." *Peace and Conflict: Journal of Peace Psychology* 16, no. 4 (2010): 415–23.

Fiske, A., and P. Tetlock. "Taboo Trade-offs: Reactions to Transactions That Transgress the Spheres of Justice." *Political Psychology* 18, no. 2 (1997): 255–97.

Fiske, S. T., and S. L. Neuberg. "A Continuum of Impression Formation, from Category-Based to Individuating Processes: Influences of Information and Motivation on Attention and Interpretation." In *Advances in Experimental Social Psychology*, vol. 23, edited by M. P. Zanna. New York: Academic Press, 1990, 1–74.

Foer, J. "How to Win the World Memory Championships." *Discover: Mind & Brain*, April 2, 2006.

Foucault, M. *The Foucault Reader*. New York: Pantheon, 1984.

Frederickson, B., M. Cohn, K. Coffey, J. Pek, and S. Finkel. "Open Hearts Build Lives: Positive Emotions, Induced Through Loving-Kindness Mediation, Build Consequential Personal Resources." *Journal of Personality and Social Psychology* 95, no. 5 (2008): 1045–62.

Freedman, M., T. Leary, A. Ossorio, and H. Goffey. "The Interpersonal Dimension of Personality." *Journal of Personality* 20, no. 2 (1951): 143–61.

Freud, S. "Negation." *Standard Edition* 19 (1925): 235–39.

———. "Beyond the Pleasure Principle." *Standard Edition* 18 (1920): 1–64.

———. "Why War? (Einstein and Freud)." *Standard Edition* 22 (1933): 195–215.

Fridja, N. "The Laws of Emotion." *American Psychologist* 43 (1988): 349–58.

Fromm, E. *Escape from Freedom*. New York: Farrar & Rinehart, 1941.

Fry, D. *The Human Potential for Peace: An Anthropological Challenge to Assumptions About War and Violence*. New York: Oxford University Press, 2006.

Gaertner, S., J. Dovidio, P. Anastasio, B. Bachman, and M. Rust. "The Common Ingroup Identity Model: Recategorization and the Reduction of Intergroup Bias." *European Review of Social Psychology* 4, no. 1 (1993): 1–26.

Gagnon, V. "Ethnic Nationalism and International Conflict: The Case of Serbia." *International Security* 19, no. 3 (1994): 130–66.

Gardner, M. "Can Time Go Backward?" *Scientific American*, January 1, 1967, pp. 98–108.

Geertz, R. "Religion as a Cultural System." New York: Fontana Press, 1965.

Gibson, J. "Do Strong Group Identities Fuel Intolerance? Evidence from the South African Case." *Political Psychology* 27, no. 5 (2006): 665–705.

Gilbert, D. *Stumbling on Happiness.* New York: Vintage Books, 2005.

Gilligan, C. *In a Different Voice: Psychological Theory and Women's Development.* Cambridge, MA: Harvard University Press, 1982.

Gilligan, J. *Violence: Reflections on a National Epidemic.* New York: Vintage, 1996.

Ginges, J., S. Atran, D. Medlin, and K. Shikaki. "Sacred Bounds on Rational Resolution of Violent Political Conflict." *Proceedings of the National Academy of Sciences* 104, no. 18 (2007): 7357–60.

Glatthaar, J. T. *General Lee's Army: From Victory to Collapse.* New York: Free Press, 2008.

Gobodo-Madikizela, P. *A Human Being Died That Night: A South African Woman Confronts the Legacy of Apartheid.* Boston: Houghton Mifflin, 2003.

Gottman, J., and J. DeClaire. *The Relationship Cure: A 5 Step Guide to Strengthening Your Marriage, Family, and Friendships.* New York: Harmony, 2002.

Greenberg, Jay, and S. Mitchell. *Object Relations in Psychoanalytic Theory.* Cambridge, MA: Harvard University Press, 1983.

Greenberg, Jeff, et al. "Evidence for Terror Management Theory II: The Effects of Mortality Salience on Reactions to Those Who Threaten or Bolster the Cultural Worldview." *Journal of Personality and Social Psychology* 58 (1990): 308–18.

Hackett, S. *Oriental Philosophy: A Westerner's Guide to Eastern Thought.* Madison: University of Wisconsin Press, 1979.

Hammond, C. *Time Warped: Unlocking the Mysteries of Time Perception.* Toronto: House of Anansi Press, 2012.

Han, S., J. Lerner, and R. Zeckhauser. "Disgust Promotes Disposal: Souring the Status Quo." Harvard Kennedy School Faculty Research Working Paper Series RWP10-021 (2010).

Harris, S., S. Sheth, and M. Cohen. "Functional Neuroimaging of Belief, Disbelief, and Uncertainty." *Annals of Neurology* 63, no. 2 (2008): 141–47.

Haslam, S. *Psychology in Organizations: The Social Identity Approach,* 2nd ed. New York: Sage, 2004.

Hegel, G. *The Logic of Hegel, Translated from the Encyclopaedia of the Philosophical Sciences by William Wallace.* London: Oxford University Press, 1817.

Hehman, E., S. Gaertner, J. Dovidio, E. Mania, R. Guerra, D. Wilson, and B. Friel. "Group Status Drives Majority and Minority Integration Preferences." *Psychological Sciences* 23, no. 1 (2012): 46–52.

Heidegger, M. *Being and Time.* 1927. Reprint, New York: Harper, 1962.

Heifetz, R. *Leadership Without Easy Answers.* Cambridge, MA: Harvard University Press, 1994.

Hendrix, H., and H. Hunt. *Making Marriage Simple: 10 Truths for Changing the Relationship You Have into the One You Want.* New York: Crown Archetype, 2013.

Herman, J. *Trauma and Recovery*. New York: Basic Books, 1992.

Heschel, A. J. New York: Farrar, Straus and Giroux, 2005.

Higginson, J. "Rocky to Knock Out Disaster News." *Metro UK*, February 7, 2007.

Himmler, K., and M. Mitchell. *The Himmler Brothers: A German Family History*. London: Macmillan, 2007.

Hitler, A. *Mein Kampf*. Munich: Eher Verlag, 1925.

Hong, K. "Soul Spectacle: The City Hall, the Plaza and the Public." In *City Halls and Civic Materialism: Towards a Global History of Urban Public Space*, edited by S. Chattopadhyay and J. White, New York: Routledge, 2014, 276–95.

Horowitz, D. *Ethnic Groups in Conflict*. Berkeley: University of California Press, 1985.

Hurlbert, A. "Learning to See Through the Noise." *Current Biology* 10 (2000): R231–33.

Iacoboni, M. "Imitation, Empathy, and Mirror Neurons." *Annual Review of Psychology* 60 (2009): 653–70.

Ignatieff, M. *The Warrior's Honor*. Toronto: Viking, 1997.

James, H. *The Letters of William James*. Boston: Little, Brown, 1926.

James, W. *Talks to Teachers on Psychology: And to Students on Some of Life's Ideals*. New York: Henry Holt and Company, 1899.

———. *The Principles of Psychology*. New York: Henry Holt, 1890.

———. *Psychology, Briefer Course*. London: JM Dent & Sons, 1917.

———. *The Varieties of Religious Experience: A Study in Human Nature*. New York: New American Library, 1902.

———. "The Sense of Dizziness in Deaf Mutes." *American Journal of Otology* 4 (1882): 239–54.

Jenkins, A., C. Macrae, and J. Mitchell. "Repetition Suppression of Ventromedial Prefrontal Activity During Judgments of Self and Others." *Proceedings of the National Academy of Sciences* 105, no. 11 (2008): 4507–12.

Johnson, Allan. *Privilege, Power, and Difference*. 2nd ed. Boston: McGraw-Hill, 2006.

Johnson, Alan, and S. Nishida. "Time Perception: Brain Time or Event Time?" *Current Biology* 11, no. 11 (2001): R427–30.

Josselson, R. *The Space Between Us: Exploring the Dimensions of Human Relationships*. San Francisco: Jossey-Bass, 1992.

Jung, C. G. *The Archetypes and the Collective Unconscious*, 2nd ed. New York: Routledge, 1968. Translated by R.F.C. Hull.

Kaufman, S. *Modern Hatreds: The Symbolic Politics of Ethnic War*. New York: Cornell University Press, 2001.

Kelman, H. "Compliance, Identification, and Internalization: Three Processes of Attitude Change." *Journal of Conflict Resolution* 2 (1956): 51–60.

Keltner, D. *The Compassionate Instinct: The Science of Human Goodness*. New York: W. W. Norton, 2010.

Kempny, M., and Jawlowska, A., eds. *Identity in Transformation: Postmodernity, Postcommunism, and Globalization*. Westport, CT: Praeger, 2002.

Kitron, D. "Repetition Compulsion and Self-Psychology: Towards a Reconciliation." *International Journal of Psychoanalysis* 84, no. 2 (2003): 427–41.

Kolb, D., and J. Williams. *The Shadow Negotiation: How Women Can Master the Hidden Agendas That Determine Bargaining Success.* New York: Simon & Schuster, 2000.

Kong, L. "Negotiating Conceptions of 'Sacred Space': A Case Study of Religious Buildings in Singapore." *Transactions of the Institute of British Geographers, New Series* 18, no. 3 (1993): 342–58.

Korostelina, K. *Social Identity and Conflict Structures, Dynamics, and Implications.* New York: Palgrave Macmillan, 2007.

Kosfeld, M., M. Heinrichs, P. Zak, U. Fischbacher, and E. Fehr. "Oxytocin Increases Trust in Humans." *Nature* 435 (2005): 673–76.

Krishnamurti, J. *The Collected Works of J. Krishnamurti.* Dubuque, IA: Kendall/Hunt, 1991.

Kundera, M., and L. Asher. *Ignorance.* New York: HarperCollins, 2002.

Laing, R. *Knots.* London: Routledge, 1970.

———. *The Politics of the Family.* London: Tavistock, 1969.

Laitin, D. "The Ogaadeen Question and Changes in Somali Identity." In *State Versus Ethnic Claims: African Policy Dilemmas,* edited by D. Rothchild and V. Olorunsola. Boulder, CO: Westview Press, 1983, 331–49.

Lambert, K., and C. Kinsley. "Disorders of Anxiety: Obsessive-Compulsive Disorder and Tourette's Syndrome." In *Clinical Neuroscience,* 2nd ed. New York: Worth, 2010.

Lamothe, R. "Sacred Objects as Vital Objects: Transitional Objects Reconsidered." *Journal of Psychology and Theology* 2 (1998): 159–67.

Laplanche, Jean, and Jean-Bertrand Pontalis. Translated by D. Nicholson-Smith. *The Language of Psych-Analysis.* New York: W. W. Norton, 1973.

Lax, D., and J. Sebenius. *3-D Negotiation: Powerful Tools to Change the Game in Your Most Important Deals.* Boston: Harvard Business School Press, 2006.

Lederach, J. *Building Peace: Sustainable Reconciliation in Divided Societies.* Washington, DC: United States Institute of Peace Press, 1997.

Lerner J. S., Y. Li, P. Valdesolo, and K. Kassam. "Emotion and Decision Making." *Annual Review of Psychology* 66 (2015): 799–823.

LeVine, R., and D. Campbell. *Ethnocentrism: Theories of Conflict, Ethnic Attitudes, and Group Behavior.* New York: Wiley, 1971.

Levs, J. "North Korea: Reality vs. The World According to Dennis Rodman." CNN, September 10, 2013.

Lewin, K. "Group Decision and Social Change." In *Readings in Social Psychology,* edited by E. Maccoby, E. Newcomb, and E. Hartley, 265–84. New York: Holt, 1948.

———. *Resolving Social Conflicts: Selected Papers on Group Dynamics.* New York: Harper, 1948.

Lewis, H. *Shame and Guilt in Neurosis.* New York: International Universities Press, 1971.

Liberman, V., S. Samuels, and L. Ross. "The Name of the Game: Predictive Power of Reputations Versus Situational Labels in Determining Prisoner's Dilemma Game Moves." *Personality and Social Psychology Bulletin* 30, no. 9 (2004): 1175–85.

Lieberman, M. *Social: Why Our Brains Are Wired to Connect.* New York: Crown/ Archetype, 2013.

Lifton, R. *The Broken Connection: On Death and the Continuity of Life.* New York: Simon & Schuster, 1979.

———. Transcript of PBS interview by Bill Moyers, September 17, 2001. See http://www.pbs.org/americaresponds/moyers917.html, accessed on November 22, 2015.

———. *Witness to an Extreme Century: A Memoir.* New York: Free Press, 2011.

Lindner, E. "Healing the Cycles of Humiliation: How to Attend to the Emotional Aspects of 'Unsolvable' Conflicts and the Use of 'Humiliation Entrepreneurship.'" *Peace and Conflict: Journal of Peace Psychology* 8, no. 2 (2002): 125–38.

Loftus, E. "Planting Misinformation in the Human Mind: A 30-Year Investigation of the Malleability of Memory." *Learning & Memory* 12 (2005): 361–66.

Lorenz, K. *On Aggression.* New York: Harcourt, Brace & World, 1966.

Lutz, A., J. Brefczynski-Lewis, T. Johnstone, and R. Davidson. "Regulation of the Neural Circuitry of Emotion by Compassion Meditation: Effects of Meditative Expertise." *Public Library of Science (PLoS) One* 3, no. 3 (2008).

Maalouf, A. *In the Name of Identity: Violence and the Need to Belong.* New York: Arcade, 2001.

Mack, J. "The Enemy System." In *The Psychodynamics of International Relationships.* vol. I, *Concepts and Theories*, edited by V. Volkan, D. Julius, and J. Montville. Lexington, MA: DC Heath, 1990.

Mahoney, A., K. Pargament, G. Ano, Q. Lynn, G. Magyar, S. McCarthy, E. Pristas, and A. Wachhotz. "The Devil Made Them Do It? Demonization and the 9/11 Attacks." Paper presented at the Annual Meeting of the American Psychological Association, Washington, DC: 2002.

———, T. Jewell, A. Swank, E. Scott, E. Emery, and M. Rye. "Marriage and the Spiritual Realm: The Role of Proximal and Distal Religious Constructs in Marital Functioning." *Journal of Family Psychology* 13 (1999): 321–38.

Mandela, N. Transcript of interview conducted on *Frontline*, PBS, May 25, 1999. See http://www.pbs.org/wgbh/pages/frontline/shows/mandela/etc/script.html, accessed on November 22, 2015.

Marcia, J. "Common Processes Underlying Ego Identity, Cognitive/Moral Development, and Individuation." In *Self, Ego and Identity: Integrative Approaches*, edited by D. Lapsley and F. Power. New York: Springer-Verlag, 1988, 211–66.

McCall, G., and J. Simmons. *Identities and Interactions.* New York: Free Press, 1966.

McTaggart, J. "The Unreality of Time." *Mind: A Quarterly Review of Psychology and Philosophy* 17 (1908): 456–73.

Mead, G. H. *Mind, Self, and Society: From the Perspective of a Social Behaviorist.* Chicago: University of Chicago Press, 1934.

Milar, K. "William James and the Sixth Sense." *Monitor on Psychology* 43, no. 8 (2012): 22–24.

Minow, M. *Between Vengeance and Forgiveness: Facing History After Genocide and Mass Violence.* Boston: Beacon Press, 1998.

Mlodinow, L. *Subliminal: How Your Unconscious Mind Rules Your Behavior.* New York: Pantheon Books, 2012.

Mnookin, R., S. Peppet, and A. Tulumello. "The Tension Between Empathy and Assertiveness." *Negotiation Journal* 12 (1996): 217–30.

Mock, D. *More Than Kin and Less Than Kind: The Evolution of Family Conflict.* Cambridge, MA: Belknap Press of Harvard University Press, 2004.

Modern Times. Motion picture. 1936. Directed by Charlie Chaplin.

Moreno, J., and Z. Moreno. *Psychodrama.* New York: Beacon House, 1946.

Morrison, I., D. Lloyd, G. di Pellegrino, and N. Roberts. "Vicarious Responses to Pain in Anterior Cingulate Cortex: Is Empathy a Multisensory Issue?" *Cognitive, Affective, & Behavioral Neuroscience* 4, no. 2 (2004): 270–78.

Neu, J., and V. Volkan. "Developing a Methodology for Conflict Prevention: The Case of Estonia." Special Report Series, Conflict Resolution Program, The Carter Center, 1999.

Niederhoffer, K., and J. W. Pennebaker. "Sharing One's Story: On the Benefits of Writing or Talking About an Emotional Experience." In *Oxford Handbook of Positive Psychology,* 2nd ed., edited by C. Snyder and S. Lopez. New York: Oxford University Press, 2009, 621–32.

Northrup, T. "The Dynamic of Identity in Personal and Social Conflict." In *Intractable Conflicts and Their Transformation,* edited by L. Kriesberg, S. Thorson, and T. Northrup. Syracuse, NY: Syracuse University Press, 1989, 55–82.

"Obama Draws Fire for Bow to Japanese Emperor." Foxnews.com, November 16, 2009.

Otto, R. *The Idea of the Holy.* Oxford: Oxford University Press, 1917.

Packer, G. "The Lesson of Tal Afar." *New Yorker,* April 10, 2006.

Pargament, K., and A. Mahoney. "Sacred Matters: Sanctification as a Vital Topic for the Psychology of Religion." Working Paper Series (02-17), Bowling Green State University, Center for Family and Demographic Research, 2002.

Paulhus, D., and D. Lim. "Arousal and Evaluative Extremity in Social Judgments: A Dynamic Complexity Model." *European Journal of Social Psychology* 24, no. 1 (1994): 89–99.

Pinker, S. *The Better Angels of Our Nature: Why Violence Has Declined.* New York: Viking, 2011.

Pizer, S. "Facing the Nonnegotiable." In *Building Bridges: The Negotiation of Paradox in Psychoanalysis.* Hillsdale, NJ: Analytic Press, 1998.

Pogatchnik, S. "Despite Peace, Belfast Walls Are Growing in Size and Number." *USA Today,* May 3, 2008.

Putnam, R. "Diplomacy and Domestic Politics: The Logic of Two-Level Games." *International Organization* 42, no. 3 (1988): 427–60.

Radcliffe-Brown, A. *Taboo: The Frazer Lecture 1939*. Cambridge: Cambridge University Press, 1939.

Raz, J. *The Morality of Freedom*. New York: Clarendon Press, Oxford University Press, 1986.

Retzinger, S., and T. Scheff. "Emotion, Alienation and Narratives: Resolving Intractable Conflict." *Mediation Quarterly* 18, no. 1 (2000): 71–85.

"Riots Over US Koran 'Desecration.'" BBC, May 11, 2005.

Rodriguez-Vila, F. "Why Reconciliation? *Poder Enterprise*, March 1, 2009.

Rosenhan, D. "On Being Sane in Insane Places." *Science* 179 (1973): 250–58.

Ross, D. "Transcript of WBGH Interview by Will Lyman," 2002. From WBGH *Frontline*, produced and directed by Dan Setton and Tor Ben Mayor. See http://www.pbs.org/wgbh/pages/frontline/shows/oslo/etc/script.html, accessed on November 22, 2015.

Ross, L., and R. Nisbett. *The Person and the Situation*. Padstow, UK: Pinter & Martin, 2011.

Rouhana, N. "Identity and Power in the Reconciliation of National Conflict." In *The Social Psychology of Group Identity and Social Conflict: Theory, Application, and Practice*, edited by A. Eagly, R. Baron, and E. Hamilton. Washington, DC: American Psychological Association, 2004.

Russell, P. "The Compulsion to Repeat." *Smith College Studies in Social Work* 76, nos. 1–2 (2006): 33–49.

———. "The Role of Paradox in the Repetition Compulsion." In *Trauma, Repetition, and Affect Regulation: The Work of Paul Russell*, edited by J. Teicholz and D. Kriegman. New York: Other Press, 1998.

———. "Trauma and the Cognitive Function of Affects." In *Trauma, Repetition, and Affect Regulation: The Work of Paul Russell*, edited by J. Teicholz and D. Kriegman. New York: Other Press, 1998.

Sadat, A. *In Search of Identity: An Autobiography*. New York: Harper & Row, 1978.

Sander, D., J. Grafman, and T. Zalla. "The Human Amygdala: An Evolved System for Relevance Detection." *Reviews in the Neurosciences* 14 (2003): 303–16.

Sartre, J., and G. Becker. *Anti-Semite and Jew*. New York: Schocken Books, 1965.

Schacter, S. "Deviation, Rejection and Communication." *Journal of Abnormal and Social Psychology* 46 (1951): 190–207.

Scheff, T. "Shame and Conformity: The Deference-Emotion System." *American Sociological Review* 53, no. 3 (1988): 395–406.

Schwartz, R. *Internal Family Systems Therapy*. New York: Guilford Press, 1995.

Schwartz, S. "The Evolution of Eriksonian and Neo-Eriksonian Identity Theory and Research: A Review and Integration." *Identity: An International Journal of Theory and Research* 1, no. 1 (2001): 7–58.

Sebenius, J., and D. Curran. "'To Hell with the Future, Let's Get On with the Past': George Mitchell in North Ireland." Harvard Business School Case 801-393, 2001; revised March 2008.

———, and L. Green. "Tommy Koh: Background and Major Accomplishments of the 'Great Negotiator, 2014.'" Harvard Business School Working Paper, 2014.

Sen, A. *Identity and Violence: The Illusion of Destiny*. New York: W. W. Norton, 2006.

"Seoul's New City Hall Opens." *Chosun Ilbo* (English edition), 2012. See http://www.pbs.org/wgbh/pages/frontline/shows/oslo/etc/script.html, accessed on November 22, 2015.

Shapiro, D. "Emotions in Negotiation: Peril or Promise?" *Marquette Law Review* 87, no. 737 (2004): 737–45.

———. "The Greatest Weapons in Iraq." *Harvard Crimson*, March 19, 2008.

———. "Relational Identity Theory: A Systematic Approach for Transforming the Emotional Dimension of Conflict." *American Psychologist* 65, no. 7 (2010): 634–45.

———, and V. Liu. "Psychology of a Stable Peace." In *The Psychology of Resolving Global Conflict: From War to Peace*, edited by M. Fitzduff and C. Stout. Westport, CT: Praeger, 2005.

Shapiro, J. "Bill Clinton Endorses Muslim Center Near Ground Zero." *DNAinfo*, September 21, 2010.

Sherif, M., O. Harvey, B. White, W. Hood, C. Sherif, and J. White. *Intergroup Conflict and Cooperation: The Robbers Cave Experiment*. Rev. ed. Norman, OK: University Book Exchange, 1961.

Shull, D. "The Neurobiology of Freud's Repetition Compulsion." *Annals of Modern Psychoanalysis* 2, no. 1 (2003): 21–46.

Siffre, M. *Beyond Time*. New York: McGraw-Hill, 1964.

Silverman, J. "'Vice' Season Finale on HBO Gives Fresh Look at Dennis Rodman's Meeting with North Korea's Kim Jong-Un." *New York Daily News*, May 29, 2013.

Singer, T., B. Seymour, J. O'Doherty, H. Kaube, R. Dolan, and C. Frith. "Empathy for Pain Involves the Affective But Not Sensory Components of Pain." *Science* 303 (2004): 1157–62.

Sluzki, C. "Transformations: A Blueprint for Narrative Changes in Therapy." *Family Process* 31, no. 3 (1992): 217–30.

Sobelman, B. "Israel: Officials Find Morocco a Tough Room These Days." *Los Angeles Times*, October 31, 2010.

Staub, E. "Individual and Group Selves: Motivation, Morality, and Evolution." In *The Moral Self*, edited by G. Noam and T. Wren. Cambridge, MA: MIT Press, 1993.

———, and L. Pearlman. "Healing, Reconciliation, and Forgiving After Genocide and Other Collective Violence." In *Forgiveness and Reconciliation: Religion, Public Policy, & Conflict Transformation*, edited by R. Helmick and R. Petersen. Philadelphia: Templeton Foundation Press, 2001.

Stets, J. "Identity Theory." In *Contemporary Social Psychological Theories*, edited by P. Burke. Stanford, CA: Stanford Social Sciences, 2006.

Stevens, A. *On Jung*. London: Routledge, 1990.

Stewart, F., and G. Brown. "Motivations for Conflict: Groups and Individuals." In *Leashing the Dogs of War: Conflict Management in a Divided World*, edited by

C. Crocker, F. Olser Hampson, and P. Aall. Washington, DC: United States Institute of Peace Press, 2007.

Stone, D., B. Patton, and S. Heen. *Difficult Conversations: How to Discuss What Matters Most.* New York: Viking, 1999.

Stryker, S. "Integrating Emotion into Identity Theory." In *Theory and Research on Human Emotions (Advances in Group Processes),* vol. 21, edited by J. Turner, 1–23. Emerald Group Publishing Limited, 2004.

Tajfel, H. *Differentiation Between Social Groups: Studies in the Social Psychology of Intergroup Relations.* London: Academic Press, 1978.

———. "Experiments in Intergroup Discrimination." *Scientific American* 223, no. 5 (1970): 96–103.

———, and J. Turner. "An Integrative Theory of Intergroup Conflict." In *The Psychology of Intergroup Relations,* edited by S. Worchel and W. Austin, 33–47. Monterey, CA: Brooks/Cole, 1979.

Tenbrunsel, A., K. Wade-Benzoni, L. Tost, V. Medvec, L. Thompson, and M. Bazerman. "The Reality and Myth of Sacred Issues in Negotiation." *Negotiation and Conflict Management Research* 2, no. 3 (2009): 263–84.

Tetlock, P. "Thinking the Unthinkable: Sacred Values and Taboo Cognitions." *Trends in Cognitive Science* 7, no. 7 (2003): 320–24.

———, O. Kristel, S. Elson, M. Green, and J. Lerner. "The Psychology of the Unthinkable: Taboo Trade-offs, Forbidden Base Rates, and Heretical Counterfactuals." *Journal of Personality and Social Psychology* 785 (2000): 853–70.

Tillich, P. *Dynamics of Faith.* New York: Harper, 1958.

Tsuruta, T. "African Imaginations of Moral Economy: Notes on Indigenous Economic Concepts and Practices in Tanzania." *African Studies Quarterly* 9, nos. 1–2 (2006): 103–21.

Turner, J. *Contemporary Sociological Theory.* Newbury Park, CA: SAGE Publications, 2012.

———, P. Oakes, S. Haslam, and C. Mcgarty. "Self and Collective: Cognition and Social Context." *Personality and Social Psychology Bulletin* 20, no. 5 (1994): 454–63.

Tutu, D., and M. Tutu. *The Book of Forgiving: The Fourfold Path for Healing Ourselves and Our World.* New York: HarperOne, 2014.

Twenge, J., K. Catanese, and R. Baumeister. "Social Exclusion and the Deconstructed State: Time Perception, Meaninglessness, Lethargy, Lack of Emotion, and Self-Awareness." *Journal of Personality and Social Psychology* 85, no. 3 (2003): 409–23.

Ury, W. *Getting Past No: Negotiating with Difficult People.* New York: Bantam Books, 1991.

Van der Kolk, B. "The Interaction of Biological and Social Events in the Genesis of the Trauma Response." *Journal of Traumatic Stress* 1 (1988): 273–90.

Volkan, V. "Bosnia-Herzegovina: Ancient Fuel of a Modern Inferno." *Mind and Human Interaction* 7 (1996): 110–27.

———. *Chosen Trauma, the Political Ideology of Entitlement and Violence.* Berlin, 2004. See http://www.vamikvolkan.com/Chosen-Trauma%2C-the-Political -Ideology-of-Entitlement-and-Violence.php, accessed on November 22, 2015.

———. *Killing in the Name of Identity: A Study of Bloody Conflicts.* Charlottesville, VA: Pitchstone, 2006.

———. *Linking Objects and Linking Phenomena: A Study of the Forms, Symptoms, Metapsychology, and Therapy of Complicated Mourning.* New York: International Universities Press, 1981.

———. "Psychological Concepts Useful in the Building of Political Foundations Between Nations: Track II Diplomacy." *Journal of the American Psychoanalytic Association* 35, no. 4 (1987): 903–35.

———. "September 11 and Societal Regression." In *Group Analysis*, 456–83.

———. "The Tree Model: A Comprehensive Psychopolitical Approach to Unofficial Diplomacy and the Reduction of Ethnic Tension." *Mind and Human Interaction* 10 (1999): 142–206.

Vroom, V., and P. Yetton. *Leadership and Decision-Making.* University of Pittsburgh Press, 1976.

Waller, W. *The Family, a Dynamic Interpretation.* New York: Cordon Company, 1938.

Walton, R., and R. McKersie. *A Behavioral Theory of Labor Negotiations: An Analysis of a Social Interaction System.* New York: McGraw-Hill, 1965.

Warneken, F., and M. Tomasello. "Altruistic Helping in Human Infants and Young Chimpanzees." *Science* 311, no. 5765 (2006): 1301–3.

White, F. *The Overview Effect: Space Exploration and Human Evolution,* 2nd ed. Reston, VA: AIAA, 1998.

Whitrow, G. *What Is Time?* London: Thames & Hudson, 1972.

Wiggins, J. "Agency and Communion as Conceptual Coordinates for the Understanding and Measurement of Interpersonal Behavior." In *Thinking Clearly About Psychology: Personality and Psychopathology,* vol. 2, edited by D. Cicchetti and W. Grove. Minneapolis: University of Minnesota Press, 1991, 89–113.

Wilde, O., and R. Ellmann. *The Artist as Critic: Critical Writings of Oscar Wilde.* New York: Random House, 1969.

Wilkinson, P., and N. Philip. *Mythology.* London: DK, 2007.

Winnicott, D. *What Is Psycho-analysis?* London and Hull: A. Brown and Sons, 1952.

Wiseman, R. *Quirkology: The Curious Science of Everyday Lives.* London: Pan Books, 2007.

Yalom, I. *The Theory and Practice of Group Psychotherapy.* New York: Basic Books, 1985.

Zak, P., R. Kurzban, and W. Matzner. "Oxytocin Is Associated with Human Trustworthiness." *Hormones and Behavior* 48 (2005): 522–27.

Zaltman, G., and R. Coulter. "Seeing the Voice of the Customer: Metaphor-Based Advertising Research." *Journal of Advertising Research* 35, no. 4 (July–August 1995): 35–51.

Zander, R., and B. Zander. *The Art of Possibility.* Boston: Harvard Business School Press, 2000.

Index

About the Author

Daniel Shapiro, Ph.D., is the founder and director of the Harvard International Negotiation Program, associate professor in psychology at Harvard Medical School/McLean Hospital, and affiliate faculty at the Program on Negotiation at Harvard Law School. He consults regularly for government leaders and Fortune 500 companies, and has advised everyone from hostage negotiators to families in crisis, disputing CEOs to clashing heads of state. He has launched successful conflict resolution initiatives in the Middle East, Europe, and East Asia, and for three years chaired the World Economic Forum's Global Agenda Council on Conflict Resolution. Through nonprofit funding, he developed a conflict management program that now reaches one million youth across more than twenty countries.

He has published extensively in the field of conflict resolution, and is coauthor of the bestseller *Beyond Reason: Using Emotions as You Negotiate.* Dr. Shapiro also has contributed to *The New York Times, The Boston Globe,* and other popular publications, and is the recipient of numerous awards, including the American Psychological Association's *Early Career Award* and the Cloke-Millen Peacemaker of the Year Award. The World Economic Forum named him a Young Global Leader. His life's joy is spending time with his wife and three young boys—who have proven to be his greatest teachers in how to negotiate the nonnegotiable.

Interested in learning more?

Dr. Shapiro offers energizing keynote lectures, intensive negotiation trainings, and personalized coaching in conflict resolution. He can be reached at integrativedynamics@gmail.com. Additionally, you can check out his website for resources to further boost your negotiation effectiveness: **www.danshapiroglobal.com.**